AMERICAN COMMUNITY

AMERICAN COMMUNITY

Radical Experiments in Intentional Living

MARK S. FERRARA

RUTGERS UNIVERSITY PRESS

New Brunswick, Camden, and Newark, New Jersey, and London

Library of Congress Cataloging-in-Publication Data
Names: Ferrara, Mark S., author.
Title: American community : radical experiments in intentional living /
    Mark S. Ferrara.
Description: New Brunswick : Rutgers University Press, [2019] |
    Includes bibliographical references and index.
Identifiers: LCCN 2019007533 | ISBN 9781978808232 (hardcover)
Subjects: LCSH: Communal living—United States—History. |
    Collective settlements—United States—History. | Utopias—
    United States—History.
Classification: LCC HX653 .F47 2019 | DDC 307.770973—dc23
LC record available at https://lccn.loc.gov/2019007533

A British Cataloging-in-Publication record for this book is available from the
British Library.

All photographs by the author

♾ The paper used in this publication meets the requirements of the American
National Standard for Information Sciences—Permanence of Paper for Printed
Library Materials, ANSI Z39.48-1992.

www.rutgersuniversitypress.org

Manufactured in the United States of America

For Liangmei Bao—how wonderful to walk with you through this transient world

CONTENTS

AMERICAN COMMUNITY

INTRODUCTION

Community of Goods in the Colonies

In THE SUMMER of 1723, Conrad Beissel, seeking solitude, gathered his scanty belongings and trekked further into the remote Conestoga frontier of Pennsylvania. He followed a narrow Native American trail that wound through dense forests of red ash, silver maple, white oak, and pitch pine. The thick underbrush of sweetfern, shadbush, and prickly ash slowed his progress. Short of stature due to the malnourishment that he endured as a child in Eberbach (Germany), we can imagine him stopping occasionally to clear the path and to rest. The quiet hush of the ancient woodlands must have seemed a world away from the continual warfare that had turned the Rhine corridor—from the high lakes of Switzerland to the Netherlands—into a field of death during the Thirty Years' War, French-Dutch War, and Nine Years' War.[1] As a young man, Beissel witnessed thousands of homeless victims of these conflicts wandering the streets. Despite his own deprivation, their suffering touched him to the quick. That sense of compassion for others never left him, and, in the fullness of time, Beissel's religious sensibilities would lead him to the American colonies. There, he founded Ephrata Cloister, one of the most successful intentional communities in American history.

Intentional communities are those "purposely and voluntarily founded to achieve a specific goal for a specific group of people bent on solving a specific set of cultural and social problems."[2] Their goals vary widely, but they represent a call to action that is simultaneously personal and communal. Intentional communities are often conceived as separate and distinct from larger societies. Researchers might categorize these communities by their location, use of land, methods of building, the actions and behaviors of residents—or define members of such communities by their shared ideologies and points of view, psychological and emotional connections, and common histories and practices. Unlike members of social movements and organizations, or tribes and villages, residents of intentional communities seek to create an entire way of life. They embrace communalism as an ethical end in itself (rather than for the value it creates), and they emphasize economic sharing as a means of achieving collective goals.

Over the centuries, intentional communities have been referred to as communal societies, cooperative communities, alternative societies, communitarian experiments, socialist colonies, communes, collective settlements, and practical utopias. Regardless of the terms used to describe—or to deride— intentional communities, they have remained a persistent part of the American cultural landscape since the early colonial period. *American Community* emerges out of a desire to throw light on experiments in intentional living eclipsed by better-known societies that practiced cooperation and collective ownership of property and resources: New Harmony, Oneida, Brook Farm, and Twin Oaks. Rather than revisit these and other intentional communities, already the subject of many fine studies, I propose a journey through four centuries of less conspicuous experiments in purposeful living as a way to highlight a long-standing American concern with social justice and cooperative business enterprise. From among tens of thousands of current and former intentional communities, I have selected forty that uniquely prioritized communal living and the sharing of resources (whether to imitate the apostles, to put into practice another social theory, to live more sustainably, or simply to save money by pooling resources)—and therefore might be regarded as expressions of communal socialism in America.

To discover more about these social experiments than may be gleaned from books and articles, I embarked on a series of road trips, logging more than 11,000 miles along the way. In some cases, as with Ephrata Cloister, sustained historical preservation efforts allowed careful explorations of community grounds, restored houses, churches, and businesses. In other instances, like that of the socialist cooperative colony Llano Del Rio in Southern California, little evidence remained of bold attempts to find alternatives to profit-driven capitalist enterprise, but gaining a better sense of place, purpose, and landscape proved invaluable to me. During these travels, I also discovered active vibrant communities dedicated to living more sustainably, such as The Farm in Tennessee and EcoVillage Ithaca in New York. When possible, I spoke with members, observed day-to-day operations, and participated in social activities.

With a few exceptions, I arranged these case studies, and the interpretive perspectives drawn from them, chronologically to highlight the myriad ways in which communalism evolved alongside American society—and to permit patterns of persistence and change to emerge that might easily be lost in a book structured to extract experiences with communitarianism to stoke social reform. In entitling this book *American Community*, I invoke a tradition of late nineteenth- and early twentieth-century writing about intentional communities less concerned with advancing arcane arguments than offering in-depth accounts of these societies through informative discussions of founding principles, membership requirements, community leaders, architectural styles, historical influences, business ventures, cultural landscapes, religious beliefs, sexual practices, relationships with nature, interactions with local populations, outsider perceptions of the group, and causes for decline (or continued vibrancy). I am thinking foremost of *History of American Socialisms* (1870) by John Humphrey Noyes (founder of a free-love society in upstate New York), *The Communistic Societies of the United States* (1875) by Charles Nordhoff, and *American Communities and Co-Operative Colonies* (1908) by William Alfred Hinds.

To trace this history briefly, American communitarianism began during the colonial era when groups led by dissenters from the traditional religions of Germany, England, France, and Sweden made their way by sea to the forested shores of the New World seeking religious freedom. The next wave of community building from the Revolutionary War (1775–1783) to the first half of the nineteenth century included social experiments by Perfectionists, Transcendentalists, Fourierists, and Harmonists—among others. A surge of communalism swept over the nation again in the interval between the end of the Civil War in 1865 and the onset of the Great War (World War I) in 1914, this time in the guise of urban and rural socialist and anarchist communities. In the 1930s and 1940s, the U.S. federal government took the lead in community building as a meaningful response to the economic devastation of the Great Depression—although a variety of private relief agencies, including the Catholic Worker Movement, joined the effort to find viable ways of living and working collectively amid the crisis. A resurgence of communitarianism during the 1960s and 1970s resulted in the formation of thousands of counterculture encampments, hippie communes, and alternative religious centers. Each of these important phases in intentional living forms the basis of a chapter that illuminates a rich legacy of socialism too often relegated to the back pages of American history.

The term "socialism," not coined until the 1830s, first denoted a political movement that arose in response to the grinding poverty generated by economic inequality during the Industrial Revolution.[3] While it is true that American soil became a principal testing ground for the ideas of such socialists as Henri de Saint-Simon, Charles Fourier, and Étienne Cabet in France, and Robert Owen in the United Kingdom, in this book "socialism" refers more generally to an economic system wherein some measure of collective or public ownership of productive property (including land and buildings) ensures that everyone's basic needs are met, while preventing great wealth from accumulating in a few hands. The term "socialism" includes an astonishing array of political and economic beliefs, many of which predate the egalitarian and meritocratic visions of the so-called utopian socialists; the publication of Karl Marx and Friedrich Engels's *Communist Manifesto* (1848); and the founding of the Socialist Party of America in 1901.

Simply put, a socialist is someone who believes in equality and freedom and who consciously uses political, social, and economic machinery to change society in accordance with those ideals. The quest for a better society by people professing such a conviction is rooted in ancient revolts of the poor against the rich, in rebellions of oppressed peoples against the ruling classes, and in the dreams of individuals everywhere for a just and egalitarian social order. I first developed an interest in utopian studies as a doctoral student at the University of Denver in the early 2000s and returned to the subject after graduation in a series of books and academic articles, but Bernie Sanders's unapologetic embrace of the Democratic Socialist label during the race for the Democratic Party nomination for president in 2016 and 2020 encouraged me to pen this book. In the wake of the election of Donald Trump, I sensed a renewed interest in intentional living and alternate forms of social organization and posited a resurgence in such communities as our own democracy frays. As the chapters which follow demonstrate, turbulent times generate heightened interest in intentional living, and radical changes in social and cultural environments produce programs for recapturing something Americans feel that they have lost.[4] The dire economic travail of the Great Depression, for instance, led to a call for shared economic prosperity that made Franklin Roosevelt's New Deal possible.

Growing interest in new and sustainable ways of living suggests that we are entering a sixth major wave of intentional community building—a supposition borne out by an explosion of cohousing communities and ecovillages across the nation. Affordable housing projects for veterans, supportive communities for special needs groups, multigenerational housing, neighborhood development for aging in place, and low impact ecological living represent just some of the ways that the cohousing model is being adapted to the needs of local populations. In examining each of the four previous waves of community building, we shall see that the intentional community movement consistently anticipated major shifts in American culture—such as emancipation and the establishment of humane working conditions in the nineteenth century and gender equality and civil rights in the twentieth.

Recent studies suggest that young Americans with dimming memories of the Cold War embrace socialism far more than do older people. A 2016 survey by Harvard's Institute of Politics found that 16 percent of eighteen- to twenty-nine-year-olds identify as socialist—and 33 percent now support socialism. Consider also that the group Democratic Socialists of America has experienced an enormous surge of interest in their platform since the election of President Trump—even in conservative states. Dozens of Democratic Socialist candidates were vying across the country (in Hawaii, Tennessee, California, and Texas) for offices at nearly every level. Many of their millennial supporters find hope in their promises to combat income inequality, to provide affordable health care, to ensure fairness in the criminal justice system, and to address rising levels of student debt. Therefore, it makes more sense than ever to reflect upon the persistence of intentional and cooperative living as part of the American experience.

In other words, we engage with the intentional living movement at a time when more Americans are exploring socialism as a viable alternative to capitalism and are returning to the land in an effort to live in ways that are less exploitative, violent, and harmful to the biosphere—people such as David Fisher, founder of Natural Roots Farm, which provides hundreds of shareholders in his harvest with fresh produce grown organically without tractors or heavy machinery. The way most human beings are living now, Fisher observes, "consuming, destroying the earth is absurd."[5] Seeking an alternative, Fisher left the suburbs of New York City for western Massachusetts to work hard and live frugally with like-minded people. The story of intentional living in America is filled with imaginative individuals like Fisher who, appalled by the existing social order and its injustices, determined to change it.

*   *   *

Ephrata Cloister may represent one of the earliest, longest-lasting, and most successful intentional communities founded during the colonial era, but several social experiments based on the Community of Goods preceded it. The Pilgrims who settled Plymouth Colony in 1620 accepted the discipline of a community of property until 1623, during which time the entire company agreed that the profits and benefits secured by "trade, traffic, trucking, working, fishing, or any other means of any person, or persons" would remain in the common stock—and members would draw "their meat, drink, apparel, and all provisions" out of it.[6] They intended that arrangement to last for seven years, after which time the "houses, lands, goods and chattels" would be divided equally among adventurers (investors) and planters (colonists). Their experiment in communitarianism was cut short after just three years when the decision was taken to assign families parcels of land—and productivity and industriousness increased as colonists labored for their own benefit. Governor William Bradford called that inclination toward selfishness "men's corruption," and he discovered no individual free from it.[7]

The Puritans founded a "Bible Commonwealth" in what is now Massachusetts, a shining City upon a Hill intended to serve as a model for the transformation of society.[8] "The eyes of all people are upon us," Governor Winthrop preached to his fellow immigrants in 1630. The colonists would have to live up to much higher standards of holiness than they had practiced in England:

"We must delight in each other; make others' conditions our own, rejoice together, mourn together, labor and suffer together," Winthrop declared, "as members of the same body."[9] Many Europeans who followed the Pilgrims and Puritans to the American colonies chose to live communally for religious reasons. Of course, many Native Americans lived in communal homes and shared resources long before the arrival of the colonists, but their compelling story must wait for another study.

Radical communal experiments in the American colonies gave tangible expression to the ancient human yearning for a better life, which usually requires a better place. Community leaders at Ephrata, Zwaanendael, and New Bohemia drew inspiration from biblical stories extolling the Garden of Eden, the Promised Land, and a coming Messiah. They knew that the Hebrew prophet Isaiah had foreseen a "New Jerusalem," a heavenly city of eternity and template for social justice; they understood that tens of thousands of men and women had retreated to monastic communities during the Middle Ages; and they studied Thomas More's fictional portrayal of a society in *Utopia* (1516) that condemned private ownership of property and advocated a form of communism in its place.[10] They remembered that Plato had imagined an ideal state based on social justice led by a philosopher king in the *Republic* (ca. 380 B.C.E.), and they were familiar with classical notions of the Golden Age. The individuals who started and those who joined those intentional communities, whether religious or secular, consciously challenged the assumptions of the existing order, and they meaningfully addressed the exploitation, violence, and inequality that have plagued humanity for millennia by creating models of alternative societies.

During the 1640s, native Dutchman Pieter Plockhoy led a Collegiant circle (an influential religious fellowship with a Unitarian outlook) in Amsterdam whose members prohibited confessionalism (adherence to a set of essential theological doctrines) and rejected formal organization of the ministry.[11] Plockhoy popularized his plans for social reformation in a series of publications, some with lengthy and revealing titles:

A Way Propounded to Make the poor in these and Other Nations happy, By bringing together a fit, suitable and well-qualified People into one Household-government, or little Common-wealth, Wherein everyone may keep his propriety and be imployed [sic] in some work or other, as he shall be fit, without being oppressed. Being the way not only to rid these and other Nations from idle, evil and disorderly persons, but also from all such as have sought and found out many Inventions, to live upon the labour of others. Whereunto is also annexed an Invitation to this Society, or Little Common-wealth (1659).

In its opening pages, Plockhoy takes stock of the "great inequality and disorder among men in the World" wrought by "evil Governours or Rulers, covetous Merchants and Tradesmen, lazie, idle and negligent Teachers, and others" who oppress the "common handy-craft men, or labourers" along with honest and good people.[12] To remedy that longstanding injustice, Plockhoy invited his readers "to lay the foundation, for the common welfare" by contributing a sum of money to "raise a Stock" and buy a piece of land whereupon "Husbandman, handy Craftsmen, Tradesmen, Marriners, and others" might live harmoniously. Plockhoy did not compel members to make their "goodes Common," but if out of a "bountifull heart" they donated land or property, it would be employed by the community—and subsequently passed on to donors' friends or children at death.[13] In the event of their departure from the community, former members would receive everything that they had donated plus any profits derived from those assets.

In *A Way Propounded* (and other works), Plockhoy outlined practical proposals for reorganizing society into small commonwealths that pooled skill and experience, and he made room for a diversity of individuals that included investors, craftspeople, and the unemployed. After failing to secure financial support in London, Bristol, and Ireland to realize his ideas, because public opinion at the time of the Restoration had shifted against far-reaching reforms, Plockhoy returned to Holland and petitioned the Dutch government to establish a colony on the North American seaboard. In 1662, Plockhoy signed a contract with Amsterdam Regents and Burgomasters eager for citizens to migrate to a Dutch colony, the New Netherlands, at the heart of which was New Amsterdam (renamed New York after English capture).[14] In return for land and a substantial advance lump sum of 100 guilders for passage, twenty-five Mennonites agreed to live along the Delaware River and to "work at the cultivation of the land, fishing, farming, handicraft, etc., and to be as diligent as possible."[15] Members of the company left undivided "land, cattle, and other common property" in order to pay off the entire loan of 2,500 guilders as quickly as possible.[16] Plockhoy planned to build a community based on equality and association that would "rest upon righteousness, upon love and upon brotherly union," and he called for adherence to the cooperative way of living practiced by the earliest Christians, a society of love in which all things were held in common.[17] For this reason, in Mennonite circles, Plockhoy is still spoken of as "the father of modern socialism."[18]

Plockhoy's prospectus stipulated that settlers work at least six hours per day at a useful occupation in return for an equal distribution of the profits among those over twenty years of age. Plockhoy provided for the election of officers by ballot each year, and he obliged children to attend a common school for half the day.[19] Eager to attract a total of one hundred colonists to improve viability and security, Plockhoy delayed emigration for nearly a year, but in May 1663 he set sail from the Netherlands with forty-one kindred souls. They landed on the shores of the Delaware River at Horekill near Lewes in late July—ominously on the site of the DeVries colony annihilated by Native Americans in 1630.[20] Swedish and Dutch colonists wisely bypassed the area to settle what would become New Castle and Wilmington, but Plockhoy mistakenly regarded Horekill, or Zwaanendael (Valley of Swans), "an excellent place for a noble experiment in communal living," and his colonists erected a small fort near the ruins of the stockade.[21]

Whereas social class determined the course of most European lives during the seventeenth century, Plockhoy spent years generating support for an egalitarian colony that permitted a diversity of religious beliefs and abolished social classes. That communal experiment might have survived longer than two years had not war between the Dutch and English brought commander Sir Robert Carr to the region. Carr singled Zwaanendael out for the kind of savage destruction not visited on other Dutch settlements—perhaps because its egalitarian ethos challenged the political status quo. Under Carr's command, the English plundered "what belonged to the Quaking colony of Plockhoy to a very naile."[22] Carr sold surviving members of Zwaanendael to various English colonial settlements as slaves. Plockhoy and his wife escaped that cruel fate, but they hid among Dutch families in the area for the next thirty years in fear for their lives.[23]

Not far from the site of the Plockhoy colony in present-day Cecil County, Maryland, a longer-lasting community sprung out of a similar vision for a communalist society. Jean de Labadie, a gifted religious leader born to an aristocratic family in France during the early seventeenth century, believed that he had been chosen by God for a special mission on Earth. A Jesuit education turned the savant with large eyes and a mustachioed face into an elegant and forceful speaker who enchanted audiences. His talent for public speaking helps explain his ordination as a Jesuit priest after only two of the traditional four years of training.[24] Years later, Labadie became convinced that God wanted him to restructure the Catholic Church along the lines of the early apostolic churches. These local churches of the Roman world, essentially small, self-sustaining communes that constituted a kind of counter-empire within the empire, were "founded upon charity rather than force" and gave expression to "a radically different understanding of society and property."[25]

Although Labadie continued to affirm Catholic views of monasticism, confession, and mystical communion with God, he converted to the Reform faith in 1650 and became pastor and professor of theology at Montauban in Geneva and later at Middelburg.[26] He worked to establish a true church within the Reformed Church for those who had experienced rebirth and wanted to live a Christ-like life. His booklet *Manual of Piety* (1668) outlined the marks of that awakening: humility, self-knowledge, disdain for the world, eradication of lust, intense devotion to God, mystical union, and child-like simplicity.[27] In Middelburg, Labadie met with reborn believers in their homes and studied scripture with them in practical and accessible ways that encouraged participants to raise questions, explore new ideas, and voice objections in the spirit of edification. He encouraged a communal study method that became one of the distinguishing features of "Labadism," but these innovations alienated him from other Reformed pastors and raised suspicions of separatism and sectarianism.

Asked to leave Middelburg, Labadie traveled to Amsterdam and founded a religious house community. As he began to attract wealthy and influential converts, members of the Reformed clergy worried Labadie might "win over the best Christians" and strip their churches "of their pearls."[28] Alarmed, Amsterdam ministers petitioned the burgomasters to silence Labadie, and the authorities responded by issuing an edict forbidding anyone not already a member of his household from attending his services—thus prohibiting him from preaching to the public.[29] Labadie and approximately fifty of his followers left Amsterdam to establish a house community in Herford, Germany. They moved next to Altona, Denmark, where Labadie died in 1674, apparently satisfied that the one true church had been founded and his life mission accomplished. "Nothing," he admitted toward the end, "remains for me to do except go to my God."[30]

Under the leadership of Pierre Yvon, Labadism became associated with mysticism, enthusiasm, separatism, chiliasm (millennialism), and ascetic withdrawal from the world.[31] Yvon returned the Labadists to Wieuwerd in Friesland, where the sect expanded so vigorously that a policy evolved for the founding of "daughter" churches to relieve overcrowding at the central colony. They attempted to settle coastal Surinam in South America, a Dutch possession, but that venture failed due to malaria and unfavorable agricultural conditions.[32] Undeterred, the Labadists sent two agents to North America to find a suitable location for a new settlement. The pair secured a title for 3,750 acres of land at the head of the Chesapeake Bay, traveled back to Friesland with the deed, and returned to America in 1683 with other settlers to take control of the site.[33]

The sprawling Bohemia Manor estate, from which the Labadie tract was parceled, belonged to explorer and merchant Augustine Herman, and it was a "noble piece of land" with thick forests of black walnut and chestnut trees.[34] Today it remains largely unspoiled by development, and walking the grounds, one is struck by the low, undulating hills, the beauty of the nearby Bohemia River, the fecundity of the vineyards, and the dark redness of the dirt roads that still crisscross the property. Regrettably, few written details survive regarding the layout of the Labadist community, so we must imagine a thriving group of one to two hundred adherents living communally on the scenic shores of the Bohemia River. Most likely, the community's first leader, Peter Sluyter, lived apart from the others with his wife on the third neck of the Labadie Tract, while the brothers and sisters occupied a large building (called the Great House) and some adjoining structures. Like the householders at Ephrata, married settlers lived in their own homes but worshipped with the congregation.[35]

In an effort to translate primitive Christianity into a blueprint for a new society, the Labadists lived simply, spurned hierarchy and authority, and viewed themselves as members of one extended family. They ate meals together, held "temporal goods" in common, and prohibited marriages between believers and nonbelievers.[36] Dress was plain, rooms were unheated, food was consumed in silence, and, even though absolute gender equality was observed, men and women lived separately.[37] New Bohemia was a communal affair from its very inception; newcomers donated their property to the group and forfeited it when they left. New Bohemians initially refused to plant tobacco or employ slaves, as was the common practice in the southern colonies, but in later years they stooped to growing that plant using slave labor.[38] The mother colony at Friesland had provided the Labadists at New

FIGURE 1. Bohemia River landing

Bohemia a social template for economic communalism, but hewing a community out of uncultivated woodlands of the New World required more people and greater coordination.

In 1685, a second party of colonists arrived to help complete a house and farm building and to clear a cemetery ground. Arduous conditions altered the type of work Ladadists performed (more carpentry than masonry), the animals they raised (cattle rather than sheep), and the plants they grew (hemp, flax, corn, and eventually tobacco).[39] Seven years later, when Labadists in Friesland suspended the requirement regarding Community of Goods, this move opened the way for private ownership of property at New Bohemia. Members of the Maryland colony held out for six years, but they eventually apportioned land to individuals, though fixed assets remained shared property. The wharf at nearby Bohemia Landing—the very spot where Johannes Kelpius disembarked in 1694 with a devoted band of followers before traveling north to Wissahickon—grew into an important regional trade route, particularly for liquor. In time, settlers of all sorts (Anglicans, Mennonites, Jesuits, and Native Americans) received land grants in the area.

The Labadists, seated on a prime tract, grew wealthy enough to purchase a schooner-like ship for transporting their produce to market and to act in prominent social positions, such as justices of the peace.[40] The population of New Bohemia peaked at about 125 people. In 1721, Conrad Beissel visited New Bohemia with a Mennonite friend who shared his religious sensibilities and happened to have relatives at the nearby manor. Beissel, still living as a recluse in Conestoga, would not establish Ephrata for another eleven years, but during his visit he was shown manuscripts by Labadie and other important figures in the movement. Although impressed, Beissel remained perplexed at the Labadist retreat from the rule about Community of Goods, and he departed with a feeling that New Bohemia was in decline. That hunch proved correct, for a spate of deaths among elders within months of each other deprived New Bohemians of effective leadership. Most of the settlers dispersed into local communities, so that according to one contemporary account "nothing of them remained of a religious community in that shape" by 1727.[41] Even so, the Labadists left behind a rich heritage in the typography of the Labadie Tract at Bohemia Manor, and they lent their name to a strain of separatist and pietistic spirituality that found sympathizers among members of established churches in the colonies.

*　*　*

Conrad Beissel's father, a member of the local baker's guild, succumbed to alcoholism and died penniless before Conrad was born. His mother, whom he remembered as a "pious and devout woman," fought to sustain the family with the help of her oldest sons, but that struggle wore her down.[42] Passed among impoverished elder siblings following her death, Beissel defied adversity and managed to achieve a notable record at the local parish school, where he developed the ability to concentrate intently for extended periods of time and to learn without direct instruction. As an adolescent, Beissel apprenticed to an Eberbach baker who taught him to play the violin. The precocious young man regularly played at local country dances and in time became an attractive showman who "drew others to him, particularly women." That charisma never abandoned him, though its impact on the sensibilities of several celibate sisters brought unwelcome attention to his experimental community at Ephrata.[43]

The only surviving image of Beissel—a silhouette in profile with his head raised, eyes lowered, and white collar loosely buttoned—reveals a mixture of confidence and humility many people found appealing. When those relatively carefree days as apprentice and popular musician came to an end, Beissel fell under the spell of the Pietist movement. By that time, Lutheranism had lost much of its original zeal, and its rigid doctrinalism opened the way for the Pietism of Philipp Jakob Spener—who in *Pious Wishes* (1675) had championed the formation of small, semi-independent lay groups within the church called conventicles. Pietists emphasized study of the Bible and Early Christianity, advocated the replacement of theological rhetoric with inner devotion, and encouraged the formation of a universal priesthood to break down church hierarchies and engage the laity. Outlawed by church and state, most of those devout little groups became secret (at least from authorities)— much like some primitive Christian communions under Roman rule.

The Pietist movement spread rapidly in the wake of the liberating influence of the Swiss Reformed Church, the rise of Puritanism in seventeenth-century England and Scotland, and the Cromwellian revolution.[44] After being promoted to the rank of journeyman by the bakers at the end of his guild apprenticeship in Eberbach, Beissel moved to Strasbourg where he encountered the mystical, occult, and millennialist underground of European Christianity, including the Inspirationalists who sought religious ecstasy, exaltation, and prophecy (possession by the Holy Spirit, visionary states of consciousness, glossolalia, and miracle making).[45] Beissel journeyed on to Heidelberg where a new bread recipe made him the city's most popular baker at the age of twenty-five. Two years later, while worshiping with a local Pietist group, Beissel underwent a profound spiritual conversion. He embraced radical millennialist views and developed a separatist inclination. When he abandoned regular church service and forsook more worldly acquaintances, Beissel fell afoul of local authorities. He alienated fellow guild members as their treasurer after he withheld funds for lavish banquets and made moral criticisms of their excesses.

Due to guild machinations, the ecclesiastical court summoned Beissel to answer questions regarding his faith and alleged membership in a secret religious society. Found guilty, stripped of his status as a journeyman, and banished from the Palatinate for refusing to reveal anything of his associations in the religious underground, Beissel eked out a precarious existence as a wandering peddler bereft of citizenship and the means of earning a living. He learned to spin wool, but malnourishment compounded by excessive fasting and penitence led him to develop consumption. In that compromised condition, he traversed the countryside visiting the homes of visionaries and Inspirationalists generally described as the Awakened—an antichurch movement of individualistic enthusiasts.[46] His deepening spirituality led him to yearn for solitude, to observe strict religious discipline as a renunciate, and to consider migrating to the North American colony of Pennsylvania.

When King Charles II of England granted William Penn a charter for Pennsylvania in 1681 (to cancel a large debt owed to the estate of Penn's father), the thirty-seven-year-old Penn, a Quaker convert and religious reformer, extended invitations to German and Dutch dissenters to settle this land. He intended to make the territory into an ideal Christian commonwealth, a "holy experiment" and a safe haven for all nonconformist sects.[47] Just four years later, as many as eight thousand people lived in Pennsylvania, most of them English, Welsh, and Irish Quakers who settled in and around Philadelphia. The German Quaker and Mennonite families who established Germantown in 1683 divided 6,000 acres into spacious lots fronting the road to Philadelphia. The first charter for Germantown, ratified in 1691, granted to corporate members the sole right of franchise, oversight of government, and the power to admit new members—and it authorized a self-appointed town council to make laws, levy fines, and try cases. Because the Germantown charter permitted, in effect, a government within a government, it was an unusual political experiment designed as a community in the image of the apostolic church.[48]

To escape indigence and political chaos in the Palatinate, Conrad Beissel emigrated to Pennsylvania in 1720. Upon arrival, he headed directly for Germantown with the aim of joining a group of forty celibate Pietistic Lutherans, who called themselves the "Contented of the God-loving Soul" (later the "Society of the Woman of the Wilderness") and settled an area known as The Ridge near Wissahickon Creek in 1694. Led by Pietist Johannes Kelpius, a contemplative mystic and composer of religious poems set to music, the Contented brethren cleared land for a garden, an orchard, an herbarium, and common living quarters. They constructed a large log structure on the high point of the ridge that included a watchtower and observatory to detect heavenly signs of the approaching millennium, and they frequently retreated to nearby caves to meditate.[49] By the time of his arrival, Beissel found that the Contented brethren had essentially disbanded, and their former members had been absorbed into Pennsylvanian culture as German emigration increased and townships spread.[50]

To survive, Beissel apprenticed himself to a weaver in Germantown for a year while he preached to reinvigorate the spiritual sensibilities of his compatriots, whom he believed had too quickly discarded the radical religious

beliefs that had led them to the New World. Determined to live a more dis-
ciplined spiritual life, Beissel trekked 70 miles west into Conestoga—a
sparsely populated area settled by Swiss and German Mennonites and other
Protestants. He built a house there with Jacob Stuntz and George Steifel—
and lived as an ascetic. He continued to preach a gospel of charity and simplicity, and his graceful demeanor and charisma attracted locals to his homi-
lies. After his housemate Jacob Stuntz sold the hut to recoup Beissel's
transatlantic fare, Beissel, once again homeless and penniless, vowed never
to borrow money again on God's account.[51] More determined than ever to
practice contemplation in seclusion, he made a lonely "pilgrimage to silent
eternity" when he migrated to Swede's Spring in 1723.[52]

The solitude, which he found blessed, did not endure, for religious seekers sought Beissel out. After several of them requested permission to join
Beissel, a small congregation took shape around the former baker apprentice from Eberbach. To those members, Beissel taught that celibacy was superior to marriage, observed a Saturday Sabbath, and gained a reputation as a
prayerful, loving man. His flock of devotees grew so quickly that in 1725 members built a new cabin for him closer to their own domiciles. When two
young and attractive women (Maria and Anna Eicher) left home to join the
group, drawn by Beissel's charisma, scandalous gossip spread throughout the
region that prompted the construction of a cabin on Mill Creek for the two
future members of the sisterhood. Soon, additional squatters' cabins, built
by members of Beissel's growing congregation appeared between Mill Creek
and Conestoga. Local wives left their husbands to be "rebaptized into virgin-
ity," and male "solitaries" likewise joined and practiced celibacy.[53] Beissel's
insistence on orthodox morality, mystical exhilaration, avoidance of "unclean"
foods, the Pauline doctrine of purity, and the spiritual necessity of poverty
proved too onerous a program for many devotees.[54] Beissel organized those
who continued to worship with him into three "orders" (married Householders, Spiritual Virgins, and the Brotherhood of Angels)—a triunal structure that persisted for two-thirds of a century at Ephrata.[55]

Surprising everyone, Beissel resigned as leader of the solitaries at Swede's
Spring in February 1732 and followed a Native American trail 8 miles north
into the unbroken forest to a crude cabin built alongside Cocalico Creek.
Once there, he took renewed delight in the solitude that had previously
eluded him, and he penned inspired hymn-poems. The coppery-brown
waters of the languorous Cocalico, and its canopy of dense foliage reaching

upward from the stony river banks, appealed to Beissel's mystical sensibilities. In one praise-poem, he wrote: "O blessed solitary life, / Where all creation silence keeps!"[56] That restive and reflective mode of being did not endure long either, for disciples yearning for his companionship followed him further into the Pennsylvania wilderness. As they increased in number, Beissel found himself at the fulcrum of a new society in need of spiritual leadership. Those who joined the new settlement referred to it as Camp of the Solitary, deliberately evoking the experiment at Swede's Spring, though it became known as Ephrata—a pre-Israelite name for Bethlehem.

Building at Ephrata Cloister commenced in the early 1730s and continued through the 1740s. Ephratans felled timber and quarried stone to construct buildings that evoked a Germanic style of architecture characterized by steep shingled roofs, brick chimneys, and dormer windows. Often built according to guidelines found in scripture, structures at Ephrata could reach three to four stories in height "with walls one foot thick, and no nails or iron used."[57] They soon added a bakery; a barn; a stable; a meeting house for worship; separate dormitories for men and women; and grist, lumber, and linseed oil mills. Bethania, a dormitory cum meeting house for the celibate brotherhood, measured 72 by 36 feet (numbers evoking the era of Philadelphian love). Its closest wall to Saron, the Sister's house, was 300 feet away—the number of years in the "Enochian age."[58] Completed in 1743, Saron had three floors and an attic; housed thirty-six sisters; and, like Bethania, included a kitchen, a room for communal meals, about a dozen sleeping chambers, and two common workrooms. The hand-cut shingle roof, stone foundation, and timber siding of Saron complemented its white plastered walls and tidy rooms sparsely furnished with items of everyday use: tables with folding leaves, four-legged chairs with high backs and no armrests, sinks carved from large fieldstones, and utensils for cooking hung neatly near the chimneys.

At its height, Ephrata Cloister included around fifty buildings on a 250-acre site. Surviving structures include the Conrad Beissel House, Sal Meeting House, Physician's House, Weaver's House, Carpenter's House, Bake House, and Printing Office. The Bake House and kitchen produced bread, the community's staple fare, and it served as a distribution point for food and clothing donated to needy residents in the surrounding area. The house that Beissel built in the late 1740s featured a simple, yet elegant, study with wide plank hardwood floors and a small desk where Beissel read and wrote. Wooden benches around the parameters of the room turned his study into

FIGURE 2. Sisters' House and Meetinghouse at Ephrata

a cozy space to welcome guests and to hold small meetings. Through a low doorway off to the right was a tiny bedroom for Beissel with a hardwood cot and a pine block for a pillow. The low doorways found in most Ephrata buildings reinforced the importance of cultivating humility, and they reminded the brothers and sisters of the narrowness of the gateway leading to salvation. Although the Ephratans expended little effort to make Beissel's home, or those of other community members, supremely comfortable, the cloister reflected the sensibilities of artistically and religiously minded people.

Initially, anyone could join Ephrata, but after 1734 Beissel required new recruits to serve a year of probation, during which inspectors scrutinized their behavior for loud talking, dawdling, and absenteeism from morning and midnight meetings.[59] In the 1740s and 1750s, the community at Ephrata included celibate brothers and sisters, as well as married householders—couples who lived on nearby farms, raised children, worshipped with Beissel and the Solitary order, and supported the vision of holiness that the monks put into practice.[60] The celibates held regular worship services and love feasts that included ritual feet washing, supper, and communion.[61] During the Saturday Sabbath, householders and celibates gathered in one of the meeting houses, and Beissel presided over a simple service lasting one to two hours

FIGURE 3. Bake House (left) and Meetinghouse (right) at Ephrata

that included readings from scripture, choir music, public testimonials, and a sermon.[62] Male and female celibates donned long white robes and hooded scapulars that covered their bodies from head to toe. Their clothing reflected a vow of poverty, and it inhibited the arousal of sexual desire in the celibate community.[63] In truth, Beissel's insistence on covering the body was an added precaution, for the daily work and worship schedule of the celibates and their austere diets combined to weaken their bodies to the point that the sexual urges of the better nourished did not assail them.

The sisters, for instance, adhered to a daily routine that began at 5 A.M. with an hour of prayer. They alternated periods of contemplation and work (tending gardens, spinning wool and flax yarn, sewing clothes, making candles, and weaving baskets) for the remainder of the day.[64] The brothers grew grain and flax, cleared land and tended orchards, raised animals, and worked in the community mills. Members set aside the 6 P.M. hour for the only meal of the day—a vegetarian repast consisting of bread, fruit, vegetables, and water. Exceptions to that meager diet were granted to Ephratans requiring more nutrition or suffering from poor health, but contemporary accounts suggest a population of exceedingly gaunt individuals. Following that single meal, the celibates studied for two more hours, rested for three, and arose at midnight

FIGURE 4. Stairs at Ephrata

for a two-hour worship service at the Saal that included music, prayer, and scriptural readings. They returned to their beds to rest from 2 A.M. to 5 A.M.[65]

A hermit and renunciate by nature, Conrad Beissel never imagined that the Ephrata community would become wealthy. It did quickly become self-sufficient in terms of food, clothing, and other necessities—so much so that Beissel donated excess grain and flour and established branch monasteries at Germantown and Snow Hill in Franklin County.[66] A man of few possessions, Beissel practiced charity to an extent that sometimes alienated others—for example when he made an "offering" to the remaining hermits of Wissahickon, while his own fledgling group was hard-pressed.[67] Perhaps because Beissel kept no accounts of Ephrata's resources, he tended to be more charitable toward others than to members of his own community, and he failed to enforce the principle of common property with any uniformity.[68] Despite the fact that cloister members consigned all property to Beissel, Ephrata remained a communist venture in which members contributed toward the common good.

When Beissel put the Eckerlin brothers in charge of a shared economy, the last vestiges of privately owned property disappeared, and a fully communal order emerged. The entrepreneurial-minded Eckerlins (Israel, Samuel, and Emanuel) organized the sale of lumber to nearby towns; constructed a paper mill and a bookbinding shop; and opened weaving and pottery workshops, a tannery, and a shoe shop.[69] Under the Eckerlin brothers' charge, Ephrata produced quality paper and the only high-grade cardboard stock in the colonies. Its tannery made superb leathers that supplied large shoe-making and book-binding operations. Its sawmill fashioned logs for community and local building projects. Its fulling mill prepared wool for weaving, and its oil mill made much of the printer's ink used in the province.[70] The sisters contributed by cultivating farm and garden produce, making clothes, managing a free school, producing sulfur matches and household remedies, and sometimes doing heavy work in the mills. Due to the frugality and simplicity of members' lifestyles and the range of their business interests, the community grew wealthy as Ephrata's products gained in repute across the region.

Ephratans engaged in a variety of artistic enterprises to support the community. On their printing press, purchased from Frankfurt in 1743, the celibate brothers published carefully crafted books (such as the German edition of *Martyrs Mirror* in 1748)—in addition to poems, mystical texts, hymns, and music.[71] The sisters illuminated manuscripts, book plates, and massive wall charts. Hymnals written in the Frakturschriften ("broken" calligraphy) style of lettering became an Ephrata specialty.[72] Music also played an essential role in the spiritual lives of community members. When Beissel (who set his and others' words to music in more than a thousand pieces) directed the a cappella choirs after 1740, rehearsals lasted up to four hours and ended with a procession through the meadow. He developed an unusual type of music involving four-part, six-part, and sometimes seven-part harmonies sung mostly by the sisters, that consisted of simple, long notes combined to suggest the sound of angels.[73]

As the American colonies moved toward a capitalist free-enterprise system, the Ephratans continued to reject the accumulation of wealth for its own sake, and they eschewed economic competition.[74] Cloister leaders aimed foremost to prepare congregants for mystical union with God, but the financial success of community businesses challenged the monastic values upon which it was founded. A growing treasury contradicted a professed belief in intentional poverty and simplicity as vehicles for spiritual awakening. Still worse, in the Eckerlin economy, cloister members came under direct pressure to produce more, which meant working longer hours at grueling tasks under the watch of foremen. Soon, little time and energy remained for the religious experience and mystical speculation that had been the original intention of the community.[75] Instead, the celibates became part of an industrial and market-oriented powerhouse that at its peak "may have been the single most comprehensive economic-industrial system in the colonies prior to the Revolution."[76]

Questions soon arose regarding the rightful division of communal resources, and some Ephratans began to interrogate the need for living so austerely given their economic prosperity. Others began to assail Beissel's leadership, and the most salient challenge came from Israel Eckerlin, the Prior of the Brotherhood. Israel procured horses to transport Ephrata commodities to market despite Beissel's avowed rejection of "animal slavery," and he and his brothers plotted to appropriate the resources of householders by luring them into the communal economy. The Eckerlins also dedicated Hebron House, where the married couples were to reside separately in propertyless chastity, with ceremony unbecoming of a semimonastic community (including a mass divorce proclamation and rebaptism in the frigid waters of the Cocalico). The mass divorce irked local civil authorities, and they started to investigate the economic behemoth in their midst. The Eckerlins' Hebron House ploy fell apart when a male community member relayed to the state governor false accounts against Beissel of infanticide from a deranged female admirer (Anna Eicher). Once acquitted of wrongdoing, Beissel returned all contributions to the common assets from the inducted householders.[77]

But the Eckerlins were not repentant: they again attempted to commandeer the spiritual leadership of the community when Beissel fell ill. The confrontation that followed led to the expulsion of the brothers from Ephrata in 1745 and the abandonment of the Eckerlin economy. Following their departure, hundreds of fruit trees planted by the celibates were uprooted in an act of vandalism. A serious food shortage ensued that winter, compounded by the abandonment of the Eckerlin economy, but the householders supplied emergency sustenance to the brothers and sisters. Likewise, in December 1747, a fire destroyed their gristmill and grain stores and spread to the fulling and oil mills. Yet the householders helped the celibates to rebuild the grist mill in a matter of months.[78] The paper mill continued at full production, and the community returned to subsistence and self-reliance in a year or so. The population of Ephrata peaked between 1745 and 1755 at more than three hundred residents (including celibates and householders). New converts arrived from Germany, including several of Beissel's relatives.[79] Such a resurgence suggests that the decline of Ephrata owes more to the death of Beissel in 1768 than to the departure of the Eckerlins in 1745. In fact, the Seven Years' War (1756–1763) slowed immigration to the region, and the fizzling out of a youth revival that was to bring enthusiastic new members proved more destabilizing to the community.

As he fought off continual Eckerlin claims to community land, Beissel fell into a cycle of illness and recovery that made him increasingly inaccessible, even to close associates. Beissel became more reclusive, fasted frequently, and practiced severe self-flagellation.[80] He withdrew from important leadership positions in the community, and as he did so, members of the congregation drifted away. As his death approached, he transferred his remaining administrative duties to Peter Miller, a highly educated and accomplished man who at the request of Thomas Jefferson translated the Declaration of Independence into seven languages.[81] As the end approached, Beissel "tried to make peace with those who had rejected or resented him and with those he himself had scorned or scolded."[82] A "living skeleton til his death," he departed the world attended by aging celibates.[83] He left a rich legacy that included

some of the most spiritually profound poetry of the colonial period; passed
on an integrated view of the arts to later generations; and demonstrated the
viability of living according to the Acts of the Apostles and the Synoptic Gos-
pels by sharing dwellings, owning all resources communally, and distributing support based on need.

After the War for Independence, Ephrata flowered artistically once more—
but American society and culture were changing rapidly. The opening of the
frontier encouraged a rugged form of individualism, and do-it-yourself free
enterprise quickly replaced older and gentler forms of agrarian cooperation
and community.[84] William Penn's "holy experiment" evaporated as the frontier stretched ever westward. Migration from the religious underground in
Europe slowed, and sons and grandsons of early American immigrants
thirsted after money more than salvation.[85] Germanic Pennsylvanians
became increasingly conservative and sought a gentle way of life on their fertile farms. With the passing of the last of the solitaries at Ephrata in 1813, the
householders—some of whom had cared for the aging celibates—gradually
appropriated cloister buildings and resources. Church members living on
cloister grounds fell into disagreement regarding the allocation of the site and
its artifacts. In 1934, a court revoked the incorporation charter for the Church
at Ephrata and placed the property under the care of a court-appointed
receiver—who sold the remaining 28 acres of the historic site to the Commonwealth of Pennsylvania in 1941.[86] The federal government designated the
entire site a National Historic Landmark in 1967, and the Ephrata Cloister
Associates now preserve attractively restored buildings from this once-
thriving religious commune.

1 ▸ REVOLUTION AND SOCIAL REFORMATION

ONE HUNDRED YEARS after the American colonies gained independence, writer and newspaper editor William Alfred Hinds visited Zoar, Ohio—a thriving intentional community organized by members of the Society of Separatists along an important corridor of the Ohio and Erie Canal. The Zoar commune had changed considerably after the death of its spiritual and economic leader Joseph Bimeler in 1853. Although the community was still economically vibrant, the Zoarites' commitment to the society's founding religious principles had waned. Hinds described immense fields of corn, wheat, oats, and other crops. He made note of 1,000 sheep; 85 cows grazing 200 acres of pasture; a new, two-story cattle barn containing 104 stalls; orchards and a community garden (designed after the seven-pointed star-shaped community seal and featuring triangular beds of petunias, geraniums, and dahlias).[1] Hinds found nothing noteworthy about Zoar's quaint German folk architecture, but a large two-story brick house built for Bimeler impressed him with its inviting balcony, cupola, and piazzas. By contrast, Constance Fenimore Woolson (great-niece of James Fenimore Cooper) was more discriminating in her appreciation of the village's aesthetic appeal. Writing for *Harper's Weekly*, she described a community that preserved a rustic Old-World charm in the rough-hewn wooden logs joined with mortar that formed the walls of its major structures.[2]

Perhaps more interested in the Zoarites than in their architecture, Hinds interviewed dozens of residents, most of whom came "from the common classes of Germany."[3] He found them exceedingly frank about the history of the community. One Zoar woman, a teacher for twenty-six years, explained to him the terms of the covenant through which 254 Zoarites worked collectively and shared resources. In return for their diligent labor, bread was distributed to members without limit—and beef, coffee, sugar, butter, and other staple foods were accorded to families based on their size.[4] She told him about the year of probation for new members, during which time newcomers received wages and retained their private property, and she highlighted the fact that Zoarites relinquished personal belongings forever upon admission to the community. As a result, the Zoar educator wryly observed that rich people seldom applied for membership, "and we are glad of it. We would rather take poor people, half naked though they may be, provided they have the right character." At the end of her conversation with Hinds, she expressed hope that Zoar beliefs would "spread all over the world," meaning that eventually everybody "would come into Communistic relations."[5] "In heaven there is only Communism," she mused, "and why should it not be our aim to prepare ourselves in this world for the society we are sure to enter there? If we can get rid of our willfulness and selfishness here, there is so much done for heaven."[6] That sensible line of reasoning notwithstanding, the Society of Separatists of Zoar formally disbanded in 1900 after eighty-seven years—unable to withstand the influx of settlers who surrounded them, or the advantages mechanization and industrialization offered to their secular business competitors.

The quintessentially American story of how the Zoarites built a communistic community worth an estimated $1 million before Joseph Bimeler's death involves escape from religious persecution in Europe and an arduous journey to a safe haven where their beliefs could be put into practice. It begins with the Reformation in sixteenth-century Germany, a time when many religious sects in the region opposed the Catholic Church. The Zoarites refused to accept the rituals of baptism, communion, and confirmation. They rejected social and religious ceremonies (including marriage) and removed their children from Lutheran clergy-run public schools.[7] Were that not enough to provoke outcry, they recognized no civil authority (believing all people equal in the eyes of God), did not swear oaths of allegiance, would not serve in the military (since murder was a sin), and left their taxes unpaid. These expressions of independence led to persecution, flogging, and imprisonment.[8]

Because they so stridently transgressed religious and civil norms, European authorities dealt harshly with them. Civil courts frequently charged sectarians with large fines that they could not pay and sometimes confiscated their homes. The first Separatist group to depart Germany for the United States followed George Rapp, a weaver and lay preacher from Württemberg, who led a band of religiously minded peasants and mechanics. The Rappites founded a Harmony Society in Pennsylvania (and later Indiana), where they owned common property and worked for the welfare of all members.[9] They opted for a communal way of life in a foreign land to escape what they perceived as the "vice and infidelity" of early nineteenth-century Germany.[10] By the time that Rapp sold New Harmony in Indiana to Welsh-born socialist and industrialist Robert Owen for $135,000, the Rappites had built it into a frontier trading town with successful core industries in agriculture, textile production, and manufacturing.

The Separatists had fled Germany and settled in the Ohio frontier at Zoar following the proclamations of Barbara Grüberman, beloved mother, mystic, and religious refugee from Switzerland, who had found sanctuary in Württemberg, home to several dissenting sects. Württembergians endured decades of violence and social unrest due to repeated invasions from France between 1688 and 1707, poor administration of the region by Duke Charles Eugene, and the negative economic consequences of the French Revolution and subsequent Napoleonic Wars. The Lutheran Church did little to help when congregants' farms and homes were destroyed and their men forcibly conscripted into the military. Many ordinary folk turned for spiritual guidance to mystics such as Grüberman, who proclaimed the imminent second coming of Christ.[11] A trance-medium and prophetess who entered visionary realms, Grüberman described a Dantesque afterworld to her followers where punishments were meted out in accordance with the severity of one's sins.[12]

Like Mother Ann Lee, the founder of the Shakers, Grüberman spent hours in alternate states of consciousness that her Separatist brethren understood as direct revelatory experiences from God. After Grüberman urged them to settle in the United States (though she was too infirm to accompany them),

her followers determined to make the voyage. Grüberman prophesized that
they would prosper in the New World if, for the length of a human life, they
banded together. She warned that should they abandon their religious devotion once safely ensconced, their community would fall into economic decline,
and strangers would purchase their property, or appropriate it through marriage. As apocryphal as her prophesy may sound to contemporary readers, the
fact that Zoar experienced more than eighty years of prosperity (a human lifetime), followed by a slow march toward dissolution that included appropriation of property, attests to Grüberman's powers of prognostication.[13]

In equal part frustrated by repeated harassment from German officials and
inspired by Grüberman's visions, the Separatists made secret arrangements
to emigrate during the winter of 1816. The following spring, after Grüberman's
death, three hundred Separatists gathered in Hamburg and embarked on a
ninety-two-day transatlantic voyage to the United States. Their destitution
meant making the crossing in steerage—the lower decks where cattle were
usually shipped. Many of the Separatists aboard the emigrant ship fell ill with
dysentery and other infectious diseases and were treated by the physician
Joseph Bimeler.[14] Had the group not received the support of the London
Quakers, who assisted the Separatists and notified their brethren in Philadelphia of the emigres' precarious situation, they might not have made it to
the Midwest.[15] Upon their arrival at port, the Philadelphia Quakers, who
sympathized with the pacifist views of the Separatists, paid about $18 per per-
son for their passage and provisioned them with food and shelter. The
Quakers also led Bimeler—who emerged as the leader of the group following the death of Grüberman—through the vast forests of Pennsylvania to a
5,500-acre plot secured on credit for the group in Tuscarawas County, Ohio.
The Philadelphia Quakers also loaned the Separatists money for the down
payment on the property and advanced them $5,000 to cover the costs of
moving.[16]

Although no portraits of Joseph Bimeler survive, because he was averse
to being reproduced in "living colors on the glowing canvas," one writer
describes him as an unprepossessing and physically imperfect person who
walked with difficulty.[17] One of Bimeler's eyes was larger and more prominent than the other, but through the force of personality and the morality of
his actions, he "held the Society together and impelled it to the zenith of its
career."[18] An astute businessman, effective doctor, and good land surveyor,
Bimeler traveled with a few men by wagon to Ohio in the fall of 1817 ahead

FIGURE 5. Bimeler Cabin (1817) at Zoar

of the rest of the group. Once arrived, the advance party surveyed their prop-erty, scouted the river from atop a wooded hill, and contemplated the seem-ingly endless expanse of forest surrounding them in every direction. Since they intended to build a refuge there from the sins of the world, they called it Zoar—the city to which Lot fled after the destruction of Sodom.[19] Bimeler and his team built a crude log hut for shelter and hired themselves out as field-workers to local farmers to generate funds. Yet they could not produce enough food to sustain themselves through the winter months of late 1817 and early 1818. Because the Zoarites lacked adequate supplies and were hin-dered by the accumulation of 4 feet of snow by February, they accepted gifts of flour and potatoes from their neighbors to avoid starvation.[20]

When spring arrived and the ground thawed, surviving Zoarites resumed construction of several homes situated around a town center, but the arrival of the Separatists who had remained behind in Philadelphia—women, children, and the infirm among them—created unforeseen inequality and deprivation in the community. The Separatists did not arrive with the inten-tion of living communally, but the addition of so many people unable to par-ticipate in agricultural production (or otherwise contribute to the econ-omy) compelled them to adopt the Community of Goods. They found support for their decision in Acts of the Apostles when disciples of Jesus, infused with the Holy Spirit, converted three thousand souls on the Day of Pentecost and established the true Church: "And all that believed were together, and had all things common; And sold their possessions and goods, and parted them to all men, as every man had need. And they, continuing daily with one accord in the temple, and breaking bread from house to house, did eat their meat with gladness and singleness of heart, praising God, and having favour with all the people. And the Lord added to the church daily such as should be saved" (2:44–47).

On April 15, 1819, 53 men and 104 women signed a constitutional agreement that abolished private property and put the resources of the Zoar community under the control of trustees. In the preamble to their articles of association, the Zoarites, based on "a true Christian love towards God and their fellow-men," pledged to "unite themselves according to the Christian apostolic sense" and to "renounce all and every right of ownership, of their present and future moveable and immovable property."[21] With the formal adoption of a Community of Goods, women gained voting privileges equal to those of men. Successive articles of agreement permitted the election of officers, and as their expertise in business evolved, the Zoarites succeeded in sustaining a commitment to communal living.

Even after that forthright embrace of Christian communitarianism and dedication to equality, forging a community out of the Ohio wilderness proved a formidable challenge. Zoarite survival remained so precarious between 1822 and 1830 that members practiced celibacy—not for religious reasons, but to improve their financial standing by avoiding the addition of new members to support through childbirth. Their fortunes improved significantly when they secured a contract to construct 7 miles of the Ohio and Erie Canalway through their land in 1833. With the $20,000 the state paid them for that grueling work, they paid off their mortgage and built a foundry, a water-powered milling factory, a stove factory, a dye house, a distillery and cedar press, and a tannery. In addition to operating two blast furnaces on the canal, they erected a general store, and across from it, a hotel with a ninety-guest capacity (at its grandest) that filled regularly with canal boat crews and their passengers.[22]

A cholera outbreak in 1834 claimed the lives of fifty-six residents and forced the Zoarites to hire outside wage laborers to keep their industries running. That decision proved economically sound: the following year the Zoarites

FIGURE 6. Zoar Hotel

produced all of their food (save coffee, tea, and rice), made most of their own clothing, fabricated the stoves that heated their buildings, crafted their own furniture, forged utensils in their tin shop, and built their farm machinery in their blacksmith shop. Zoar women worked side-by-side with the men in the fields and in shearing sheep. They controlled cultivation, harvest, and spinning of flax, though they also worked at more traditionally gendered tasks, such as home gardening, meal preparation, and candle and soap manufacturing.[23] With the assistance of the Quakers and their Tuscarawas neighbors, and due to their diligence and adherence to an ethic of altruism and mutual benefit, the Zoar commune thrived. By 1838, the Zoarites owned 12,000 acres of land and had an estimated net worth of $2 million.[24]

They lived communally in twenty-seven multifamily houses that contained centrally located rooms for sharing meals. Each house sent representatives to the communal storehouse, dairy, and bakery to pick up goods as needed. The Zoar Store sold supplies (including foodstuffs and other goods, such as bacon, coffee, potatoes, flour, eggs, butter, blankets, leather products, axes, and sawlogs) to farmers and wage laborers in the local area.[25] The Zoar Hotel, which still stands, became nationally renowned for clean well-appointed rooms, country hospitality, and delicious fresh foods from its farms. Restaurant staff at the hotel waited on millionaires and paupers alike—though those guests sat at opposite ends of the hostelry. Beggars ate the same wholesome fare as more celebrated guests, including President William McKinley and the state governor, though they worked for meals by filling empty coal hods.[26] When Zoar became accessible by train, coach, private conveyance, and canal after 1833, the focus of the hotel gradually shifted from serving a clientele of transient laborers and travelers to attracting tourists.

The industrious residents of Zoar worked at a variety of smaller collective enterprises too, many of them short-lived affairs, like their operation of a pottery and silk mill, but because they had "a mind to work," they prospered.[27] In the dairy, for instance, diligent milkmaids learned to balance wooden pails on their head, while carrying a milk bucket in each of their hands.[28] The Zoarites ran a butchery that distributed meat to the community twice a week, and they staffed a smokehouse, brickyards, a small print shop, a planing mill, a saddler shop, a foundry, and a bee house.[29] One Zoar visitor in the late 1890s remarked on the "trim and swept appearance" of the village, a tidiness that he attributed to a "characteristic of the German habit."[30] Twenty-first-century visitors to Zoar may explore placid tree-lined streets, surviving frame houses, and log outbuildings. Walking northward along Main Street through the diminutive village (seven blocks long and four blocks wide), the Zoar blacksmith shop on the right is distinguishable by its large bay doors for fabrication and machinery repair, and by three chimneys and an adjacent A-frame wagon shop with attic windows. In positioning the blacksmith shop on the outskirts of the village, Zoar residents kept the noise and heat associated with those work-intensive enterprises far from shops and residences.

Farther up Main Street stands #23 House—a two-story structure with five windows on the second floor and four on the first, white stucco walls, and a steep roof facing the street. Continuing northward, the Zoar Store comes into view with its narrow white columns and broad covered porch; directly across the street, the Zoar Hotel with its distinctive third-story widow's walk observatory. In the center of town stands the grand brick and sandstone house built in 1835 that became Bimeler's residence. Nearby stands Garden House, with two-story windows reaching from the ground floor to the roofline, and

FIGURE 7. Zoar Garden and Garden House

the redbrick Assembly House. At the end of Main Street, a thoroughfare still unspoiled by stoplights, stand the Bakery and Weaving House. Across from them, a Meeting House was constructed with handmade bricks and locally quarried stone and furnished with benches and pews suggestive of the sparse elegance found in Shaker woodworking.

Yet the most remarkable feature of Zoar culture was not entrepreneurial, architectural, or aesthetic—it was the community's democratic organization. The 1819 constitution established communal ownership of property and stipulated the election of three directors (who served three-year terms). In the Articles of Agreement of 1824, the community created an executive arbitrator position; formalized the process by which youths became full members; outlined an admission procedure for outsiders; and refused disgruntled or excommunicated members' demands for goods and services. The 1833 amendment of the constitution came in response to passage of an act by the Ohio legislature to incorporate the Society of the Separatists of Zoar as a "body politic."[31] It permitted the community to function as a corporation that could pass laws and hold property in common. The Separatists provided a

rationale for their decision "to renovate" the articles of "our hitherto existing Constitution" in its introduction:

> In order furthermore to secure to our consciences that satisfaction, proceed-
> ing from the faithful execution of those duties which the Christian religion
> demands, and to plant and establish the Spirit of Love as the bond of Peace and
> Unity for a permanent foundation of social order for ourselves and our poster-
> ity forever, we, therefore, seek and desire, in accordance to pure Christian princi-
> ples, to unite our various individual interests into one common stock and con-
> formably with the example of the Primitive Christians, all inequalities and
> distinctions of rank and fortune shall be abolished from amongst us, and, con-
> sequently, to live as brethren and sisters of one common family.[32]

The new constitution established democratic governance of the community
through elections, and it permitted a majority of two-thirds of voting members to amend the constitution. Zoar women held the same voting privileges
as men, and while they did not serve in administrative posts, they were not
expressly prohibited from doing so.[33]

In addition to electing directors who controlled property, managed community affairs, and provisioned members with adequate food, clothing, and
housing, residents after 1833 selected a five-member Standing Committee to
act as a court of appeals in cases that the directors could not resolve. Members elected an agent general to conduct business transactions with the outside world. This most important post Bimeler held until his death—a strong
indication of the faith that his followers had in his business acumen and integ-
rity.[34] When community members failed to live up to group expectations or
acted contrary to duty and good order, the society reserved the right to
excommunicate them. Members could depart at any time, but they forfeited
all claims to community property. In practice, however, departing Zoarites
could appeal to the Standing Committee and receive an indemnity based on
their contributions.[35] Over more than eight decades, the Separatists of Zoar
admitted only a few hundred new members, with marriage being the most
common means for outsiders and foreigners to gain admission. Applicants
usually brought with them property worth around $200, and they had to
share the community's religious beliefs.[36]

Zoar did not suffer the suspicions and accusations from the outside world
as Ephrata did, but neither did the Zoarites escape conflict and controversy.

Discontented members sometimes took their grievances to outside courts, though such complaints were generally lodged by expelled members. For example, the Standing Committee once charged John Goesele and his wife Anna Maria, operators of the canal tavern, with the misuse of community funds and tolerance of inappropriate behavior, including drunkenness. When Goesele and his wife continued to run the tavern after the Society shut it down, they were expelled from Zoar. In March 1845, the Goeseles, along with several other malcontents, filed suit in county court against the Separatists. They likened their former condition in the community to slaves who received just enough sustenance to survive, and they accused Bimeler of living luxuriously and maintaining his position by keeping the German-speaking Zoarites ignorant of their civil and political rights as Americans.[37] Based on kinship with John Goesele, a member of the original migration in 1817, they demanded an inventory of community property and payment of their share.

When the Seventh Circuit Court of the United States ruled in favor of the Separatist Society of Zoar, Goesele and his group appealed to the Supreme Court. The high court ruled that, according to the Zoar constitution, John Goesele had renounced individual ownership of property when he agreed to work for the community with others. Since individual rights of property merged into the general right of association, Goesele and the others held no individual rights to community property—and could transmit none to their heirs. "It is strange," remarked the Court, "that the complainants should ask a partition through their ancestor, when by the terms of his contract, he could have no divisible interest. They who now enjoy the property enjoy it under his express contract."[38] The high court also vindicated Bimeler, calling his decision to hold the land in trust "above reproach" and "wise and judicious, to secure the best interests of the association."[39] Although many people questioned his leadership and motives over the years, most reached the same conclusion as the Supreme Court, namely that Bimeler was an honest, hardworking man who served the community effectively as its physician, spiritual leader, and chief economic officer.

During the summer of 1853, at the age of 75, Bimeler fell ill and died. Good to his word, the society's property held in trust reverted to the community after his passing. Subsequent leaders did not measure up to Bimeler, and absent the charismatic founder, many young people left the community. The Civil War lured another fourteen youngsters away to fight in opposition to slavery, even though the society regularly paid the $200 fee that exempted men from the draft. Zoar manufacturing did not benefit financially from the war, since its small mills could not handle large government orders for cloth and yarn.[40] In any case, industrialization obviated the need for many of the community's small industries, including its shoe shop, woolen factory, and stove foundry. Although the railroad station established at Zoar in 1884 opened the community to the larger world, the expansion of the hotel permitted long-term stays by individuals who sometimes challenged central community beliefs. As Zoar prospered, younger members also grew lazy just at the moment older residents began to find arduous tasks more difficult to undertake (thus necessitating additional outside laborers).[41] Calls arose for the society's dissolution, and members voted to disband in 1898. That process would take a couple of years to complete, but in the end, 222 members split most of the land and property. Each claimant received $250 in cash and a share of the property worth $2,000.[42] Today, the Ohio Historical Society operates Historic Zoar Village as a tourist site.

* * *

The communitarianism practiced by Zoarites and other American experimentalists in intentional living represent concrete expressions—working models—of just and democratic ways of living in community. Many communitarians fully expected that once operational, their intentional societies would strike a balance between authoritarianism and freedom and create harmonious social relations that could be "infinitely reduplicated" across the land.[43] One such optimist, anarchist Josiah Warren, worked to establish unregulated communities that preserved individualism (too often diminished in cooperative societies) through a system of voluntary membership and labor exchange. Anticipating the dramatic levels of income inequality that characterized the Gilded Age decades later—and the soaring wealth inequity of our own time, Warren wrote in 1827, "Already have we in this country made alarming progress in the road to national ruin; and unless some effort be made to prevent the accumulation of wealth of the country, in the hands of a few, we instead of setting to the world an example of republican simplicity, of Peace and Liberty, shall soon add one more to the catalogue of nations, whom aristocracy has blasted, and whom inequality of wealth, has precipitated from a comparatively prosperous situation to the lowest grade of degradation and misery."[44] At the heart of Warren's plan to solve income inequality, while preserving the autonomy of the individual, was a system of labor exchange based on time—*that which, above all things, is most valuable.*

Born in 1798 to a distinguished Boston family that traced its American ancestry to English Dissenters on the Mayflower, Warren earned a reputation in his teens as a capable musician and multi-instrumentalist, and he played in several successful Boston bands. A short, thickset man with a large forehead, bushy hair, and scraggly sideburns that ran to his throat, Warren married at age twenty-one, moved his family to Cincinnati, led the local orchestra, and taught music. An inveterate tinkerer, Warren designed a lard-burning lamp; a speed press; a self-inking cylinder press fed from a continuous roll of printing paper; a process for making stereotype plates more easily and cheaply; and a remodeled structure for written music.[45] Warren patented the lamp and established a profitable factory in town to produce it. After hearing a lecture by Robert Owen, who briefly considered creating a socialist community in Cincinnati, Warren sold his factory after two years of operation and moved his family into the Welsh industrialist's New Harmony community in Indiana.[46]

Robert Owen first arose to world prominence as the owner and operator of a large mill in New Lanark, Scotland, that he organized according to cooperative and communitarian principles, rather than commercial ones. Owen sold goods in his store just above wholesale cost, rather than bilking workers with a truck system, which paid employees in store vouchers for overpriced goods instead of money. The young reformer also established quality schools for children, rather than employing them in the mills at New Lanark (as was common practice at the time), and he improved conditions for adult workers by instituting an eight-hour day. Determined to maximize efficiency and productivity, while creating a contented workforce, Owen met worker demands for lodging, implemented a "silent monitor" system to rate worker performance daily, and opened the Institution for the Formation of Character to address theft and alcoholism among employees.[47]

Owen strove to make New Lanark into a model-planned community that demonstrably benefited the poor and working classes. He redesigned the mills with a focus on health and safety, created footpaths and walking grounds on company property, and paid wages weekly (minus store purchases). When his workers bought on credit from the New Lanark store, they were issued one-shilling tokens or paper vouchers, known as "tickets for wages," in place of cash advances.[48] Proceeds from the store, estimated at £3,000 between 1818 and 1823, went entirely to fund New Lanark schools (including student fees, teacher wages, and equipment). In that way, the store contributed to the creation of a moral economic system that encouraged self-sufficiency, created proximity, and fostered interpersonal financial relations in the village.[49] Owen realized that in intentional agricultural and manufacturing villages of cooperation, surpluses (the result of manual labor that made factory owners wealthy) could be redirected to residents. He "freely permitted" every resident "to receive from the general store of the community whatever they may require. This, in practice," Owen argued, would "prove to be the greatest economy."[50] During the first two decades of the nineteenth century, curious people from throughout Europe and the United States flocked to see his "industrial paradise" firsthand.[51]

Inspired by the success of Shaker, Rappite, and Moravian movements in America, Owen began searching abroad for an appropriate location to launch the first cooperative community of his social movement. After an agent for George Rapp arrived in New Lanark in hopes of selling the Rappite communal township in Indiana, Owen set sail from Liverpool. In mid-December 1824, Owen inspected the ready-made town with orchards and 2,000 acres of land already under cultivation. He agreed to buy New Harmony a few weeks later. The 180 buildings on the property included dwellings and community homes for eight hundred people, two churches, four mills, numerous shops, a textile factory, a tanyard, distilleries, and a brewery.[52] Despite the advantageous start offered by a ready-made town, Owen's non-sectarian community was quickly bedeviled by class differences, ill-considered divisions of labor, the absence of meaningful admission criteria, and the lack of a single governing instrument beyond a few months. Additionally, there were repeated and prolonged absences by Owen. As a consequence, that experiment lasted only three years and nearly bankrupted Owen, yet the social movement that bore his name continued unabated and inspired an array of experimental villages across the nation from 1825 to 1863.

One feature of Owen's experiment at New Harmony was to introduce "labour notes," or "time money," based on hours worked as a medium of exchange. This innovation did little to improve community production, yet one other pioneer in communal living was deeply impressed. That man was Josiah Warren, who advanced different ideas.[53] A thoroughgoing individualist with communitarian sympathies, Warren grew disillusioned by the problems Owen encountered with freeloaders and unskilled workers. Warren felt that the Community of Goods at New Harmony diminished individual responsibility, and that the communal and conformist nature of that experi-

FIGURE 8. Rappite cabin (1814) at New Harmony

ment contributed to its speedy demise. Warren later observed "during the great experiments in New Harmony in 1825 and 1826, every thing went delightfully on, except pecuniary affairs! We should, no doubt, have succeeded but for property considerations. But then the experiments never would have been commenced but for property considerations. It was to annihilate social antagonism by a system of *common property*, that we undertook the experiments at all."[54] After the collapse of New Harmony, Warren drifted away from Owenite socialism and embarked on a series of social experimentations on his own. He pioneered innovations in simplified printing to publish the periodical *The Peaceful Revolutionist*, opened Time Stores, and established several intentional communities. His activities were "designed at once to reverse and to make good Owen's utopian vision."[55]

FIGURE 9. Beal House (ca. 1829) in the Owenite community at New Harmony

The economic philosophy that Warren developed over his lifetime, and enumerated in various ways, was based on the principles of individualism, self-sovereignty, the cost limit of price, and the labor note as the circulating medium.[56] One of the extreme individualists in a turbulent era of radical social reform (e.g., Ralph Waldo Emerson and Henry David Thoreau), Warren felt that laws and constitutions invited exploitation since they were open to interpretation by different people at different times and tended to deindividualize people by treating them en masse or in classes.[57] Believing that any form of collectivism impinged upon individual responsibility and personal liberty, he came to oppose all organizations founded on joint ownership and shared responsibility. Warren's radical notion of self-sovereignty called for people to exercise absolute control over their own bodies and their own actions—but at their own cost and responsibility.[58] The true spirit of self-sovereignty meant equal rights and natural opportunities for all, but it also implied noninterference in the affairs of others and obligation for one's own support (i.e., self-reliance). In this sense, Warren's doctrine of self-sovereignty represented a pure expression of American individualism that finds a correlate in the abolitionist movement and its rejection of claims to ownership of persons.[59] Although the ideal of self-sovereignty became something of a euphemism for license (particularly in regard to polyamory or "free love"), for Warren it was much more about personal responsibility and freedom from social institutions, customs, and public opinion that demanded conformity.

In regard to the cost limit of price, Warren argued that social harmony and cooperation could be achieved, without sacrificing individual sovereignty, by simply pricing goods and services at cost—and not what they would fetch on the open market.[60] He believed that the profit motive encouraged unnatural greed that devoured people and wrecked the economy by creating hoards of useless wealth that coexisted alongside grinding poverty, homelessness, food insecurity, and exploitation. Warren proposed a modified form of capitalism that removed profiteering as a motivation for conducting exchange and replaced it with self-interested aspiration for living a decent life of useful work and moderate ownership (even of capital) without greed.[61] The time-labor system that he invented used the labor note (introduced at New Harmony) as a circulating medium in the Time Stores to ensure that individuals retained control over their own labor by equitably exchanging it for goods and services. In his conception of the equitable return of labor for labor, we discover Warren's "socialism" (i.e., his way of addressing classism, income inequality, and wage slavery through the deletion of layers of inflated costs associated with commodities bought and sold in a capitalist economy).[62] Warren also put equitable commerce, the cooperative exchange of goods and services, at the heart of his social vision since it eliminated money along with profit.[63] Equitable commerce reduced economic life to its simplest terms and made social interactions related to commerce voluntary and self-evident.

Josiah Warren set forth on his first Time Store (an integral component of a new form of economic relationship based upon equitable exchange) located on the corner of Fifth and Elm in Cincinnati, after the collapse of New Harmony in 1827. That business establishment provided a nexus around which a small cooperative economy formed, and it provided an illustration of his labor theory of value in practice. Cincinnati emerged as a major city in the late 1820s because of its strategic location on the Ohio River, and Warren situated his Time Store directly across from the Cincinnati Chamber of Commerce and within easy walking distance of Union Central Station, Government Square, and the Hotel Netherland.

Customers who entered his Time Store found all commodities marked in simple plain figures representing their actual cost—plus a nominal percentage over it to cover freight, rent, and other expenses (usually about four cents on the dollar). Beyond that transparently calculated price, Warren charged customers for the time spent by the salesperson making each exchange, which was calculated using the large clock in the store. In payment for his services, a customer might issue Warren a labor note similar to this one: "Due to Josiah Warren, on demand, ten minutes of needle work—Mary Brown."[64] By agreeing to exchange his time for an equal amount of his customers' time, Warren avoided taking a traditional profit on anything. In "Plan of the Cincinnati Labour for Labour Store," published by the *Mechanics' Free Press* in 1828, Warren explained the rationale for the cooperative exchange of goods. He began by asking readers to consider the problems that established laws and customs regarding property had created in the world, namely "Ignorance, Want, Wretchedness, to the majority of mankind."[65] In European countries, where inequitable economic arrangements had persisted longest, Warren discovered "the labouring and useful" members of society "starving in the streets for want," while others "are rendered equally miserable from the anxieties of speculation and competition."[66]

In order to validate his assertion that time is "above all things most valuable," and therefore should constitute the real standard of economic value, Warren's Time Stores operated according to a "single and simple" principle: that "all exchanges of articles and personal services are made, so that he who employs five or ten hours of his time, in the service of another, received five or ten hours labour of the other in return."[67] Easily ascertainable labor rates per hour (regulated by the cost—in time—of learning a trade) ensured that customers knew the real cost of products and services purchased from farmers, doctors, merchants, and artisans. Anyone who wanted to sell a product or service that took, for example, ten hours to complete could take an item from the store *of equal production value*—or receive a Labour Note. For the sake of transparency, the shopkeeper exhibited "the bills of all of his purchasers to public view" so that the cost of every article might "be known to all."[68] Such a system prevented the needless waste of a vendor's time, did away with the frustrations of haggling, and promoted mutual respect and confidence in place of sharp dealing and distrust.

A Time Store magazine permitted the deposit of saleable products in demand by Warren and his outside vendors, and the shopkeeper posted an updated list of desired goods and services every morning. Once Warren accepted their products, sellers could take in exchange goods of equal value or one of Warren's labor notes (with value expressed in hours, not dollars).[69]

Those seeking employment might refer to the daily posting for job opportunities. Although there were other terms and conditions too tedious to enumerate, Time Stores ran smoothly in the absence of formal contracts between parties, and they provided small-scale models for spontaneous cooperation.[70] The first Time Store in Cincinnati broke even after two years in business, and Warren opened stores in other cities and towns to demonstrate that the voluntary exchange of labor could peaceably supplant the profit system. Several of those stores became economic centers in the intentional communities that Warren founded at Equity in Tuscarawas County, Utopia outside of Cincinnati, and Modern Times on Long Island in New York.

Equity never grew to include more than six families of approximately twenty-four people, for the location selected proved malarial and the community disbanded after less than two years.[71] Having learned from that mistake, Warren used the proceeds from his successful printing operations to purchase a village on the Ohio River in 1847, 30 miles outside of Cincinnati, from the Fourierist Clermont Phalanx. Warren parceled out lots in Utopia according to the cost limit of price to demonstrate that people given free access to natural resources could build their own houses, supply their own prime necessities, and attain comfort and prosperity without dependence on capitalists or other authorities—by simply exchanging their labor on equitable terms with each other using labor notes.[72] The population of Utopia grew over five years, and the community persisted after Warren returned to the East Coast in 1848.

Three years later, Warren began collaborating with sociologist Stephen Pearl Andrews on the Modern Times community situated on 700 to 800 acres on Long Island, then deemed wasteland (now Brentwood). Modeling self-reliance, Warren surveyed the property, manufactured bricks, and built the first house. It sold quickly, and from that modest beginning, the community reached one hundred residents within a decade.[73] Warren also helped establish important community institutions following his cost limit principle, including a theater, a gymnasium, a library, a school, and a fire company. The Time Store at Modern Times coordinated labor exchanges, and visitors paid for their food and lodgings with time money. An emphasis on sovereignty safeguarded the right of Modern Timers to live as they saw fit.[74] There were critics: John Humphrey Noyes, socialist author and founder of the Oneida Community, observed that Modern Times, "where all forms of social organization were scouted as unscientific, was the electric negative of New Harmony."[75]

Warren's insistence on cooperative individualism preserved liberty and autonomy at Modern Times, and it generated a society with few rules, no formal leadership, and virtually no crime.[76] However, when Fourierists Thomas and Mary Nichols arrived advocating free love, plural marriage, and sex education, Warren objected to their views on the grounds that they diverted attention from the central point of their experiment in cooperative living and pandered to media sensationalism. Warren feared that a reputation at Modern Times for free love—just one way, among many, that its denizens could order their relationships—would eclipse the emphasis on self-sovereignty.[77] His intuition proved correct. The gradual association of Modern Times with free love attracted all sorts of eccentrics, and the community became a center for American spiritualism and a sanctuary for nearly any form of quackery.[78] Warren exercised his own self-sovereignty and departed. Nonetheless, Modern Times inspired reformers around the world, including John Stuart Mill, who developed a theory of "self-sovereignty" on utilitarian grounds.[79] Ultimately, the Panic of 1857, as well as public opposition to the Modern Times commune based on rumors of its transgressive doctrines regarding diet and sexuality, undermined the community's manufacturing enterprises and contributed to its demise in the mid-1860s.

* * *

Contemporaneously with Josiah Warren's experiments with equitable commerce and individual sovereignty, the tireless pacifist and reformer Adin Ballou and his Christian socialists sought to "perfect *individuality*" in a religious community where members cooperated in a manner that preserved "unabridged individuality of mind, conscience, duty, and responsibility."[80] The joint-stock commune that Ballou and several other former Universalist ministers formed in 1842 sought a balance between the communalism advocated in the Sermon on the Mount and a more secular spirit of American individualism and self-reliance. Ballou's 1851 prospectus for the community stipulated no religious qualification for membership beyond a "simple declaration of faith in the religion of Jesus Christ" and acknowledgment of its moral obligations.[81] Otherwise, members remained "free, with mutual toleration, to follow their own highest conviction of truth and religious duty," knowing that the Practical Christianity adopted by the society was premised on "supreme love to God and man" and "the harmonization of just individual freedom with social co-operation."[82]

In *History of the Hopedale Community* (1897), Ballou observed that the decade of the 1840s stood out in American history for the general humanitarian spirit which pervaded it, and for the numerous efforts to "put away existing evils and better the condition of the masses of humankind."[83] Fired with a zeal in keeping with the times, Ballou and his Practical Christian Socialists signed a declaration that required them to refuse participation in all military and civic activities (including the vote), to abstain from using alcohol as an intoxicant, and to eschew gambling. Under no pretext could members "kill, assault, beat, torture, rob, oppress, defraud, corrupt, slander, revile, envy or hate any human being—*even my worst enemy*," and they vowed "never to aid, abet, or approve others in anything sinful."[84] Ballou initially limited membership in Fraternal Commune No. 1, later renamed Hopedale, to approximately one hundred persons who purchased joint stock shares at $50 each. After drafting the constitution, bylaws, and regulations, the Executive Council identified two estates for sale on Mill River in Milford, Massachusetts, adjacent to the Mendon town line.

Both sites, about a mile apart, boasted respectable mill privileges. One consisted of 258 acres of woodland, sprout land, and pastures that came with a two-story dwelling house (30 × 38 feet in ground measurement) in poor repair, a couple of barns, and various outbuildings.[85] Following the purchase of both properties for about $4,000, the Hopedale community commenced as "a practical attempt to realize in individual and social life a grand idea of fraternal unity, co-operation, harmony, peace, on the broad Christian basis of 'love to God and man.'"[86] The Practical Christians made the "honest acquisition of individual property" a basic tenet, but they limited that "property" to shares in the Christian joint-stock concern that would own the land, residential properties, and productive enterprises of the town. Since members could buy or sell shares (and receive profits proportionate to them), all shareholders had good reason to contribute their talents to the enterprise. Collective control of the property helped to ensure that individual efforts served the well-being of the entire community.

In April 1842, Ballou and his followers moved into the Old House on the former Jones property. The Hopedalians hired a surveyor to lay out village streets following the fashionable grid system. The main thoroughfares in Hopedale—Water, Main, and High streets—intersected six inspiringly named cross streets (Freedom, Chapel, Social, Union, Peace, and Hope).

Following an appeal for donations of money, cattle, books, and building materials, Hopedalians constructed houses on half-acre lots in the designated residential blocks between Chapel and Hope and Main and High streets, and they reserved the area along the river for industrial use due to their dependence on water power. By June, twenty-five adults and twenty children had settled into existing structures on site and began the daunting work of creating a Christian paradise. The farmers, artisans, and small-town businesspeople who settled in Hopedale put nearly 20 acres under cultivation, repaired decrepit buildings, and erected a multiuse structure that served as a dormitory, schoolroom, and printing office for the biweekly newspaper *Practical Christian*. They also began work on a two-story water-powered mechanic shop and planned a combined chapel and schoolhouse.[87]

After just six months of communal living, Ballou scrapped the idea of shared houses and also of collective work. He endorsed a provision allowing individual members to build their own houses and to run their own businesses, so long as their activities remained consistent with the principles of association and a clearly defined code of conduct animated by Christian love. In an effort to create the revenue-generating industries needed to sustain their miniature commonwealth, Ballou allotted monies to recruit skilled workers (including a carpenter and a shoemaker), to establish a hatting business, and to secure equipment for a blacksmith shop. In place of equal wages and living conditions, working members could now earn up to $1 per day—though dividends on joint stock were limited to 4 percent (with the remainder of any profits divided equally among workers or given to the community for collective use).[88]

In less than three years, the once dilapidated farms showed promise of becoming a prosperous industrial village that integrated three forms of property: individual possession of houses and personal items; joint stock control of the land and most productive assets; and a limit on wages and dividends to ensure that any surplus profit could be used "for the benefit of the needy, for education, and for the general good."[89] Labor and capital alike reaped just returns from their cooperative businesses, and members and their dependents benefited from cooperative living by being shielded from common economic adversities. This arrangement also denied "idlers and loafers" any right to wealth generated by productive members—allegedly without limiting individual freedom.[90] However, by opening the door to individual enterprise in 1842, Ballou inadvertently weakened the collective joint-stock businesses of the community. Nevertheless, in socializing property, Ballou found the means to subordinate private ownership to human needs and humane ends.[91]

At its apex in the early 1850s, Hopedale included nearly two hundred people residing in thirty-one houses, and they worked in shops and mills, various service buildings, and the printing office. Hopedalians graded and graveled streets and sidewalks, laid pipe to bring water to the village from a nearby spring, constructed a burial ground across the river, and built a wood-shed and icehouse for common use. Although they did not intend to become a farming community, additional land purchases guaranteed access to sufficient water power and doubled the size of their property. Along with farms, orchards, and gardens, they sustained a number of cottage industries, including lumber, boots and shoes, cabinetry, painting and glazing, printing, hardware, and the manufacture of temples for power looms. As a result of coordinated effort, the joint-stock enterprise at Hopedale, which began with less than $4,000 in assets, increased in value to over $60,000.[92] Men, women, and children contributed to that success, and even Ballou, their elected president, labored manually for the community (in addition to serving as minister, missionary, and editor of the *Practical Christian*).

Ballou's vision for the village remains evident in the placement of the town hall, commons, post office, library, churches, and schools along what today is Hopedale Street. The small, plain homes (measuring 25 × 21 or 30 × 14 feet) in which they lived were built using lumber from the community mill.[93] A village policy stipulated that homeowners grow fruit trees or shade trees on the frontage of their properties. With the nursery that sold trees, plants, roots, and garden seed, Hopedale at midcentury resembled a beautiful garden village. Ballou encouraged those aesthetic improvements, for he believed that the main task of the community was "to restore land and man to their Eden-like condition."[94] A genial and courteous fellow with bright eyes, a cleft chin, and receding hairline, Ballou described Hopedale in his writings as "a village of practical Christians, dwelling together by families in love and peace" who intended to ensure for themselves the "comforts of life by agricultural and mechanical industry" and to devote their moral, intellectual, and physical resources to the "general welfare of the human race."[95]

Ballou insisted on absolute equality among members, irrespective of sex, color, occupation, wealth, or rank. Seventeen women, for instance, served on important community committees responsible for relief, morality, and

FIGURE 10. Adin Ballou statue in Hopedale

education from 1850 to 1856. Hopedale resident Abby Price observed that in the "little commonwealth where I live all persons have equal rights in public deliberations," and she proudly noted, "here woman has no restrictions imposed because she is a woman, but has a fair chance of being all she is capable of doing."[96] A year later, the *Practical Christian* published Price's demand that the State of Massachusetts eliminate the word "female" from its voting requirements. All permanent residents served in the Hopedale Industrial Army, which formed in 1849 to make further physical improvements to community grounds. Army recruits planted a widow's garden, drained wetlands, laid out a playground, and dug a swimming hole for the children. Other communal ventures included the creation of a community savings bank (that paid 4 percent interest on deposits), the establishment of the Mutual Fire Insurance Company to guarantee against fire loss, and the collection of a small property tax to start a poverty relief fund.[97]

Treasurer Ebenezer Draper reported in 1852 that the miniature Christian republic ended the prior fiscal year with a profit, and he predicted few future deficits, lest fire or flood should visit. Ballou resigned as president that watershed year, believing the move would facilitate creation of a "system of social machinery" that could operate "under the superintendence of any fairly honest and intelligent management."[98] Draper succeeded Ballou as president of Hopedale, and matters went fairly well over the next few years with the regular dividends on the joint stock nearly earned. Like the Zoarites (and Ephratans before them), Hopedalians found it difficult to manage the rapid pace of the village's growth without hiring outside laborers. By 1853, only 76 of 223 Hopedale residents were Practical Christian Socialists.[99] Among those counted as nonmembers were a couple of dozen probationers and their children, but 52 hired laborers in Hopedale were essentially outsiders who were increasingly regarded as a threat to those who had sworn to abide by the dictates of Practical Christian morality. After Ballou relinquished the presidency, new members grew lax as religious enthusiasm waned. Draper instituted monthly meetings "for Christian discipline and improvement" to admonish and correct those bad habits and customs.[100]

After that revival of moral discipline, the community lost several members, though Hopedale continued to prosper. In 1854, Draper estimated that the value of communal and private property had risen from less than $12,000 to more than $90,000 over ten years. In the previous year alone, the community had added more than $17,000 to its assets, chiefly new houses, shop buildings, and equipment. Two years later, their holdings included nearly 600 acres of land, fifty houses, a cooperative grocery store, a sawmill and gristmill, and several water-powered mechanics shops.[101] Draper, an original founding member unquestionably dedicated to Practical Christianity, purchased most of the joint stock issued by the community to fund the

FIGURE 11. The Little Red Shop where Ebenezer Draper manufactured loom temples (foreground) and the Draper factory complex (background)

construction of a school and a barn and to make infrastructure improvements. In doing so, he made himself the town's largest stockholder and creditor. When Draper's brother George became a member, a fellow whom Ballou described as "a natural born man of the world" inclined toward money, his presence altered the trajectory of Hopedale forever. It did not take George long to learn that, due to nonresistant aversion to government, the Hopedale joint-stock had never been legally incorporated. With his brother heavily invested in Hopedale, George sensed an opportunity to acquire control of a successful village whose productive assets exceeded the value of its stock. As a developing town with a manufacturing base, water power, and skilled labor, it also held considerable potential as an industrial center.

George Draper publicly questioned Ballou's vision for an egalitarian society where the rewards for everyone's talents and contributions were low wages and dividends limited to 4 percent. Taking advantage of a financial crisis in the community in 1856 that generated a $12,000 deficit, George persuaded Ebenezer to join him in buying up joint stock at par and assuming the debts of the town, in exchange for its productive assets at a fair appraised value. Community members surrendered, rather than attempt to resist by voting to dissolve, and the Hopedale commune ceased to exist. The Drapers moved quickly to consolidate control of the town's manufacturing facilities by forming the Hopedale Machine Company and selling house lots and farm tracts ranging from 2 to 20 acres.[102] After the takeover, Ballou and his Christian Perfectionists became a small, marginalized enclave, but their emphasis on social amelioration persisted in the form of paternalism, a set of beliefs

FIGURE 12. Hopedale Community House (1923)

about business management widely held among mill owners in the Black-stone Valley during the nineteenth and twentieth centuries. That creed emphasized the need for owners of enterprise to provide for the economic, civic, spiritual, and recreational needs of their employees. Many buildings sponsored by the Drapers (including the large brick Hopedale Community House, the Unitarian Church, and the two-story brick and stone Town Hall) speak to that management practice.[103]

Although the Practical Christians survived as a diminished presence in Hopedale, gone were its savings bank, Industrial Army, Mutual Fire Insurance Company, and Council of Religion. Ballou confessed to being deeply pained by the way that events had unfolded, and he abandoned hope for the reinstatement of a cooperative association. The loss of these productive properties to the Drapers devastated the economic foundation of Practical Christianity, and Hopedale grew into a secular town known for pleasant homes on tree-lined streets.[104] The Civil War initially caused local businesses (including Hopedale textile and machine shops) to suffer, but during the final years of conflict it became clear that war had boosted the fortunes of the Draper family and further weakened those of the old community. Ebenezer sold his shares to his brother and departed for Boston, so that by the mid-1870s

George had acquired commanding interests in Hopedale Machine Company, Dutch Temple Company, and George Draper & Sons.[105]

Ballou continued to serve as pastor of the Hopedale parish, but only fourteen Practical Christians were left by 1876. Four years later, Ballou retired on a pension donated principally by the Draper family, but he continued to tout the formation of an ideal society based on Christian socialism in which wealthy community members voluntarily limited the personal use of their private property to their basic needs and reserved the surplus for the less fortunate. When Hopedale was incorporated as a town in 1886, the Drapers owned $150,000 in personal property and real estate. They practiced welfare capitalism (industrial paternalism, or what today we might call corporate social responsibility) and paid decent wages, provided worker housing at low rents, supported the town's school and library, and cut the workweek in their shops to fifty-five hours.[106] Draper family members also helped to fund a local hospital, a gymnasium, and a community center. The Drapers still own substantial parts of Hopedale, but the abandoned Draper factory complex near the river looms over the town like an old ghost. Adin Ballou outlived George and Ebenezer (who both succumbed to kidney disease) by three years. On his deathbed, he asked his daughter Abbie to read aloud passages from the Bible, as well as from his own account of the "profoundly impressive" vision that spiritualist Thomas Lake Harris (founder of the Brotherhood of the New Life) revealed to him in 1856.[107]

While never as important a thinker as Ralph Waldo Emerson, or so interesting a personality as Amos Bronson Alcott, Ballou was revered as much as those lights—and he remained a major force in New England during his lifetime.[108] Ballou always contended that economic competition (in any field of endeavor) resulted in class distinctions, gross inequalities, and unacceptable extremes of poverty and wealth—and thereby engendered discontent, ill-will, animosity, and sometimes violence. Indeed, no one "with any sense of human dignity could quarrel with Ballou's conception of a harmonious society," for he dreamed of freeing people from exploitative models of social organization.[109] In that endeavor, he won the admiration of many prominent people, including Robert Owen and the abolitionist Frederick Douglass. Ballou, a staunch advocate of suffrage, recounts in his autobiography an inspiring visit by Douglass to Hopedale. According to Ballou, Douglass stayed for several days and helped "to break into floating fragments much of the proslavery ice of Milford and vicinity."[110] When Owen returned to the United

States in 1845, nearly twenty years after the collapse of New Harmony, he spent two days at Hopedale and "won much admiration for his character but not for his cause."[111]

In *History of American Socialisms* (1869), John Humphrey Noyes asserted that had Americans not been so preoccupied with utopian importations from England and France in the years leading up to the Civil War, Ballou's scheme would have commanded "as much attention as Fourier's and a great deal more than Owen's. The fact of practical failure," Noyes added, "is nothing against him in the comparison, as it is common to all of them." Noyes, the leader of an influential commune of free-love Perfectionists at Oneida in New York, concluded that should he ever again attempt community building "by paper program, we should use Adin Ballou's scheme in preference to anything we have been able to find in the lucubrations of Fourier and Owen."[112] Ballou's work at Hopedale also encouraged John Anderson Collins to found a community in Skaneateles, New York, following a disagreement with the Hopedale founder over the impact of environment on personal and social amelioration.

*   *   *

Of the fifty-two utopian communities founded in the United States in the 1840s, ten were situated in New York.[113] When Frederick Douglass arrived in Syracuse during the summer of 1843 to promote abolition, he faced two major challenges: finding a place to hold meetings and working with the abolitionist agent John Anderson Collins. The Massachusetts Anti-Slavery Society had sent Collins to assist Douglass in organizing One Hundred Conventions to advance the abolitionist cause and to increase society membership. When Collins failed to secure a proper venue (so unpopular was their cause), Douglass delivered a historic address at Fayette Park that began in the morning with a handful of listeners and grew throughout the day to around five hundred souls. By evening, an abandoned Congregational chapel on East Genesee Street became available to the forceful speaker, and there Douglass engaged impromptu audiences over the next three days.

In his speeches, Anderson glossed over emancipation and chose to rail instead against individual property, to advocate utopian socialism, and to promote his own communalist project in the hamlet of Mottville near Skaneateles. Perturbed that Collins used those speaking opportunities to advance another agenda, Douglass wrote to his superiors at the Boston office of the Anti-Slavery Society to inform them that Collins took little part in the convention at Syracuse and used the meetings as "a mere stepping stone to his own private theory of the right of property holding."[114] The celebrated social reformer threatened to resign. In the end, however, Collins chose to quit, refusing any salary for his work during the year. That decision seemed to satisfy his detractors, for the Society paid him tribute and wished Collins the best in his new endeavors.

A native Vermonter who had studied at Middlebury College and Andover Seminary, Collins became enthused with the new spirit of communitarianism spearheaded by George Ripley's transcendentalists at Brook Farm, at the Ebenezer Community (later Amana) in New York, and at the Phalansterian Associations inspired by the writings of Albert Brisbane (an enthusiastic disciple of Charles Fourier). During the spring of 1843, months before the fiasco with Douglass, Collins held preliminary meetings in Skaneateles and Syracuse to discuss plans for his own putatively Fourierist community. Those gatherings drew large audiences that included editors from Onondaga and Skaneateles newspapers, who published the proposed constitution for the community.[115] Initially envisioned as a joint-stock organization that would pay interest on shares after two years, membership depended upon owning at least one transferable share ($50), abjuring liquor, and possessing a sound moral character. By June, the solicitation of subscriptions began and prospective members were interviewed.

Representatives from the proposed community decided that the three-hundred-acre Elijah Cole farm would make an ideal site and could be purchased for just $15,000. One editor from a Skaneateles paper noted that the location was perfect for up to three hundred families aiming to live in harmony with each other in "a blooming Eden stretching down the Outlet, containing not two only but fifteen hundred joyous, happy beings!"[116] Collins planned a convention on the property to generate funds for its purchase. In the barn, the largest structure, he argued passionately and persuasively that the current organization of society could never eliminate the "evils existing in the world," and he intrigued many in the audience with the commercial possibilities of a location accessible to the Skaneateles Railroad and the Erie Canal. Collins raised approximately $18,000 in personal property, real estate, and cash to jumpstart the Skaneateles commune, and he secured a deed for the property with a down payment of $5,000.[117]

Like Ballou, Collins believed that he could establish a "community of property and interest, by which we may be brought into love relations, [and] through which plenty and intelligence may be ultimately secured to all the inhabitants of this globe."[118] In fact, it never spread beyond Skaneateles. Collins, called by a Syracuse newspaper "a thorough-going radical, whose views will be far from pleasing all," mistakenly imitated Robert Owen and issued a general invitation to the public to join him.[119] Communal operations commenced in January 1844 with 150 members and the publication of the first issue of the community newspaper, the *Communitist*. In "Articles of Belief and Disbelief and Creed," Collins denied revealed religion and the authority of the church and Bible; banned individual property; forbad the consumption of meat, narcotics, and alcohol; and repudiated the right of any government to use force to uphold the law—meaning Skaneateles Community members did not vote, pay taxes, serve in the military, or testify in courts. When five members dissented, Collins issued a less stringent set of principles that simply read: "We repudiate all creeds, sects, and parties in whatever shape and form they present themselves . . . our principles are as broad as the universe, and as liberal as the elements that surround us. We estimate a man by his acts rather than by his particular belief, and say to all, 'Believe what you may, but act as well as you can.'"[120]

The Skaneateles Community attracted freethinkers united around the broad principles laid out by Collins. They favored an absolute community of property, raised children collectively, worked on the Sabbath, deemed the clergy an imposition, and made marriages and sexual relationships a matter of consent. For these and other views, locals called the community No God, and a dangerous prejudice grew up against them among residents of central New York.[121] In the face of mounting opposition, the motley crew fronting this socialist experiment prospered. The editor of the *Onondaga Standard* visited the community during its first summer, and he noted its favorable location, fine growth of 70 acres of timber, and the well-fenced and cultivated land that made up the other 230 acres of the estate. Members grew wheat, corn, oats, barley, beans, pumpkins, cabbages, and other garden vegetables, and they tended an apple orchard and operated a fruit tree nursery.[122] The property included a well-furnished, two-story stone house with a 30-foot extension; a log house and rough two-story dwelling; two large and two small barns; and a 40-foot shed, all located on an elevation with a fine view of the surrounding country. A steady stream supplied the communitarians with ample waterpower, and they built a two-story sawmill to cut lumber and power lathes for turning iron and wood. The ninety or so people in residence

FIGURE 13. Restored Skaneateles Community home (ca. 1821)

that first summer were usefully employed, so far as the editor and his colleagues could tell, and their efforts in the span of eight months suggested
that they might prove themselves successful after all.[123]

The Skaneateles Community doubled in value in just three years. One visitor in early 1845, a successful iron merchant from Liverpool and disciple of
Robert Owen, estimated that the Skaneateles farm and sawmill generated
close to $9,000 per year—while its expenditures scarcely exceeded $3,800.[124]
In May, Owen spent four days at Skaneateles and addressed a large community meeting. He found the little society much more congenial than he had
expected, declaring at last that he would be delighted to "end his days" with
them.[125] Owen discovered that their labor was free and voluntary, yet sys-
tematized and diversified, so as to accommodate the skills and preferences

of each member. Collins ingeniously divided community industry into five categories (agriculture, mechanical, domestic, educational, and publishing) and placed a foreman over each division. Those five individuals formed an advisory committee to handle all outside business. By the fall, the sawmill ran day and night, with the help of fifteen hired laborers. Collins urged members of the collective to "work diligently so that additional buildings could be erected, new machinery purchased, and a school-house with philosophical equipment constructed."[126] He warned that constant toil would be required, but their hard work and dedication did not shield "No God" (or Community Place) from its share of troubles.

Collins claimed the right to reject or eject undesirable characters, but as a believer in nonresistance who refused to appeal to outside authority, such cases proved challenging. Take, for example, the Syracuse lawyer whom Collins bought out in frustration and persuaded to leave.[127] Collins ousted other dissatisfied members and many more voluntarily withdrew. When a common zeal could no longer prevent the petty squabbling, personal jealousies, and rival ambitions that inevitably erupted, this propensity for dissention within the rank-and-file contributed to the dissolution of the community. Nearby bustling Syracuse also drew members away, but in the end, Collins tired of community building. He ceased publishing the *Communitist* in March 1846, and in May, he called a meeting of the membership. Collins explained that his plan could not be "practicably executed," donated his portion of ownership to them, and departed "like one who had lost his nearest and dearest friend."[128] Most residents followed Collins—and the property was sold shortly thereafter. At the time of this writing (summer 2017), a restored two-story stone house and a large barn once belonging to Skaneateles Community constitute the main buildings of the Frog Pond Bed & Breakfast. The ruins of a log house (today a roofless structure with two windows and a wooden door), along with several other decaying buildings, are plainly visible. Ironically, given Collins's beliefs about marriage, the Frog Pond is a preferred site for local weddings.

Much more survives of the Bishop Hill community in Illinois founded by a group of Jansonites—Separatists from the Church of Sweden and led by the controversial reformer Eric Janson. The Jansonites deplored the worldliness of the church with its liturgical formalism, rigid hierarchies, strict laws and regulations, and intemperate and negligent pastors. Following a man with a magnetic influence over people, they emigrated from a country with a rich

FIGURE 14. Skaneateles Community ruins

religious heritage to the prairies of Henry County, Illinois. The son of peasant parents, Eric was sent to work as a young lad, his ill health and love of solitude notwithstanding. One scholar describes the young Swede as a strikingly ugly individual of "middle height, pale with sunken cheeks, long prominent teeth, and a scarred forehead, hypnotic blue eyes, and twitching facial muscles."[129] At the age of twenty-two, the emaciated and rheumatoid community builder fell from a horse and heard God ordain him a "vicar of Christ" destined to found a New Jerusalem. Four years later, he read scripture, composed verses, and preached that converted individuals had no sin because Christ had taken it away.[130]

His public burning of Lutheran devotional books in Sweden landed Janson in jail. Once freed, he suffered repeated arrest, and the group's enemies broke up Jansonite meetings—sometimes violently. In fear for their lives, Janson and his wife went into hiding as ugly rumors regarding the prophet's relations with women circulated alongside sordid stories of his followers' moral shortcomings. In desperation, the community sold all this real estate, personal property, and handicrafts (sometimes at a loss), and the proceeds were put into a common fund to purchase transportation and provisions for the long voyage to America.[131] Those transatlantic crossings, which brought 1,500 Jansonites to the United States between 1846 and 1848, were dogged by disaster. Passengers suffered shortages of food and water and frequent outbreaks of deadly pestilence. One ship was lost with all onboard and two others were wrecked (though all lives were spared).

The first four hundred or so settlers, weakened by the arduous journey, arrived in Illinois in 1846 too late in the season to plant crops. They had money, but there was almost nowhere to buy food on the frontier. On unbroken land with only a single farmhouse within miles, they passed a bitter first winter in which almost every morning "a fresh corpse was pulled out from the reeking death-traps" where they huddled.[132] As additional colonists arrived, the community experienced greater difficulty securing sufficient food and adequate shelter for everyone. Hundreds of colonists of all ages and classes sheltered out of necessity in caves and earthen dugouts until more suitable dwellings could be constructed.[133] The situation grew so dire that more than a third of the members perished before the spring of 1847, and no proper burials could be managed. Many left to try their luck elsewhere. When the weather finally broke, those who remained began to manufacture adobe houses. As lumber became available, frame structures followed.

It seemed miraculous that by late 1847 the Jansonites had survived the starving time and constructed mills, a tannery, and shops of all sorts—and they had sown nearly 800 acres of wheat, barley, oats, and potatoes; built eighteen houses and a large church; and constructed a 4.5-mile earthen wall to protect fields from their livestock.[134] For the sake of economy, they fasted often, advocated celibacy, and discouraged new marriages during the first two years, though these policies were reversed when their economic fortunes improved. Janson called nearly one thousand believers living in makeshift log and canvas structures to devotion every day at 5 A.M., and he held a second gathering every evening. In between those prayer meetings, worshippers toiled in the fields during the spring and labored indoors during winter months.[135] Despite their straitened circumstances, Janson appointed twelve young men as apostles of Jansonism in North America, and after a few months of English language training, they ventured out of Bishop Hill to proselytize.

In 1849, a cholera epidemic struck the community and claimed the lives of 150 members, including Janson's wife and two of their children, but the colonists persevered and brought $10,000 to $15,000 worth of gold into circulation, built a massive brick building four stories high and 200 feet long

FIGURE 15. Bishop Hill home (1855)

(the largest structure west of Chicago), and successfully adopted farming innovations, such as the grain cradle, to increase production.[136] Four years after its founding, Bishop Hill took its place alongside thriving intentional communities at Oneida, Amana, and Zoar. Tragically, Janson was murdered just a few years into construction efforts at Bishop Hill. He mistakenly permitted his cousin to marry John Root, a veteran of the Mexican War, on the written condition that should he ever wish to leave the commune, he would not compel his wife to go with him. No Pietist, Root soon departed and contrary to his word twice resorted to kidnapping his unwilling wife—who had to be rescued from Chicago 150 miles away. Seeking revenge, Root initiated legal proceedings against Janson, and on the day of the trial in May 1850, he entered the courthouse, called Janson's name, and shot the pastor through the heart with a pistol.[137]

Control of the community passed to Jonas Olson, and the Bishop Hill colony entered its most successful phase. The *Practical Christian* reported in 1856 that 780 people lived communally on 8,500 acres, and that they made at least $36,000 from a crop of broom-corn and between $150,000 and $200,000 from contract railroad work.[138] That period of prosperity ended when too much power was granted to community trustees—one of whom speculated wildly on real estate and mortgaged the entire colony. His financial investments fared terribly during the Panic of 1857. On the verge of bankruptcy, the members of the Bishop Hill colony took an inventory of property and holdings (estimated at nearly $850,000) and legally dissolved the community by 1869.[139] Only about two hundred Jansonites remained in town. Those who departed lived as Americans or joined other religious communities, such as the Pleasant Hill Shakers. In 2003, under the auspices of the Bishop Hill Heritage Association and with state and private support, the coordinated reconstruction of the village began in earnest. Brick buildings, historic homes, two museums, and the Bishop Hill Colony Store speak today to some of the town's former glory.

*   *   *

A new surge of interest in socialism developed in France among followers of Étienne Cabet—lawyer, writer, and political activist whose best-selling utopian romance *Voyage to Icaria* (1840) inspired the formation of several intentional communities in the United States. An ardent reformer whose stinging criticisms of the French government led to accusations of sedition and earned him five years of exile in England, Cabet believed that wealth inequality generated most social ills. For that reason, he made his fictional community an egalitarian democracy where no money, no private property, no courts of law, no secret police, and no crime existed. An efficient system of mechanized workshops and scientific agriculture facilitated the daily delivery of food, clothing, and other essentials, to every person, "each according to his needs."[140] The fictional revolutionary Icarius divided the country into one hundred provinces (with ten communes each), nationalized property and natural resources, established a communist government, and guaranteed absolute equality among all citizens. The city of Icaria contained wide, straight streets and beautiful gardens kept meticulously clean and free from polluting industries. Icarians enjoyed universal education from five to eighteen years of age and adhered to a code of ethics based on their version of the Golden Rule. Icarians worked six to seven hours per day and retired at the age of sixty-five, and they elected their own community officers, dressed alike, and practiced monogamy.[141] The fictional state promoted arts and leisure, and Icarians gathered on promenades for community events and attended free concerts and theater productions.

Inspired by the reception of his novel, Cabet framed a constitution for an actual Icaria, and he sought the means to finance it and the people to build it. Of course, conjuring an imaginary model city is one thing, real community building is quite another. Nevertheless, for seven years following the

FIGURE 16. Bishop Hill Colony Store

unexpected success of *Voyage to Icaria*, Cabet wrote to propagate his social-ist views and gradually built up a following of 400,000 readers. Many of them clamored for Cabet to actualize his theory of *communisme* ("communism", a term he coined in *Voyage*). Conceding to those calls in May 1847, this French lawyer (with a protuberant chin, straight nose, and unruly hair) announced a plan to build communist cities and villages in America.[142] He projected that ten to twenty thousand working people would participate in the creation of those communities, and that a million more would join them thereafter. Although that groundswell of interest never materialized, from 1849 until his death in St. Louis in 1856, Cabet established a total of five communal settlements—in Texas, Missouri, Illinois, Iowa, and California.[143]

Robert Owen, whom Cabet met briefly while in exile, convinced the French communitarian that a tract of land along the Trinity River in Texas would make an ideal location for an Icarian community since that state, recently admitted to the union, sought immigrants to populate its vast territories. Cabet did not know that Owen and his son Robert Dale stood to financially benefit by receiving shares of stock in that settlement plan, which called for the Icarians to establish homesteads on a 3,000-acre site along the Trinity River by July 1, 1848, in return for free land.[144] Once built, each family would receive a warranty deed to 320 acres (single men over age seventeen a deed for half that amount). Unluckily for the French writer, the State of Texas insisted on retaining one-half of the tracts on the property, resulting in "a disjointed, checkerboard parcel of land where the self-sufficient community Cabet had in mind would be impossible to build."[145]

In spite of misgivings about the layout of the community, Cabet unwisely accepted the terms of the prospectus and enthusiastically recruited new converts for the Texas Colony (due to growing animosity toward the Icarians in France after the proclamation of the Second Republic). As acting managing director of the colony, Cabet selected sixty-nine men and designated them the First Advanced Guard. They landed in New Orleans in late March 1848 but could venture only as far as Shreveport by steamboat. Traveling from there to Icaria meant purchasing two wagons and oxen teams, and then trekking more than 300 miles across the unmapped prairie. They made it—and managed to plant crops, erect a few small buildings, and construct a 15- by 20-foot refectory before the July 1 deadline. Then malaria and cholera struck the camp, and by the end of August, everyone was ill. Four men died, another was hit by lightning, and the only physician went insane and deserted the settlement.[146]

After Cabet docked at New Orleans in late January 1849, he made his way to two rented houses around which some 480 Icarians awaited his arrival. Some were surviving members of the first and second advance parties, and their harrowing tales of suffering and deprivation in Texas led to rebellion and schism. For nearly a month, the Icarians pondered their future before 280 restless souls decided to make another go with Cabet on the site of a former Mormon enclave of 12,000 at Nauvoo, Illinois. Forcibly expelled by local mobs and vigilantes, the Mormons abandoned brick homes, stores, workshops, and farmsteads on a river accessible by steamboat. In late February 1849, 142 men, 74 women, and 64 children boarded a steamship with their baggage, tools, supplies, and less than 60,000 francs for the week-long trip up the Mississippi River.[147] Once established at Nauvoo, the Icarians flourished as they cultivated leased land, established workshops and mills, and organized schools. Initially, Icarians arriving from France paid an admission fee of $80 and brought four years of clothing, but soon thereafter members instituted a Community of Goods, raised their children collectively, and worked for each other's mutual benefit.[148]

When production in the fledgling community failed to cover expenditures, dissension and discontentment broke out over mounting debts. Cabet furiously resisted making changes to the communalist organization in order to spur industry, and when residents began deserting in protest, his credibility diminished as he became increasingly despotic. Cabet and a minority of those at Nauvoo departed for Saint Louis, carrying away what they could. Cabet fell ill and died during the winter of 1856—leaving those at Nauvoo little choice but to liquidate their debts and relocate to Corning, Iowa (an Icarian community founded in 1852 as the Illinois group started to weaken).[149] Proceeds from the sale of real estate and personal property failed to cover their debts, and so they put up 3,100 acres in Iowa as security to cover those liabilities. Still remote and accessible only by dirt road today, in the 1850s getting to the Corning colony meant hiking sixteen days on crude footpaths through the wilderness. Like the unfortunate First Advance Guard in Texas, early Icarians at Corning cooked meals over campfires and lived in log huts with dirt floors covered by straw, or slept under the stars.

By 1853, the Icarians at Corning had cleared 56 acres and brought in a small harvest of 80 tons of hay, and they started work on a kitchen-dining hall, a fruit cellar, and smokehouse. They finished ten more buildings by the spring of 1854 and furnished those living quarters in rudimentary fashion.[150] One year later, sixty settlers lived together frugally and put nearly 400 acres under the plow collectively. By the turn of the decade, they added nearly 3,000 acres of timber and prairie valued at $31,000 and livestock (horse, cattle, oxen, sheep, and pigs) worth $4,100 to those holdings. In September 1860, the Iowa

FIGURE 17. Restored Icarian communal dining hall (1852) at Corning, Iowa

community received an official charter of incorporation from the state des-ignating it an "agricultural society."[151] Although Icarians at Corning produced corn, oats, wool, butter, hay, and sorghum molasses, they could not find any-one to buy those commodities, and within two years their debts exceeded $15,000.[152]

The Civil War provided some reprieve from their financial burdens. Begin-ning in 1863, Union troops moving between the Des Moines and Missouri Rivers regularly stopped at Corning for supplies, and the wartime price infla-tion on wool allowed the community to generate enough revenue to pay off creditors by 1865. Five years later, with more than 700 acres under tillage, a railroad connected them, along with their goods, to Omaha. In the absence of a powerful president like Cabet, settlers practiced a form of "pure democ-racy" with carefully defined and circumscribed roles for the general assembly, president, and "a Gérance [management] in charge of industry, agriculture, lodging, and clothing."[153] Such moves failed to prevent schisms from reemerg-ing in the 1870s; only this time they took place between older Icarians and younger ones who styled themselves "progressives." In 1878, the community split into two proximal "autonomous branches" (New Icaria and Jeune Icarie, respectively).[154]

The progressives at Jeune Icarie adopted a new constitution that abolished the office of president and extended suffrage to women, but new members weakened that ethos and the community fell into decline. Some of those who withdrew from Jeune Icarie set up a new colony in Sonoma County, California, in 1881, but it fizzled out by mid-decade. The New Icaria community established on the Corning site was formally disbanded in 1898, but collectively the five Icarian colonies constituted one of the longest-lived, nonreligious, communal experiments in American history.[155] The reasons that prompted the founding of the Icarian colonies were similar to those that spurred hundreds of other intentional communities during the first half of the nineteenth century: the allure of free or inexpensive land on frontiers far from the distractions of civilization, government interference and censorship, the dehumanizing and exploitative aspects of industrialization, and the travails of the economic panics.[156]

The acceleration of mechanization and the rise of giant corporations following the Civil War made it harder for small groups of like-minded individuals to build settlements and small-scale enterprises (such as mills) that could compete with industrial mass production. Achieving basic sustainability from farming and tending to livestock, so-called back-to-nature movements, remained a viable option in the postbellum United States, but most intentional communities needed one or more cottage industries to generate revenue to purchase items not made on site or sold locally. Moreover, the frontier shrank as the young nation stretched toward the Pacific Ocean and cooperative homesteads became more difficult to sustain as land prices increased. For that reason, members of the next generation of American communalism pioneered new models of social organization that responded meaningfully to Reconstruction and Jim Crow, to the yawning income inequality of the Gilded Age, to the continued exploitation of labor by capital, to corruption in government and industry, and to urbanization and segregation.

2 ▸ SLEEPING CARS, SPIRITUALISM, AND COOPERATIVES

CHICAGO ENTREPRENEUR GEORGE Mortimer Pullman made a fortune manufacturing sleeping cars, "luxurious hotels on wheels," that revolutionized long-distance rail travel following the Civil War.[1] In the 1880s, Pullman oversaw construction of a company town for his workers—a profit center in the spirit of New Lanark. Prior to Owen's socialist reforms, New Lanark had struggled to import workers from Glasgow and resorted to the forced labor of pauper children, "of which there was at that time an unexpectedly large supply," to fill many of nearly two thousand positions required for operation.[2] Expected to toil *thirteen or more hours per shift—six days a week*, these impoverished children endured hot, unventilated workplaces and slept several to a bunk in shifts so tightly scheduled that barrack beds never had time to cool. Yet, because David Dale, the mill's original owner, fed these children, provided them with clean clothing, and taught some of them to read, he was considered a remarkably enlightened and humane man by the standards of the day.[3] When Owen took over operations at New Lanark Mill in 1800, he stopped employing pauper apprentices bound out by local churchwardens, improved work and living conditions for employees and their families, and turned New Lanark into a profitable model community that later inspired his work at New Harmony. Owen believed that, with proper education from preschool to adulthood, radical social transformation could be achieved in a relatively brief span of time.[4]

Whereas Owen endeavored to apply the lessons he learned at New Lanark across Scotland and throughout the world by lecturing and writing about community building, George Pullman wanted to address worker poverty and quell labor unrest to maximize productivity and increase profits. The situation faced by American laborers in the nineteenth century was unenviable and only grew worse following the Civil War: remuneration remained inadequate; commodity and housing prices outpaced wage growth (so that food and shelter became increasingly expensive); and men, women, and children worked extended hours in dangerous and unsanitary conditions.[5] Before 1865, most American businesses operated on a small scale, but a process of consolidation in later decades led to the absorption or annihilation of many small businesses by aggressive, well-heeled competitors. Many of the giant monopolies that emerged from those consolidations capitalized with tens of millions of dollars and were led by shrewd business tycoons, such as Cornelius Vanderbilt, who crushed competitors, manipulated stocks, bribed legislators, violated laws, and corrupted courts in the pursuit of profit.[6] In this respect, George Pullman, who in his industry achieved success comparable to Vanderbilt's in railroads, avoided many of the corrupt business practices perpetuated by other industrialists of his era. He built a company town for his workers and practiced paternalism, but those laudable acts could not mask corporate greed or prevent worker strikes.

Born in Brocton, New York, in 1831 to a mechanic barely able to provide a living for his wife and ten children, George Pullman's formal education was limited to a few years at the village school. Obliged to secure employment at fourteen years of age, he worked in a small store for a salary of $40 per annum. Three years later, he joined his brother in the cabinet-making business in Albion, and the knowledge that he gained in that trade later proved invaluable in the sleeping-car industry. Unfortunately, the two siblings found the cabinet-making trade unprofitable, and when New York State advertised for bids to move warehouses and other structures in order to widen the Erie

Canal, George secured a contract. After this work, he moved to Chicago to assist in elevating that city eight feet to improve drainage. Over the next three years, Pullman raised a number of stone and brick structures and accumulated $20,000 in capital.[7]

His rail travels between Buffalo and Chicago convinced Pullman of the need for superior locomotive sleeping accommodations, such as those found on some steamboats. In average railcars of the 1840s and 1850s, light came from candles and heat from smoky coal or wood stoves; sheets and blankets were often soiled. Recognizing an opportunity to reinvigorate an industry lagging behind ongoing innovations in transportation, Pullman purchased two ordinary coaches for remodeling and readied them for service in the fall of 1858. When they failed to generate the public interest he anticipated, Pullman moved to Colorado and prospected for gold. He returned to Chicago in 1864 and began designing another luxury sleeping car known as the Pioneer. Sumptuously appointed throughout, it included a wider and higher carriage, and it introduced a stowable hinged upper-berth that collapsed during the day and provided more cabin space. The selection of the Pioneer to convey the body of Abraham Lincoln from Chicago to Springfield after his assassination in 1865 assured Pullman's success by drawing attention to his brand.[8]

Designs for a "hotel" car and a "parlor" car soon followed, and the steady growth of his business allowed Pullman to absorb competitors. By emphasizing comfort and safety, and protecting his patents, Pullman kept rivals at bay, and his sleeping car service soon dominated the industry. An urgent need for larger production and repair facilities occasioned the purchase of more than 4,000 acres of prairie 14 miles south of Chicago's business district in 1880. Pullman believed the site would prove proximal enough to attract skilled workers, and that miles of prairie would discourage visits by union organizers who filled the city's working-class districts. He would concentrate the major works of the Pullman Palace Car Company in one central location where he could "create the perfect environment for producing unorganized skilled workers by building a new town."[9] He fashioned it in the image of his sleeping cars—beautiful, clean, substantial, and orderly—and he named it after himself.

By 1892, fifteen thousand people lived in Pullman, and it became one of Chicago's premier tourist attractions. Visitors from across the country took the Illinois Central train from downtown Chicago to Pullman—a forty-five-minute ride. They stepped off their railcars onto a modest station platform that fronted an elm-bordered boulevard leading to Lake Calumet.[10] Many who came admired the town's brick apartment houses, tidy tree-lined streets, and decorative flower beds. On clear days, they marveled at the ripples of light from the lake that reflected on the two-story waterfront apartments. A grand hotel, a limestone church, and a brick Arcade Building (containing a post office, a savings bank, a library, a theater, and a variety of shops) were conveniently situated near the station. From the upper floors of the Arcade Building, tourists enjoyed a grand view of the sculptured gardens in Arcade Park.[11] Behind the towering Pullman Company administration building stretched blocks of brick industrial structures matching the slate-roofed cottages and apartments.[12] Pullman established a free kindergarten and created excellent schools to stimulate minds, and on Athletic Island he built one of the finest sports facilities in the country. One London reporter declared Pullman "the most perfect city in the world," and American newspapers urged "distressed socialists and vague visionaries of the world" to study it.[13]

Such adulation for his community notwithstanding, Pullman made no pretense of philanthropy; his city was foremost a profit-driven enterprise. For instance, he leased (never sold) homes to workers, knowing the rents generated additional revenue, and as soon as he realized the public relations value of Pullman, he used it effectively to advertise products and services and to bolster his company's image. Consistent with his entrepreneurial vision, he centrally located the main shops, the repair department, and the administrative offices of the Car Works and made them virtually self-sufficient. The town included a rolling mill to produce iron and steel, a foundry, a wheel-making factory, huge lumberyards, and drying houses as well—which meant that workers of all skill levels could find jobs there.[14]

In that carefully designed environment, the railcar entrepreneur endeavored to shape his employees into a tractable labor force. To that end, he restricted employees' freedom after work (even prohibiting them from sitting on the steps of their homes in short sleeves), and he banned saloons. One neighbor described him as a handsome man with a high complexion, a chin beard, and very bright eyes—but called him "one of the most rigid, pompous autocrats I have ever seen."[15] In any case, Pullman understood the relationship between a contented workforce and increased productivity, and he practiced high-principled oversight of his city in the belief that the "labor problem" could be solved through enlightened paternalism. For that reason,

Pullman made every job applicant take a formidable written examination that elicited a good deal of personal information, and he kept union organizers out of town by denying them licenses to speak in public places.[16]

Such extraordinary levels of oversight soon rankled residents, and Pullman's authoritarian paternalism began to grate. Persistent surveillance by officials and numerous restrictions on tenants stirred antagonistic feelings toward the Pullman Company, and the abuses of blacklisting, arbitrary dismissal, nepotism, favoritism, and tyrannical foremen in the shops only strengthened resentment.[17] Starting in the mid-1880s, many Pullman workers (carvers, cabinetmakers, wood machine workers, blacksmiths, hammer smiths, and car builders) started to join labor unions, such as the International Working People's Association and the Knights of Labor.[18] Nationwide strikes took place in May 1886, as workers walked out in support of the eight-hour day. Seven years later, the Panic of 1893 plunged the country into the worst economic depression of that century as three million workers lost their jobs. Managers at the Pullman Car Works laid off almost a quarter of the workforce, cut the hours of those who remained, and slashed wages by an average of 28 percent—while keeping rents high.[19] Workers and their families soon faced hunger and deprivation.

In the absence of a meaningful response from management to their grievances, workers organized again, this time in greater numbers. Many joined the American Railway Union—an organization with a racial bar that excluded Pullman's two thousand black porters. The fact that no black men labored at the Pullman Car Works certainly reflected racial ideology, but also the fact that African Americans represented only 1 percent of Chicago's population in the 1880s.[20] Nonetheless, George Pullman regularly hired black men as sleeping car porters (and white men as conductors) believing that smiling, polite black porters would "increase the comfort level of his clients and that comfort was linked to *seeing* porters—black men—as servants."[21] During the early twentieth century, his porters became celebrated national figures, and they organized their own labor union, the Brotherhood of Sleeping Car Porters, during the 1920s to advance their own interests.

One founding member of the American Railway Union, Eugene Victor Debs, proved a particularly effective champion of labor. This future leader of the Socialist Party of America (and its candidate for the presidency of the United States in five elections) secured railroad employment at the age of fourteen, working first as a car cleaner, then as a car painter, and finally as a locomotive fireman. Debs won election as a Democrat to the Indiana General Assembly representing Terre Haute in 1884 and served for a single term. That experience so disgusted Debs that he abandoned the pursuit of public office for some time thereafter. Frustrated that railroad unions too often pursued their own agendas rather than those of workers, Debs called for the formation of a new organization that would unite rather than divide. He made the case for an American Railway Union before the Cincinnati convention of the Brotherhood of Locomotive Fireman, declaring with passion, "there is nothing I would not do, so far as human effort goes, to reach and rescue perishing humanity. I have a heart for others and that is why I am in this work. When I see suffering about me, I myself suffer, and so when I put forth my efforts to relieve others, I am simply working for myself."[22] Should his quasi-mystical notion of the unity of self and other be understood and put into practice, many believed that it would radically transform society.

Because the Pullman Company owned and operated a few miles of track, its employees could join the American Railway Union. The union's statement of principles expressed a belief in making reasonable demands, and acting honorably in order to resolve differences with management without recourse to lockouts, strikes, boycotts, and blacklists.[23] However, when the leaders of the American Railway Union presented their grievances to George Pullman and other officials, company leaders proffered no expressions of sympathy and proposed no solutions. As a result, more than three thousand employees took the initiative and walked out of the Car Works (without the expressed consent of union leadership) and went on strike in May 1894.[24] Had the American Railway Union's racial bar not excluded black members, and had Pullman's two thousand black porters joined the strike, workers might have successfully pressured the company to capitulate to their demands.

During the first month of the strike, Pullman workers gained support from many Chicagoans. American Railway Union delegates initiated a boycott of the company in June by persuading cardholding members to refuse to add or remove Pullman cars to trains. Within days, unionists disrupted daily operations at a coalition of twenty-four railroad corporations when they walked out in solidarity with coworkers fired for supporting the boycott. As the strikes spread, the national media increasingly portrayed Debs as an authoritarian union boss with the country at his mercy. Chicago meatpackers called for help as their production plummeted when the boycott disrupted rail traffic, and the federal government entered the fray.[25] A federal court granted an injunction that made the strike illegal, and President Grover Cleveland sent in troops. Strikers, infuriated by the presence of federal and state authorities, destroyed hundreds of railcars in Chicago and provoked a counterattack by soldiers who wounded and killed workers. The train boycott collapsed, and by early August many employees (including several hundred Dutch workers who broke with the union) returned to their jobs. Debs and other American Railway Union leaders were arrested during the violence and subsequently jailed for violating the injunction by communicating with striking workers. The Pullman company and the federal government successfully crushed the strike and destroyed the American Railway Union.

Although some striking workers decided against returning to Pullman, many who did go back were denied employment, and strike leaders were summarily blacklisted. The United States Commissioner of Labor estimated that three quarters of boycotters lost their jobs.[26] In response to the forceful crushing of the strike, an outcry arose among Democratic politicians in the state who had vehemently objected to the deployment of federal troops. The Illinois attorney general brought suit against the Pullman Company alleging that it held no legal right to own a city and had overstepped the terms of its charter. His reputation as a business reformer in tatters on account of the strike, George Pullman spent his final years fighting attempts to take away his community. Yet his embrace of corporate paternalism inspired other community builders as interest in intentional living spread westward in the decades following the Civil War.

*   *   *

As the nation gradually shifted from a manufacturing-based to a service-based economy, a movement indicative of postindustrial societies, intentional living took many new and increasingly secular forms. Like-minded people, people who rejected the central ethical, religious, and economic codes of their time, continued to follow charismatic leaders and carve out new communities. Thomas Lake Harris, mystic and founder of Brotherhood of the New Life, made a series of communal experiments from New York to California in order to create a new society—a "matrix of world redemption" wherein human and celestial beings could unite.[27] At the age of five, Harris had emigrated from Fenny Stratford in England with his Calvinist family to Utica, New York, where his father worked as a grocer and an auctioneer.

Thomas's mother died before he turned ten, and unfortunately his step-mother treated him shabbily.

Forced to work to help support the family, he was befriended by a local Universalist minister who later remembered him as "a quiet, bashful, unassuming young man, of very delicate physique, in very delicate health" who "showed a good deal of vivacity, even brilliancy, of conversational gifts."[28] Under his tutelage, Thomas became preoccupied with religion, embraced Universalism, and joined the ministry at the age of twenty-one. He served the Fourth Universalist Society in New York City for nearly two years before discovering solace in Spiritualism after the untimely death of his first wife in 1850. Over the next few years, Harris worked with trance-medium James L. Scott to organize a spiritualist community at Mountain Cove, north of Fayetteville, West Virginia; it attracted one hundred seekers.

During the second half of the nineteenth century, Americans increasingly embraced Spiritualism (with its séances, spirit guides, and trance-mediums) as an exciting alternative to traditional religious practices. Participants in the Mountain Cove community lived in private homes, but they put communitarian values into practice while they waited for the second coming of Christ (predicted to take place in their area).[29] The commune disbanded after only three years when an attempt at complete communal ownership of property collapsed and Jesus failed to return. While in residence, Harris wrote poetry and formulated a theory of "theo-socialism," which blended mystical Christianity and the egalitarianism of Fourierism with Swedenborgianism and Harris's own visionary cosmology.[30] Harris left Mountain Cove to preach to a small Swedenborgian congregation in New York City, and he entered into a celibate marriage with his second wife, Emily.

Sometime around 1857, a profound mystical experience led Harris to the discovery of "Divine Respiration," a technique (derived from Swedish mystic Emanuel Swedenborg) that made apparent the Lord God breathing through each of us. Focusing on the breath, "reverently and sacredly as a gift of God," explained Harris, transformed the body into a single "conscious form of unified intellectual and physical harmony" in which "the spirit, the real or higher self, is absorbing the lowly naturehood, yet meanwhile nourishing it with the rich and vital elements of a loftier realm of being."[31] The conscious cultivation of this inner vital force brought forth such energy and eternal delight that Harris traveled to England in 1860 to proclaim the Brotherhood of the New Life. Harris returned one year later with the financial backing of writer and parliamentarian Laurence Oliphant to establish an intentional community. Harris made a first attempt in Dutchess County, New York, at Wassaic, and a second one at Amenia, before settling on 2,000 acres of excellent farmland and vineyards on the shores of Lake Erie near Brocton in Chautauqua County.[32] Harris explained that the Brocton purchase "made by myself and friends" included the plat "at the junction of the Lake Shore and Alleghany Valley railroad, where we are laying out a village which we have named Salem-on-Erie, designing to make it an industrial and business center."[33]

In addition to important figures from England, the settlement on Lake Erie attracted several eminent American women, as well as a contingent of about twenty Japanese converts, headed by Kanaye Nagasawa, who were among the first Japanese immigrants to the United States. The generous gifts of these and other benefactors, worth hundreds of thousands of dollars, permitted the construction of a spacious main house and a large winery.[34] In 1873, Harris explained that besides "the usual operation in agriculture, and vine-culture, we are engaged, first, in the wholesale pressing and shipping of hay; second, in the general nursery business; third, in the manufacture and sale of pure native wines. At the village," he boasted, "we also carry on a hotel and restaurant, and have just enlarged our operations by erecting a steam gristmill and operating an exchange for transactions in produce and general merchandise."[35] Ultimately, though, it was his imposing personality and striking appearance, which gave the impression of awakened alertness—not his peculiar religious notions and remarkable business savvy—that attracted so many men and women to Thomas Lake Harris. Photographs of Harris reveal a vital man of moderate height and slight build with penetrating eyes, jutting eyebrows, a narrow nose, and a long flowing beard that gave him the appearance of a Biblical patriarch.

Harris made the first objective of the Brotherhood of the New Life "the realization of the noble Christian ideal in social service" to "demonstrate that the ethical creed of the Gospel is susceptible of service as a working system, adapted to the complex and cultured nineteenth century and containing the practical solution of the social problems of the age."[36] Members of the Brotherhood, a congregation that professed all life resulted from a divine inflowing "of one pure and living God," regarded themselves as "Socialists" who believed individual regeneration led to a regenerate society.[37] They embraced Harris's unorthodox religious ideas (for example, that God was male and female, "Two-in-One," and Christ a "Divine Man-Woman").[38] Seekers interested in testing his Divine Respiration meditation technique as a means of achieving union with God were also attracted to the religious commune. That quest for mystical unity provided a theological basis for their decision to live communally.

The Brocton community disbanded after Laurence Oliphant, perhaps feeling duped by the conjured "juggling fiends" of the spirit world, became absorbed in promoting Jewish colonization of Palestine and demanded that Harris return considerable sums of money.[39] Harris deeded the Brocton property to Oliphant and in 1875 purchased 700 acres 2 miles north of Santa Rosa, California, for $21,000. A few years later, Harris acquired an additional 1,000 acres. Construction began promptly on a large frame home surrounded by eucalyptus trees, hedges, gardens, and ponds.[40] Although initially only a select group of people joined Harris, within six years his devotees in New York had moved to the Golden State. Harris maintained that this gradual transcontinental relocation took place without dissension or disunion, and that it coincided with a shift toward a "modified Socialism" that permitted the payment of weekly wages for transforming the California dairy farm into a vineyard. The new wage system proved a boon to the ledger balance, but it left the communal spirit "not fully satisfied."[41] As a result, Harris abolished wages and instituted a system under which everyone lived together as one family that shared work and resources.

Harris named the estate Fountain Grove, and his disciples planted its fields with Cabernet, Pinot Noir, and Zinfandel grapes. Harris deftly marketed their wine as "divine liquor" infused with celestial energy.[42] He sold bottles in England and Japan, as well as in the United States, and the community prospered. Harris lived with several community members in a palatial mansion house with a wide porch, high ceilings, sunrooms, stained-glass windows, and plush carpeting, set among golden hills and stands of hardwood trees. A comfortable two-story apartment house, replete with paneled rooms of polished redwood, housed other members of the Brotherhood.[43] Harris built a brandy house a quarter mile from those residences and constructed an iconic round red barn that survived until wildfires tore through Santa Rosa in 2017. Since Harris interpreted Jesus as a "super Socialist" who wanted everyone to share resources equitably, he called Fountain Grove a "Theo-socialist community," a phrase that he defined in no fewer than fifty-four books and pamphlets.[44] Harris justified making a profit as a reasonable goal for a coopera-

FIGURE 18. Round red barn (1899) at Fountain Grove

tive society, since the material benefits of successful business practices permitted intentional communities to multiply and to form trusts to share their common wealth. Although he did not measure industrial production of the community (viewed essentially as a spiritual gift from God), Harris maintained discipline by assigning tasks in accordance with each person's "use" or special genius.[45]

At first, curious newspaper editors described Thomas Lake Harris as a respectable squire developing a California spa for wealthy easterners. They praised his library and commended him for his restaurant and coffeehouse that served free food and drink to visitors. They noted that members of Fountain Grove observed strict celibacy; ate communally in a large dining hall; and joined hands, sang, and danced in worship during the evenings. In place of carnal union, Harris taught an esoteric doctrine of "sexual mysticism" through which his "adherents aimed at realization of an angelic androgynous unity and ultimately at union with God."[46] Writers and journalists, who misunderstood that doctrine, accused him of sexual depravity. One professional agitator claimed that Harris permitted heavenly counterparts to take material form "in whatever women he may see fit to designate as the affinity of the disciple."[47] Rather than respond to those charges (in his view, a futile task), Harris left the community. He married longtime follower Jane Lee Waring in 1892 (Emily died in 1883), and following the wedding, the couple departed for New York City. Harris never returned to Fountain Grove, but before his death in 1906, he sold his shares in the property to five former members on the condition that the one who lived longest inherited the estate. Kanaye Nagasawa became sole owner of Fountain Grove during the 1920s, and he operated it as a winery through Prohibition until his death in 1934.

For Harris, the Brotherhood of the New Life represented a practical attempt at "the substitution of 'altruism' for egoism, of mutuality for competition, in social life."[48] Once called "America's best known mystic" by influential psychologist William James, Thomas Lake Harris is little remembered today.[49] That oversight is unjustified, and his writings deserve reexamination by contemporary scholars of history, culture, religion, and literature. Likewise, Englishman Thomas Hughes, who founded a cooperative colony in Tennessee, too often escapes note, despite his distinctive focus on education and Christian socialism. Sixty years old at the time of its founding, Hughes thought that Rugby Colony might prove the crowning achievement in a long and distinguished career of public service as a lawyer, writer, parliamentarian, and social reformer. The second son of a country clergyman, Thomas, and his brother George, studied at the renowned Rugby School under Thomas Arnold, known for "muscular Christianity." He championed opening the best schools to the working classes.[50] Following eight years at Rugby School, Hughes attended Oxford University and discovered Christian socialism.

After completing his studies, Hughes practiced law successfully in London, and he became interested in cooperative movements as an alternative to highly competitive laissez-faire free enterprise (since they encouraged voluntary public ownership of nonprofit enterprises for the benefit of stockholding members of a collective).[51] He based his first novel, *Tom Brown's School Days* (1857), on his experience at Rugby, and its success won Hughes the wide acclaim that catapulted him to Parliament. As a Liberal in the House of Commons from 1865 to 1874, Hughes used his pen to advance progressive causes, such as improving the legal standing of cooperatives and legalizing trade unions. In the company of Fireside poet James Russell Lowell, Hughes embarked on a two-month tour of the United States in 1870. During that excursion, Hughes received a warm welcome from audiences and met important public figures, including Emerson, Longfellow, and Oliver Wendell Holmes.[52]

Upon his return to England, Hughes began planning a Christian cooperative community in America that would engage his many social and political interests: reconciliation of the North and South, trade unions and cooperatives, public education reform, and the plight of young Englishmen (upper and working classes) who finished school with few options for meaningful employment.[53] Hughes hoped to attract to Rugby young men disinherited through the custom of primogeniture (by which the eldest son inherited everything), along with the sons and daughters of tradesmen, farmers, and handicraftsmen likewise lacking opportunity and victimized by the ruthless competitiveness of capitalism. After a providential meeting with Boston financier Franklin W. Smith made possible an option on a beautifully situated, heavily wooded property on a high plain overlooking two deep river gorges in northeastern Tennessee, Hughes enlisted the support of a wealthy British railway magnate and a prominent London lawyer to create a Board of Aid to Land Ownership to purchase the site as a commercial venture.[54]

Hughes heavily publicized the Rugby Colony in the United Kingdom. He lauded the advantages that the States offered as a location for his cooperative venture, noting that participants could own their own farms, establish common schools for their children, and enjoy an overall higher standard of living. Hughes assured prospective members that although they would toil during the day, in the evenings they would find themselves in cultivated company. He promised a central "store and mart, open to all" run by shareholding members, a church with no single denomination, and cheap rates for meals and living quarters.[55] While he sold lots at reasonable prices, the Board of Aid developed bridle paths and trails; set aside parklands and common areas; and built a schoolhouse, a commissary, a hotel, a sawmill, a stable, and a barracks for single men. Although construction had begun months earlier, the resort-like town officially opened on October 5, 1880.

From the veranda of the new hotel, Hughes outlined his aspirations for the community, as he also provided a philosophical foundation. He rejected the paternalism of business leaders such as George Pullman and the European state communism represented by Karl Marx, and he encouraged instead a mixture of public and private enterprise to finance the construction of simple public buildings at Rugby and to preserve the environment. Rugby Colony, Hughes declared, would rid society of "the evils which have turned

FIGURE 19. Rugby Schoolhouse (1907)

retail trade into a keen and anxious and, generally, a dishonest scramble in older communities" through the use of "common interest and common property."[56] He endorsed private housing but encouraged Rugbeians to buy shares in the commissary and livestock pasture, and he recognized the necessity of common goals to bind a community together. Hughes's eloquent advocacy of the virtues of cooperative living and religious freedom, and his prescient admonitions about the need to protect consumers and the environment from unrestrained commercialism, still resonate. However, his vision of British and Americans, Yankees and Southerners, whites and blacks, men and women, refined schoolboys and rough mountaineers, all working together for the common good, proved easier to conjure than to sustain in the real world.

Within three weeks of the opening ceremony, the population of Rugby colony reached 120—and by January 1881, 200 people lived on site. True to Hughes's vision, the community included Britons, Scots, and Americans, and it was equally divided between men and women.[57] After surviving a harsh first winter, the coldest in more than two decades, residents worked together during summer months to construct a café, a school, a boardinghouse, a three-story hotel, private homes, and a cooperative commissary. Public facilities at Rugby included a library (with a collection of seven thousand books), tennis courts, bowling greens, and a gentleman's swimming hole. The community also printed a weekly newspaper called the *Rugbeian*.[58] Since he had cofounded the London Working Men's College, run by Christian Socialists to educate adults during the 1850s, Hughes served as the Rugby School principal for eleven years. Once he banished individual indebtedness and bankruptcy through coordinated cooperation, and assured personal liberty through freedom of worship, Hughes believed that a new social order would spring into existence "in which the humblest members, who live by the labour of their own hands" would generate a sustainable society of diligent individuals at once humble and highly cultured.[59]

Tragically, a typhoid epidemic struck the community in August 1881, less than one year after Hughes had presided over the opening ceremony. The *British Medical Journal* reported twenty cases of the disease among residents caused "without doubt," according to Dr. James Whittaker, by drinking water from the shallow well near Tabard Inn or from a filthy cistern.[60] The inn closed, and the outbreak was quickly contained, but not before the disease claimed the lives of seven people. The population of the community plummeted to sixty persons in December as frightened residents fled for fairer climes. Compounding those woes, land purchasers sometimes faced months of litigation to clear property titles, and cutting heavily timbered land in the foothills of the Cumberland Mountains took true grit. The farmland under it also proved less fertile than anticipated. Worse still, the closest railroad depot lay 7 miles down a graded dirt road, and a promised railroad spur to Rugby never materialized, making it difficult for the community to reach regional and national markets. In addition, only a few of the Tennessee pioneers possessed the manual skills, business acumen, or agricultural experience required to succeed—and drought killed most of the crops planted the first year.[61] Moreover, Rugby attracted married Englishmen, some with large families, who had resided in the United States prior to joining. Hughes did not anticipate that particular demographic, nor did he relish having to find new homes in Rugby for so many overeducated and underemployed Englishmen and their families.[62]

In spite of these and other setbacks, the population of Rugby rose to between 400 and 450 residents in 1884. By that time, Rugbeians worked and lived in sixty-five buildings, and they operated a variety of commercial enterprises (including a canning operation, a drugstore, and blacksmith shops), which, with summer tourism centered around the hotel, provided a range of work opportunities.[63] Sustaining such a large population proved difficult when some members failed to contribute their fair share to the community, and the odds for Rugby's survival grew longer as a prolonged economic depression swept across the nation. Strikes and boycotts spread, wages declined, bankruptcies multiplied, and commodity prices fell. Ultimately, though, blame for the dissolution of Rugby may reside with the British and American investors who ran the Board of Aid to Land Ownership, since they never fully embraced the idealism of the project and succumbed to the single-minded pursuit of profit that Hughes called "the great disgrace of our time."[64] The town survived for seven more years as a colony, and thanks to multiple state government preservation efforts that began in 1966, Rugby entered the National Register of Historic Places in 1972. It remains a worthwhile destination for those attracted by the charms of a Victorian English village set in the mountains of Tennessee.

*   *   *

Many reasons other than profit, spiritualism, and lifelong learning drew Americans together and compelled the formation of new cooperative communities. Death, for instance, seemed to be stalking Martha White McWhirter as she walked home one hot August night in 1866 following a raucous revival meeting in central Texas. The recent deaths of a brother and two of her five children weighed heavily. McWhirter, a longtime Methodist active in Belton's nonsectarian Union Sunday School, interpreted the loss of those family members as a warning from God to reexamine her life and to reevaluate her religious community. Before she reached her doorstep, Martha heard a voice that demanded she probe her conscience to determine if the revival meeting she had just left (with its shouting, singing, and jubilation) was actually the devil's work. She prayed all night for the Lord to deliver her from evil—and the next morning in her kitchen, dustpan in hand, she experienced a "pentecostal baptism."[65] In a flash, she understood that the voice from the previous night belonged to God: the Lord had called her to new work. Thereafter, she professed sanctification and set out to do the Lord's bidding.

Martha McWhirter and her husband George had relocated from Tennessee to Bell County in Texas eleven years earlier to homestead. In the small settlement of Belton, 60 miles north of Austin, her husband George operated a small store and established a local flour mill. He fought for the Confederacy, returned home safely at the rank of major; then resumed his business pursuits. George built a three-story limestone house for his family with the profits from those endeavors, and he taught at the Union Sunday School alongside his wife.[66] Martha had given birth to twelve children (only half of whom survived to adulthood), and although past her childbearing years by the time George returned from war, she felt entitled to refuse his carnal advances in light of her conversion and sanctification. Martha moved her bedroom down the hall, commenced calling on the churchgoing women of Belton (regardless of denomination), and led regular Bible study meetings in her home and in those of other sanctified women. McWhirter never planned to form a separatist group, nor did she ever put in writing a charter or rules to live by. Nevertheless, she and her supporters "essentially created a new religion" when they formed a community around the central principles that sanctification comes from God alone; that the Lord speaks through dreams and visions; and that sanctified women were under no bond to live with abusive husbands.[67] These were dangerous notions in small-town Texas during the 1880s.

McWhirter's nondenominational group of townswomen further challenged conservative values and traditional gender roles when they attempted to solve several issues that made frontier life especially difficult for women, including the prohibition against women owning property (even that brought by them into marriage); the absurdity of needing to petition husbands for money to run their households; and the behavior of men who became overbearing when drunk.[68] As a consequence of these and other challenges, McWhirter's prayer support group for married women encouraged participants trapped in unhappy marriages to openly acknowledge that fact—and to take action. As McWhirter argued in 1880, "I have always advised wives to live with their husbands when they could, but there is no sense in a woman obeying a drunken husband," especially if it means "giving up all our religion."[69] McWhirter believed that the sanctified partner best raised the children, and she built a common fund out of the little money that came the women's way to help ease the hardships associated with separation or divorce from abusive husbands.

The independent women's commune, later known as the Belton Woman's Commonwealth, took shape in the McWhirter home when one sister, long brutalized by a drunken spouse, found shelter there with her child and worked for room and board. Martha used common reserve funds to address instances of legitimate need among the sisters, and in the decade preceding George McWhirter's death, members of the commonwealth dedicated their wages to a shared treasury—an arrangement that permitted the sisters to live in a state of financial independence from male relatives. The Sanctificationists established their own businesses by marketing the household skills they possessed: they hauled wood, sold dairy products, and hired themselves out as domestic servants to make money. With so many enterprises to operate, the sisters rotated duties. They generally earned between $8 and $10 per day selling wood, $1.25 a day (per worker) for domestic work, and about $200 a month from their lucrative laundry business.[70] In 1883, the Belton Woman's Commonwealth purchased materials for a new headquarters (situated on McWhirter land), and the sisters, together with their sons, supplied most of the labor required for its construction. The group purchased three additional houses so more women might find refuge from dysfunctional marriages.

As tiny Belton grew into a prosperous county seat with a courthouse, an opera house, and a women's college, membership in the Woman's Commonwealth approached fifty.[71] American society was rapidly changing too. Increasing industrialization between 1851 and 1891 raised the percentage of urban dwellers from 45 to 68 percent of the total population; the divorce rate doubled between 1870 and 1890; and women found new opportunities in the workforce as teachers, social workers, nurses, clerks, doctors, and lawyers.[72] In 1886, the Sanctificationists opened the Central Hotel in Belton. Three wide porches, one for each level, graced the front of the three-story brick structure, offering shade during the day and a cool spot to enjoy the evening. Most Belton townsfolk dismissed the chances of success for a large enterprise run by women, but despite their skepticism McWhirter grew their hotel business so fast that by the second year of operation, all hands were required to run it. From that time onward, the sisters ceased doing outside domestic work to support themselves.[73] Although no definitive list survives, Sanctification-ist membership seems to have included numerous children and several men (both married and unmarried).

The death of George McWhirter in 1887 briefly overshadowed the social and economic successes of the sanctified sisters. Years earlier, George had retreated from his home (as bedrooms and attic living quarters filled with desperate women) and relocated to several rooms over a store building that he owned on the north side of the courthouse square. He died there, alone, without ever calling for Martha, who by rule did not "go calling" on the unsanctified.[74] Local outcry sparked by the solitary manner of his pass-ing could only be placated by George's will (drafted a year earlier) that named Martha sole executor and left her half of his property. Meanwhile, the Central Hotel gained popularity for its good food and stellar service with traveling salesmen riding the Missouri–Kansas–Texas Railroad. Emboldened by their success, the sisters formed two holding companies to manage their business affairs: Central Hotel Company and Belton Invest-ment Company. The control of these women over their own assets was sig-nificant, since Texas granted husbands legal oversight of their wives' prop-erty until 1913.[75]

The Sanctificationists completed work on a new hotel in 1894. Three years later, they leased and operated the Palmo Boardinghouse and the Royal Hotel in Waco. They made monetary contributions to Belton's limestone and brick Grand Opera House, helped to finance the town depot, and donated the core collection for the town's public library. Martha McWhirter became the first woman invited to join the Belton Board of Trade.[76] As their fortunes grew, the Sanctificationists tired of parochial Belton, and they took group trips to places like Michigan and New York. The sisters also demonstrated a contin-ued interest in expanding their businesses, and they invested heavily in New York City properties run by Robert McWhirter, Martha's son. In the waning years of the nineteenth century, the Sanctificationists formally searched for a new headquarters, in part due to growing dissatisfaction with Belton among younger members. The group planned to run a boarding house or hotel in Denver, San Francisco, or Mexico City, Mexico—and they inspected prop-erties and priced houses. Eventually, they decided on Washington, D.C., as an ideal location, and the Sanctificationists sold or leased their Belton properties (valued by contemporaries at between $100,000 and $250,000) in 1899.[77]

Martha McWhirter loved the nation's capital city and enjoyed the cultured life that proximity to power brought: Saturday evening concerts on the White House lawn, day trips to House and Senate chambers, and the possibility of meeting the president and first lady at social gatherings. The sisters purchased a sprawling, ten-bedroom house on Kenesaw Avenue (now K Street) and reluctantly took in a few boarders to make ends meet. Perhaps with the Ruskin Commonwealth Association in mind, McWhirter suggested that the group call their new home The Commonwealth. She announced that individual and communal property would be put into a common fund to "be held by trustees for the benefit of the whole, and no part will belong to an individual, as long as they stay with the body, or family. All will receive the same benefit, and if they choose to leave, they will have to trust to the honor and justice of those that are left what they shall have, and now is the time for each to make their choice."[78] Defections followed her ultimatum, but enough new members joined with several people who worked outside of the communal home to guarantee the group's survival. Sanctificationists supported socialist and suffragist causes, and in the tradition of the Central Hotel, the sisters used their Washington home as a platform for advancing progressive causes. The group also purchased a 120-acre farm in Montgomery County, Maryland, in 1903.

Now in her late seventies, Martha McWhirter began to suffer from poor health. The matriarch wore her gray hair parted down the middle and tied it back tightly in a short pigtail. The corners of her mouth drooped, and creases ran outward from nose to chin, but her skin remained taut. While pondering ideas to make the newly acquired Maryland house more conducive to visitors, McWhirter tripped and fell down a flight of stairs. In 1904, she died of pneumonia, and afterward the ranks of the Commonwealth dwindled to just nine members (who managed to keep the boardinghouse on Kenesaw Avenue open until 1914, the Maryland farm intact until 1918, and a Florida property subsidized until 1945).[79] The last surviving member, Martha Scheble, died in the sisters' Maryland home in 1984, at age 101. In the history of American intentional communities, Belton Woman's Commonwealth stands out for its longevity, as well as for its use of communal labor characterized by equal reward and no wages. The Sanctificationists shaped their own destiny, on their own terms, at a time when most American women labored under the yoke of patriarchy. In doing so, they anticipated cultural shifts in social attitudes toward women and minorities that inspired later generations of community builders.

* * *

By the time Isaiah Montgomery and his cousin Benjamin Green founded Mississippi's—and the South's—first all-black town in 1887 at Mound Bayou, slavery had been abolished for more than two decades. White Mississippians nevertheless were determined to keep blacks from achieving any position approaching equality in southern society. The record of whites keeping former slaves as subservient agricultural workers and thwarting black attempts at economic and intellectual progress, Isaiah Montgomery argued, demonstrated that African Americans in the South needed to seek peace and prosperity in segregated communities.[80] His conviction that all-black cities and towns could provide a platform for opportunity and advancement may have stemmed from his being born a slave to Joseph Emory Davis, the older brother (by twenty-three years) of Jefferson Davis, president of the Confederacy. Joseph Davis, like many reform-minded plantation owners, took an interest in Robert Owen's experiments at New Lanark and at New Harmony.

The son of a decorated Revolutionary War hero who had migrated to Kentucky with his family, Joe—as he was known—had dark curly hair rakishly combed forward toward a long face with large expressive eyes, tight narrow lips, and a prominent chin. As a young man, Joe apprenticed at a variety store before studying law under the flamboyant politician William Wallace in 1808 and 1809. Something of a libertine, Joe sired three to nine children out of wedlock during his lifetime.[81] Most likely to avoid marrying one of his paramours and to escape the scandal of an out-of-wedlock pregnancy, Davis and his family sold their property and settled on a small farm in Wilkinson County, Mississippi, in 1811. After earning admission to the bar, Joe Davis helped that territory achieve statehood as a delegate to the constitutional convention with a notably libertarian (almost progressive) bent, and he reluctantly served as the state's attorney general.[82]

Davis also became engrossed in finding better ways of organizing southern plantations, and to test some of his ideas, he purchased extensive acreage 15 miles south of Vicksburg in 1818. The property ran along a sweeping curve of the Mississippi River known as Palmyra Bend. Subsequently renamed Davis Bend, it included some of the Mississippi Delta's most fertile farmland. At the time of purchase, however, it was a dense swamp filled with malaria-carrying mosquitos, alligators, scorpions, and other wildlife. The task of clearing it fell to more than two hundred slaves.[83] Joe may have been the most benevolent slave owner that Frances Wright, the young Scotswoman who founded the short-lived Nashoba Community in Tennessee, ever met, but Davis, of course, required forced labor for his own profit.

In place of the typical conditions found in most southern slave communities during the first half of the nineteenth century, Davis Bend resembled what we might recognize today as a blue-collar town.[84] Well-built row houses that included yards where families could grow vegetables or construct henhouses lined the streets. At a time when the swift and punitive discipline of slaves was common, Davis drew inspiration from Owen's model of labor at New Lanark, and he instituted slave self-governance (including trial by jury), nearly abolished corporal punishment, provided vocational training, encouraged self-sufficiency, and endeavored to achieve full literacy through childhood and adult education.[85] One scholar suggests that Joe's presence in the slave community "was more often welcomed among the laborers as it generally meant that he was there to pass out gifts, offer kind words, or just visit, which alone paints as odd a picture as one might conceive two centuries removed from slavery."[86] Davis cultivated an extraordinarily skilled labor force of three hundred hands, and he invested in steam technology to better compete in the booming cotton business. By mid-decade, "the Bend" had its own blacksmith shop, corncrib, cotton gin, grist mill, and sawmill.

Out of this slave "community of cooperation," designed to be profitable and, under the circumstances, just, Benjamin Thornton Montgomery, Davis's favored manservant, raised himself into one of the most influential black men in the state's history and amassed improbable fortune and authority given broader trends in the antebellum South.[87] As Davis's business agent, Benjamin Montgomery, a talented and energetic jack-of-all-trades, gained proficiencies in farm management, applied mechanics, and general merchandizing. He learned to read and write, married Mary Lewis, and raised four children. He opened a combined variety store and house along the riverfront of the Davis property in 1842. Montgomery & Sons, as that establishment became known, sold to black and white customers who did not want to make the journey to larger towns for their everyday needs.[88] Although he frequently succumbed to scurrilous business practices (such as altering credit terms, padding ledger accounts, and running up prices), he and his family remained slaves—as evidenced by Joe Davis's appropriation of Benjamin's ten-year-old son Isaiah as a houseboy.[89]

Fearful of Union troops, the Davis family fled from the Bend during the Civil War. Benjamin initially stayed behind to oversee the nearby Hurricane and Brierfield Plantation slaves as they continued to plant and harvest crops, but he and his kin escaped the fighting in 1863. They settled in Cincinnati where Benjamin found work at a canal boatyard.[90] When the war ended two years later, Montgomery returned to Davis Bend to resume his leadership role among the recently freed slaves, only to discover that Union troops had destroyed home sites and ravaged their cotton fields. Given the potential for backlash against Davis and his family, Joe had no desire to rebuild, so Montgomery wrote to him and asked to lease the Hurricane and Brierfield Plantations. Over objections from his younger brother Jefferson, Joe offered to sell Montgomery his plantation holdings for $300,000, and yearly interest-only payments of $18,000, with the principle due in nine years.[91] Quite probably, the sale meant that Benjamin Montgomery owed more money than any other ex-slave in the country.

Montgomery stepped into his new role as a southern planter with alacrity. Less than a week after signing the sale paperwork, he placed an advertisement in the *Vicksburg Daily Times* proposing to "organize a community composed exclusively of colored people, to occupy and cultivate said plantations," and he invited "the cooperation of such as are recommended by honesty, industry, sobriety, and intelligence" to join him.[92] Montgomery successfully reorganized Davis Bend without the use of slave labor. With the assistance of his nephew and two sons, Isaiah and William, Montgomery made Davis Bend into the third largest cotton producer in Mississippi by the 1870s.[93] Yet raising cotton on former swampland proved perilous business when the Mississippi River flooded, and Montgomery often found it impossible to pay the yearly interest installments (though he did make partial payments). The death of Joe Davis in 1870 left the Montgomerys without white support, and institutional racism, plummeting commodity prices, and poor crop yields meant the Bend soon reverted to its original owners. Happily, the Montgomery & Sons grocery and dry goods business continued to flourish, and one estimate put Benjamin's net worth in 1873 at $230,000 (placing him among the top 7 percent of all southern merchants and planters).[94] Severely injured when a wall fell on him during the demolition of a house in 1874,

Benjamin Montgomery died three years later having never fully recovered from the accident.

Like his father, Isaiah Montgomery became a community builder and seminal figure in the history of black entrepreneurialism in America. Isaiah struggled to sustain family businesses in the midst of labor shortages, falling land prices, infestation of crops by insects, and hostile political conditions. When representatives from a regional railroad, anxious to appeal to black settlers and purchasers, approached him about selling company lands on a contract basis as their agent, Montgomery explored the county's uninhabited wilderness for two days before choosing a site in Bolivar County 10 miles north of Cleveland, Mississippi. He sold 40-acre parcels to family and friends around a 40-acre town site called Mound Bayou. Efforts began to clear those lots and build rustic cabins in 1887, and within a few months, the town included forty residents and a completed storehouse.[95] Isaiah Montgomery and his cousin Benjamin Green formed a legal partnership to open a sawmill that turned felled lumber from their clearing operations into building timber. Both families opened stores, engaged in land speculation, and participated in large-scale cotton production. Isaiah traveled through Mississippi, Alabama, Arkansas, Louisiana, and Texas selling town lots and farmland on a commission estimated at 12 percent.[96]

The population of Mound Bayou grew steadily during the 1890s and into the opening years of the twentieth century. Its black citizens owned businesses that grossed $113,000 and garnered a total value of $144,000 in 1902.[97] A local newspaper, the *Demonstrator*, helped to advance the political and promotional aims of town leaders, but the influential writer and founder of the prestigious Tuskegee Institute, Booker T. Washington, most effectively extolled the town as a model black enclave and boosted interest in the community as a social experiment. In a series of books and articles, Washington championed agricultural and industrial education and cooperative economic development for blacks as a way to achieve racial advancement without challenging the status quo.[98] In articles about Mound Bayou (e.g., "A Town Owned by Negros"), Washington described "a self-governing community" with a mayor, three aldermen, a constable, and a town marshal—all of whom were black.[99] He noted that the town, incorporated in 1898, attracted ambitious people prepared for the hardships of pioneering in the Mississippi Delta. When Washington visited Mound Bayou in 1908, six thousand people turned out to hear him speak.[100] Four years later, the town had forty-four commercial establishments, two banks, and a variety of public works (including water, electricity, and post).[101] An array of religious organizations testified to the importance of spirituality in the community, just as the proliferation of schools reflected a focus on education.

Undoubtedly, the success of Mound Bayou undermined white suprema-cist assertions of black retrogression.[102] When asked in 1907 whether he feared that someday "whites will be moved to wipe out Mound Bayou with violence," Montgomery, who avoided racial confrontation at all costs (and even supported the 1890 state constitutional convention that disenfranchised black voters), replied in the negative—because the black residents "who have shaped and controlled the destiny of Mound Bayou understand conditions too well to allow any radical or indiscreet policy to prevail here."[103] Economic hardship brought slow, inexorable decline to Mound Bayou, as it had to many southern communities. A pre–World War I economic depression put the Bank of Mound Bayou in jeopardy, though a 1914 state banking law (later acknowledged as racist) allowed state examiners to close that institution— ostensibly for having too many outstanding high-risk loans.[104] When Booker T. Washington died the following year, Mound Bayou forever lost the national visibility it had enjoyed for almost two decades. Several businesses folded, and more than two hundred residents departed. When the sense of solidarity among town leaders dissipated after World War I, the attempt to build and sustain a major town with a predominantly black population in the Deep South came to an end. Once a communal refuge for blacks, as well as a money-making venture based on racial pride, Mound Bayou "became just another sleepy Delta town plagued by poverty and ultimately marginalized by its neighbors and the state."[105]

* * *

The surge in communalism during the 1840s and 1850s, charted in the pre-ceding chapter, ebbed in the post–Civil War era as labor unions and the socialist movement captured much of the communitarian spirit. People who before the war called themselves communists were now known as socialists. The Oneida Community in New York, for instance, commenced in 1848 as an experiment in "Bible Communism," but by the time of its dissolution in 1881, it published a weekly periodical called the *American Socialist.*[106] The explosion in cooperative stores, cooperative manufacturing, cooperative homes, and joint stock ventures across the country, together with the forma-tion of the Socialist Labor Party, speaks to a widely held desire among the general public to improve social and economic conditions. Through the works of Henri de Saint-Simon, Charles Fourier, Robert Owen, and Karl Marx, works that attributed social ills to private ownership of property and the exploitation of labor, Americans drank deep from the wellspring of European socialism.[107] The economic Panic of 1873 deepened interest in socialist communities and cooperative colonies of workers and managers as alternatives to the "wage slavery" of laissez faire capitalism.[108]

In the late nineteenth century, American political economist Henry George attempted to shed light on the social origins of wealth and poverty, and novelist Edward Bellamy touted the power of solidarity and fraternal love. George and Bellamy energized American socialists with trenchant critiques of Gilded Age inequities and the corrosive influence of competition in the capitalist system. Followers of Bellamy's Nationalist movement, so named for the writer's vision of national ownership of production and distribution in *Looking Backward* (1888), supported a cooperative community in Visalia, California, led by Burnette Haskell. A well-respected San Francisco labor leader, Haskell attended Oberlin College, the University of California, and the University of Illinois without earning a degree from any of those prestigious institutions. Admitted to the bar in San Francisco, he practiced law for a short time before assuming the editorship of his uncle's journal, *Truth*, and turning it into a publication for city workers and trade unions. In that periodical, Haskell reprinted selections from the writings of Bellamy, George, and other reformists, and he encouraged the establishment of cooperative settlements to quicken the perfection of humankind.[109] After reading a popularization of Marx entitled *Cooperative Commonwealth* (1884) penned by lawyer and political activist Laurence Gronlund, Haskell decided that nothing short of the establishment of a separate society of workers would spare the laboring classes from exploitation by industrial capitalists.

Haskell located cheap public timberland in the San Joaquin Valley of California for a settlement and set up a "Co-operative Land Purchase and Colonization Association" in 1885.[110] He traveled to Visalia with fifty-three men to file a collective application for 160 acres of land under the Timberland Act of 1878 and the Homestead Act of 1862. Suspecting the buyers of acting as a front in a Southern Pacific Railroad scheme to build rail lines connecting federal forests to San Francisco, federal land officers in Washington, D.C., blocked the sale. Convinced that their application would win approval after a thorough investigation, and the proper warranty deed obtained, Haskell leased the property when it became available. He named the site Kaweah after the river that traversed it. He advertised $500 memberships to residents and nonresidents that included voting rights—and he raised more than $53,000 (including donations) for the co-op.[111] Having striven unsuccessfully to create unity among socialists and anarchists as a labor leader in San Francisco, Haskell, a thin man with a full mustache and light, close-cut hair, described the community as an experiment in "Christian anarchy."[112] Those who joined it agreed to adhere to principles outlined in Laurence Gronlund's *Cooperative Commonwealth*. Although the Danish-born American lawyer and writer lived in Boston, Gronlund joined Kaweah as a nonresident and was elected general secretary of the collective in 1890.

Members of the Kaweah Cooperative Commonwealth organized themselves into three divisions and thirteen departments, employed a time-check system of labor reminiscent of that found in Josiah Warren's Time Stores (with checks issued in dominations ranging from 10 to 20,000 minutes), and provided free health care using the services of a doctor who lived nearby.[113] Because Kaweah lands included magnificent redwood forests, Haskell thought the colony would enjoy easy access to a highly marketable commodity and rapidly attain self-sufficiency. However, in addition to the problem of securing a deed, a road needed to be cut deep into the inaccessible forest to get the timber out. After four years of hard work "without proper tools, powder, or other appliances," Haskell called the completion of an 18-mile road in 1890 that reached an elevation of 8,000 feet "stupendous work."[114] One contemporary portrayed the plucky residents of Kaweah as a colorful group composed of "dress-reform cranks and phonetic spelling fanatics, word purists, and vegetarians," while another observer described them as "assorted cranks of many creeds and none."[115] In fact, they were mostly skilled artisans with trade union backgrounds, musicians, artists, and businessmen.

At first, Kaweahans lived in large white canvas tents with reinforced roofs, but they steadily constructed rustic cabins—along with a community store, a blacksmith shop, a print shop, a barn, and some sheds. At its height, three hundred people lived at Kaweah, though its population generally averaged between fifty and seventy-five persons (most Bellamites).[116] By the time the press turned on the community, a diversity of outlooks had already bred factionalism at Kaweah, and the energy for the social experiment waned. Such San Francisco papers as *The Chronicle* and *Report*, attacked Haskell and the Kaweah colony, and the broadsides that followed in 1891 urged public

FIGURE 20. Squatter's Cabin at Kaweah

protection of the giant Sequoias and ancient redwood groves.[117] Member-ship at Kaweah dropped below fifty as local residents filed criminal charges against the colony for illegally felling trees on federal land. The confisca-tion of Kaweah property under eminent domain to create Sequoia National Park put an end to Haskell's dream. He legally dissolved the community in January 1892 but allowed a couple of families to remain.[118] Disillusioned, he returned to San Francisco and published an account of the colony for the magazine *Out West*. In it, Haskell lamented the absence of a ready-made rem-edy for social and economic misfortunes that afflict the poor. Nearly a century and a half later, we still lack such an antidote—and only Squatter's Cabin in Huckleberry Meadow at Sequoia National Park memorializes the socialists at Kaweah.

Nevertheless, social experimentation in the United States continued unabated. Native Indianan Julius Augustus Wayland, who had made a mod-est fortune in the printing industry, founded a short-lived cooperative asso-ciation in Tennessee named after the enormously influential English art critic and social theorist John Ruskin. Born to a middle-class southern Indiana family that fell into dire poverty after the death of his father during a cholera outbreak, Wayland received only a few years of formal education before being forced to work. Such limited opportunity for schooling did not prevent him from apprenticing with a printer, founding several periodicals in Indiana and Missouri, and moving to Colorado to speculate in real estate. Sometime around 1891, he embraced Populism, supported the Populist Party in the Pueblo area, and edited the *Coming Crisis* newspaper.[119] Returning to Indiana with his family, Wayland established a bi-weekly periodical called the *Coming Age*, an eclectic publication full of anecdotes and epigrams that proved popular enough to gain sixty thousand subscribers (in the United States, Britain, and Australia) during the summer of 1894.[120]

In the *Coming Age*, Wayland endeavored to convince readers that socialism was a venerable American tradition, one that stood in stark contrast to the competitive and individualistic values of capitalism. In Wayland's estimation, the Civil War had released a "usurpation" of capitalism that permitted trade, industry, and capital to be privately owned and operated for the sake of profit, an arrangement that imperiled the nation by concentrating massive wealth in the hands of a few individuals.[121] Drawing upon a wide range of thought (from Gronlund and Bellamy to Ruskin and the free-labor republicanism advanced by antislavery reformers), Wayland made the case for a more equitable distribution of wealth, and he advocated the creation of a new social order based on cooperation that would eliminate competition and the exploitation of labor. Wayland urged his fellow Americans to form cooperative commonwealths to thwart the "wage masters" who perpetuated social inequality.[122] He described self-regulating cooperative associations, consisting of honest producers with no special privileges and utterly simple in their workings, whose ennobling surroundings would elevate their moral and political endeavors into concrete demonstrations of "practical socialism."[123]

Wayland's sketchy but favorable opinion of the rich American tradition of communitarianism provided him with compelling historical precedent. He began to draft plans for a functioning socialist colony before the *Coming Nation* was a year old. In its pages, he described a cooperative community in which the equitable sharing of goods created the basis for a new moral order, and the equal wages paid "for all grades of labor" permitted residents to create a classless society composed of citizen-producers acting in concert for their own mutual benefit.[124] Only such absolute equality, Wayland argued, could foster a truly democratic society in which everyone, not only the wealthy, had the time and the means to lead enriching cultural lives centered upon self-improvement. In his colony, everyone would devote leisure hours to "elevating influence of association" in the community library, civic meeting hall, and auditorium.[125] Wayland vowed to forever banish the consuming drudgery of wage labor and the struggle to merely survive. He brought to life for readers an idealized image of a community that in essence diagnosed the pathology of predatory capitalism, to which he offered an alternative.

In the July 21, 1894 issue of the *Coming Nation*, Wayland announced the selection of a site for such a community 50 miles west of Nashville, Tennessee. He and his assistants purchased 1,000 acres of land in a sparsely populated area that featured convenient access to a post office and a railroad depot and cost just $2.50 an acre (they discovered later due to the poor soil quality). Wayland invited anyone who bought stock subscriptions at $500 per share, or who recruited two hundred new subscribers to the paper, to join him. After securing a capital investment of over $17,000 in stock, Wayland drew up a charter for the Ruskin Commonwealth Association.[126] The first forty socialists in residence welcomed Wayland and his family when they arrived in August of the same year. The Ruskinites may not have anticipated the grueling work required for clearing timbered land, and the lack of safe drinking water on the densely wooded property compelled them to dig shallow wells wherever feasible.

Determined to succeed, Wayland and his followers surveyed the hills and ravines and attempted to lay out an orderly town site, with street names like Liberty Hill and Ruskin Avenue, from late summer 1894 to fall 1896.[127] However, as the population of the colony neared 250 residents, families built out of necessity wherever they struck water. As a result, Ruskin never became the tidy planned town Wayland envisioned; instead, houses and outbuildings speckled the steep hillsides. Recognizing the futility of continuing to build without an ample water supply, community leaders began scouting for new settlement locations in Tennessee, Kentucky, and Pennsylvania. They eventually purchased a 383-acre farm known as Cave Mills just 5 miles north in the fertile Yellow Creek Valley. Half of the property, bounded by limestone bluffs and undulating hills, was already cleared and tillable, and 75 acres of it ran along the rugged banks of Yellow Creek.[128] Subsequent land acquisitions brought their total holdings to more than 800 acres.

Over the next eight months, the Ruskinites dismantled their buildings and moved them up the road to Cave Mills. The existence of several structures on the farm (including houses, barns, a mill, and a country store) eased that transition, as did the construction of a temporary boarding house and a large three-story brick building called Commonwealth Hall.[129] Two large natural caves provided an elegant solution to the community's need for natural refrigeration (for produce storage and a fruit cellar). By 1898, almost three hundred people lived in seventy small rustic homes surrounded by young shade trees and colorful flower beds. Dotting the hillsides like mushrooms, community buildings housed a variety of shops and services: a steam laundry, a tin shop, a bakery, a coffeehouse, and a school.[130] Ruskinites ran a cannery, raised livestock, finished lumber for the railroad, manufactured leather goods and chewing gum, and published (on contract) union pamphlets and books. Their cultural lives included dances and picnics, concerts and lectures held in Commonwealth Hall, and regular musical performances by their brass band.[131] Their grade school proved so successful that plans were made, though never realized, for the nation's first socialist university: Ruskin College of New Economy. The *Coming Nation* proclaimed it would be built by "people who have so few institutions that they are free from the blight of commercialism and the influence of the arrogant wealthy."[132]

As the community grew, it attracted folks with very different political, religious, and social conceptions, so much so that when newcomers outnumbered chartered members, disagreement and petty squabbling broke out. Wayland, a better newspaper man than community leader, bristled under criticism of his operation, particularly regarding the for-profit press that he operated. Wayland could be defensive and controlling, and sensing an attack opportunity, his opponents accused him of being an individualist who lined his own pockets with money from the community newspaper.[133] Wayland demanded ownership of the newly acquired perfecting press (that allowed printing on both sides of a sheet of paper) in the summer of July 1895, and he cited his many contributions to the community. But members balked, and at a special meeting, they voted to terminate his lease.

A settlement reached between the warring factions specified that Wayland and his brother would each receive $1,000 in return for giving up "all interests, rights, title, and equity" in the *Coming Nation* (including machinery, press, type, mailing list, the building, and all stock on hand).[134] Wayland shrugged his shoulders, accepted the deal, and in August started *Appeal to Reason*, which within ten years became the leading socialist newspaper in the country with a worldwide circulation of over 150,000.[135] Among his other

FIGURE 21. Ruskin Cave entrance

notable accomplishments, Wayland introduced Eugene Debs to socialism, convinced Upton Sinclair to write a book about the Chicago stockyards (*The Jungle*, 1904), and attacked monopoly and free enterprise with unflagging zeal in *Appeal to Reason*. Yet, the Socialist Party failed to win in the 1912 election. Depressed by the death of his wife, scurrilous attacks from the conservative press, and his own failure to persuade Americans of the many advantages of socialism, Julius Wayland took his own life on November 10, 1912.

The Ruskin colony survived Wayland's departure in 1895. Stockholders turned over the editorship of the newspaper to a former associate of Wayland's, and circulation held steady for a time. The tumultuous succession of subsequent editors that followed brought to the surface long-simmering tensions among Ruskinites that were reflected in the quality and appearance of the *Coming Nation*. Subscriptions fell precipitously. In the absence of surviving business records, it is difficult to determine the financial soundness of the colony, but the quality of life at Ruskin certainly fell short of depictions in Bellamy's *Looking Backward*. Essentially an undercapitalized town with one major industry (the newspaper), Ruskin colonists mistakenly bought more land than they needed, and some of it fell fallow. They squandered limited capital on mortgaged land that failed to produce income. Houses were also shoddy or left unfinished.[136]

As their fiscal situation worsened, tempers grew short. Ruskinites argued over the status of women, political and economic stewardship, and the latitude for ideological dissent. Attrition took its toll, and the quality of life in the community diminished further. Squabbles between chartered and unchartered members erupted, and litigation began among the colonists that ended in dissolution of the community.[137] A court-approved sale on June 22, 1899, liquidated Ruskin Commonwealth Association property, but assets valued at $94,000 brought only about $17,000 at auction. Mortgage settlements reduced that figure to just under $10,600—and court costs, creditor obligations, and attorney fees claimed another $5,200.[138] In the end, 138 stockholding colonists divided approximately $5,400 (meaning they received about $39 of their $500 investment). Most resumed their former lives in the Midwest and West, but a few Ruskinites lingered in the area, and they formulated plans to join a floundering cooperative known as the Duke Colony near Waycross, Georgia.

Founded by the American Settlers Association of Dayton on the site of a former lumber mill and turpentine mill, the property included seventy buildings on 768 acres, only a small portion of which was under cultivation.[139] With both groups facing few viable alternatives for survival, the Ruskinites assumed Duke debts, and Duke colonists dissolved their association to become members of a Ruskin Commonwealth dedicated to principles almost indistinguishable from those of Wayland's Tennessee colony. Within a few months of the court-approved auction of Ruskin property in Tennessee, 240 Ruskinites and their belongings, packed into four passenger coaches and nine freight cars, and headed for Georgia. Based on their own scout reports, they anticipated finding an ideal settlement, but the new location lacked most of the attractions that made life in Tennessee enjoyable. It was flat as a floor, there was no running water, and wild pigs and alligators periodically wandered through the dusty streets. Lizzy McCoy summed up the general consensus regarding the Georgia settlement describing it as "a HELL of a place."[140] Making matters worse, sales of the *Coming Nation*, the only real hope for financially supporting the new cooperative, further slumped.

By the end of the first year in Georgia, attempts at broom making had also faltered, and although revived Tennessee industries fared better, the community's misfortunes multiplied. Membership dropped by half, and food shortages ensued. A withering of the spirit of cooperation put an end to communal dining, education, and laundry services—and rampant illness prevented the labor force from maintaining its full strength and put heavy demands on community resources.[141] Dissension increased with disillusionment, and remaining members began to scatter. With the auction of community assets in 1901, Ruskin joined a long list of short-lived communitarian experiments during the second half of the nineteenth century. At the heart of the Ruskinites' troubles lay exaggerated expectations for the elimination of poverty and squalor and dashed hopes of abundance and leisure.[142] Yet the expansion of communitarianism in the 1890s, at levels not seen since the 1840s, stimulated the establishment of intentional communities in the early twentieth century, including the Theosophical community at Lomaland, which persisted from 1900 to 1942.

3 ▸ THEOSOPHY, DEPRESSION, AND THE NEW DEAL

Helena Petrovna Blavatsky, plump, middle-aged, and exotically robed, looked every bit the eastern European mystic with her black hair half-veiled by a long shawl. Occultist, writer, and cofounder of the Theosophical Society, Blavatsky became intrigued with the spread of Nationalist (or Bellamy) Clubs that appeared across the nation following the publication of *Looking Backward* in 1888. In that popular novel, Edward Bellamy described a humanized system of publicly owned capital in which the government oversaw production and distributed national output equally among citizens. In 1889, Blavatsky endorsed the novel as the interim social goal of Theosophy and a basis for social and spiritual renewal. She explained that the "organization of Society depicted by Edward Bellamy, in his magnificent work *Looking Backward*, admirably represents the Theosophical idea of what should be the first great step toward the full realization of universal brotherhood."[1] Although her support for the Nationalist movement waned, the success of its Bellamy Clubs encouraged her to conceive a living community based purely on Theosophical principles.

Born in Ukraine in 1831, Blavatsky married a forty-year-old Russian military officer and provincial vice governor at the age of seventeen. She fled that unhappy marriage after a few months and traveled the world for nearly two decades, supporting herself as a journalist, pianist, and circus performer. During that time, Blavatsky claimed to have visited monasteries in Tibet, studied magic with a Coptic magician in Cairo, and joined a Spiritualist society in Paris. She eventually reached New York City and in 1875 helped to establish the Theosophical Society, an organization dedicated to the study of Spiritualism. In several books that drew upon a mixture of transcendentalism, Buddhism, Hinduism, and Spiritualism, Blavatsky postulated the existence of an omnipresent Eternal Principle that created and sustained the material world.[2] Her articulation of Theosophy proved a dynamic alternative for people holding progressive and reformist values, as traditional forms of religious expression lost much of their appeal in the wake of science and industrialization. During the zenith of the movement between 1890 and 1930, Blavatsky and her colleagues attracted many to Theosophy who were intrigued by the Spiritualism, Asian philosophy, and indigenous religions deemed unorthodox by mainstream American Protestant culture.[3]

The Theosophists set out to investigate the "unexplained laws of nature and the psychic powers latent in man"; to advance the study of "ancient and modern religions, philosophies, and sciences"; and to forge a Universal Brotherhood of Humanity "without distinction of race, creed, sex, caste, or color."[4] The decor of Theosophical Society headquarters, an apartment at 47th Street and Eighth Avenue in New York City, reflected that eclecticism with its golden Buddha, potted palm trees, and preserved owls, snakes, and lizards in bookcases, and, in the corner of one room, a stuffed baboon with spectacles reading a journal article on Darwin's *On the Origin of Species* (1859). Ordinary folk, journalists, and even celebrities such as Thomas Edison flocked to séances held in the apartment (during which Blavatsky made rapping sounds emanate from under the table and pictures appear on blank slates).[5] However, continued accusations of charlatanism dogged Blavatsky and diminished her reputation, and three years after cofounding the Theosophical Society, she departed to establish Theosophical headquarters in India. She left behind a small, disorganized group that would later build the Lomaland community in San Diego. Blavatsky returned to Europe in 1885 and died six years later during an influenza outbreak in London. By that time, the Theosophical movement consisted of more than one hundred chartered lodges across the globe, many of them in South Asia.

Schism followed Helena Blavatsky's death. Annie Besant became her designated successor in Europe and India, and she oversaw the lodges of the Adyar branch of the Theosophical Society. The leadership of the Theosophical Society of America fell to Katherine Tingley in 1896. Tingley convinced Besant to unify the lodges, to organize an international convention in Chicago, and to build a Universal Brotherhood for social reform. Together, the two women pushed Theosophy toward communalism as a vehicle for humanitarianism. Besant developed a variety of programs to help the poor in India, while Tingley planned a model community in America to realize a Theosophical way of life that would also serve as a platform to launch a world crusade.[6] An intuitive and charismatic leader, Tingley belonged to an era and lived in a nation abounding in utopian schemes (with no fewer than forty-eight utopian romances published between 1884 and 1900). She held public meetings in Boston and New York City and then departed for England, Scotland, Ireland, Austria, Italy, Greece, Egypt, India, Australia, and New Zealand on a mission to advance the Theosophical cause.[7]

As Tingley and her companions crossed the Pacific on their way home, word reached the group that a 132-acre school site at Point Loma in California had been secured, along with an option on an adjoining 40 acres. In February 1897, the Theosophists set a temple cornerstone in an elaborate ceremony that brought a procession of nearly a thousand San Diegans to the northern and westernmost land-arm protecting San Diego Bay. Although the grounds proved unsuitable for agriculture, they featured panoramic views of the mountains to the east and the Pacific Ocean to the west. Two years elapsed before the vanguard of the Lomaland community arrived from New York and built the first structures. The Society held its annual convention in New York City in April 1897, and a few days later Tingley organized an International Brotherhood League, headquartered it at Point Loma, and appointed herself lifetime president. The Lomalanders aspired to the following ideals:

1. To educate children of all nations on the broadest lines of Universal Brotherhood and to prepare destitute and homeless children to become workers for humanity

2. To ameliorate the conditions of unfortunate women and assist them to a higher life
3. To assist those who are or have been in prisons to establish themselves in honorable positions of life
4. To help workingmen to realize the nobility of their calling and their true position in life
5. To bring about a better understanding between so-called savage and civilized races by promoting a closer and more sympathetic relationship between them
6. To relieve human suffering resulting from flood, famine, war, and other calamities; and generally to extend aid, help, and comfort to suffering humanity throughout the world[8]

The first charitable operation of the Universal Brotherhood, International Lotus Home, took in twenty-five uncared-for tenement children from the East Side of New York City during the summer and provided them with physical, moral, and spiritual training.

A United States population census found 95 people at Lomaland in 1900. Ten years later, the population had increased to 357 (67 percent of whom were adults) before declining slightly to 320 in 1920.[9] True to Tingley's vision for the city, the design of the central buildings at Lomaland evoked the palaces of the Rajahs in South Asia. The grounds included a resplendent white hotel-sanatorium (referred to as the Homestead and later used by the Raja Yoga school) with an inner patio covered by a massive dome of aquamarine glass and surrounded by smaller domes set on the towered corners of the building. Nearby, a perfectly round white temple rose on arches that held aloft a dome of amethyst-colored glass. Adjacent to those structures, a white two-story building provided offices for the Brotherhood. Clustered among them were several round, canvas-topped cottages, which were later rebuilt out of wood.[10] Temporary tents and bungalows (collectively referred to as Camp Karnak) sheltered members of the staff, and below that makeshift village stood the first Greek theater in America, sloping gently toward the Pacific Ocean. Newly planted eucalyptus trees graced the once unwooded property and elegant private homes complemented the exotic appeal of the setting.

Anyone who endorsed Theosophy could join the Point Loma colony on probation after agreeing to the rules and paying a fee averaging $500 (though in practice rich petitioners paid more than poor ones). For their work on

FIGURE 22. Spaulding Home (1901) at Point Loma

rotating household tasks, members received no remuneration, but larger projects involving heavier work were hired out.[11] In any case, members had
scant need for personal funds, since the community took care of most living
expenses (from medical bills to plumbing fees). Theosophists at Point Loma
lived in a large, communal Homestead, or in any number of bungalows on
the property, and they took meals together. Visitors reported martial-like discipline in the community that included wearing military-style uniforms and
saluting superiors. The community's Raja Yoga School enrolled thirty-two
pupils its first year and averaged around one hundred students per year thereafter. Tuition ranged from nothing to $2,000 per annum, depending on the
financial need of the student. Parents and educators at the school strove to
create a "pure moral atmosphere" that inspired goodness, nobility, and
wholesomeness.[12] Orphans, and students recruited during Theosophical
Society outreach efforts in Cuba, filled out the school ranks. Although a number of children attended free of charge, tuition from the school provided an
important revenue stream for the community.

    Lomalanders raised children born into the community collectively (with
the help of an on-site nursery), and parents permitted older children to grow
up in group environments and were contented to see them on a weekly or
biweekly basis. Community members endeavored to instill in young people
a "moral nature and character" discernible in their "self-control, alertness,

obedience, health," and even-temperedness.[13] In addition to pioneering new methods of moral education, Tingley reformed the founding ideal of Universal Brotherhood into a "utopian vision of the Theosophical Society of America spearheading a worldwide cultural and ethical renovation of the next generation through education."[14] The quest for self-sufficiency at Lomaland led to the cultivation of a highly productive garden that provided much of the community's food, but the bulk of financial support came from tickets for dramatic performances, school tuitions, sale of Theosophist literature printed by the Point Loma press, and well-heeled Theosophists around the world. The community attempted to sustain a variety of cottage industries, including planting mulberry trees and raising silkworms, but residents had more luck with beekeeping and selling handicrafts made by members.[15]

Unfortunately, Lomaland never attained economic self-sufficiency, and rarely, if ever, did it find itself clear of debt.[16] Although their theatrical and musical troupes traveled the world and brought in needed funds, it is doubtful they ever turned a profit. At times, Tingley sold prime plots of land for considerable sums, but an excess of outlay over income continued.[17] In spite of that untenable situation, Tingley publicized the Raja School as a prototype for a Theosophical education, and she established branch campuses in Cuba (as early as 1902) and later in Sweden, Germany, and England. Tingley drew together the wealthiest and ablest members of the lodges in England and the United States to effect social renewal on a global scale. Despite those efforts to raise funds and an awareness of her cause, community indebtedness required floating a $400,000 bond issue in 1927.[18] Two years later, Point Loma announced the tragic death of Katherine Tingley. In May 1929, the eighty-two-year-old founder of Lomaland suffered life-threatening injuries in an automobile accident while on a European lecture tour. Her passing created a tremendous vacuum in Loma leadership that Sanskrit scholar Gottfried de Purucker never entirely filled. Nor could he reverse the financial trajectory of the community when the stock market crashed three months later and the country entered the Great Depression. In light of those financial straits, Purucker reached out to eighty-three-year-old Annie Besant in another effort to unify disparate Theosophical groups worldwide, but to little effect. Lomaland membership fell to 130 by 1941. Half of the surviving members were over sixty years of age, and more than a third were over seventy.[19] Classrooms closed and public concerts were abandoned.

FIGURE 23. View of the Pacific Ocean from Point Loma Nazarene University

With the onset of World War II, more military installations moved into the area, and the Lomaland community capitulated to the demand for wartime housing and liquidated its remaining property holdings. The last seventy-five residents moved to a (debt-free) secluded spot in the orange groves of Covina.[20] Today, visitors find surviving Lomaland buildings (including Spaulding Home, Greek Theater, Beaver Home, Lotus Home, and Madame Tingley Home) scattered in and around the Point Loma Nazarene University campus.[21] Despite the closure of Lomaland, Theosophy—as a part of a larger stream of esoteric thought—directly influenced the spread of Eastern religious traditions in California and elsewhere, and it contributed to the flowering of New Age movements during the 1960s and 1970s.[22] Subsequent Theosophical communities sprang up in California, for instance the Temple of the People and Krotona (still in operation), but none of them recaptured the renown and influence of Tingley's Point Loma.

* * *

In the opening years of the twentieth century, California drew westward many people in search of sunlight and communalism. Farm boy, ordained minister, and progressive politician, Job Harriman, believed that he could build a functioning cooperative town that would convert Americans to socialism. To prove it, he established Llano del Rio Cooperative Colony, one of the largest secular intentional communities in California's history. Raised in the Midwest until eighteen years of age, Harriman studied for the ministry at North Western Christian University (now Butler University) in Indianapolis. After graduating, he found his chosen vocation unsatisfying. A capable, intelligent, and handsome man, Harriman subsequently gained admission to the Indiana bar. Harriman moved to California in 1886, joined the Nationalist movement in the early 1890s, and petitioned for a charter to start a local unit of the Socialist Labor Party in San Francisco. Working his way up the party ranks, he stood as the socialist nominee for governor of California in 1898, but he polled poorly (winning only around 5,000 votes out of more than 280,000).[23]

Undeterred by that defeat, Harriman ran for vice president of the United States with the Social Democratic Party in 1900 on a ticket headed by Eugene Debs. During the campaign Harriman foresaw that the socialist movement in America needed an economic base, not just a political one, in the form of a functioning cooperative. "It became apparent to me," he wrote, "that a people would never abandon their means of livelihood, good or bad, capitalistic or otherwise, until other methods were developed which would promise advantages at least as good as those by which they were living."[24] A decade later, while practicing criminal law in Los Angeles, he assisted local socialist units in their efforts to aid striking metal workers on the Pacific coast. Harriman thought their coordinated cooperation "an excellent economic base for politics,"[25] and labor unions united with socialists to support Harriman's candidacy for mayor of Los Angeles. He nearly won that election in 1911, but Harriman's support for the unionist McNamera brothers (who confessed to bombing the *Los Angeles Times* building just five days before municipal polling) cost him the election and ended his career in politics.

Forced to change course, Harriman decided to create the economic base for the socialist movement that he first envisioned in 1900. Harriman persuaded a group of idealists (labor leaders, a banker, an architect, and a journalist among them) to develop a detailed plan for an intentional community— and to build it. They selected a site on the western tip of the Mojave Desert northeast of Los Angeles, owned by the Sunset Colony, which had been founded twenty years earlier by a short-lived group of communal farmers.[26]

"I proposed to organize a joint stock company in which each member would purchase two thousand shares," Harriman remembered, "paying for the 1000 in cash or property, and paying for the other 1000 shares by labor." Anyone who purchased shares agreed to reside in the colony. Llano residents worked for $4 per day, though $1 of that amount went toward payment of the one thousand labor shares. Community resources were pooled in a "common storehouse," out of which members drew only as much as needed to feed and clothe themselves.[27] By living simply and sharing, Harriman and his partners hoped that an economy based on equal pay and equitable ownership in the colony would be firmly established.

Equal ownership, equal wages, and equal social opportunity became defining principles of Llano del Rio. That profession of equality notwithstanding, the Llano Del Rio Cooperative Colony, like many intentional communities (including Ruskin Commonwealth Association), did not admit African Americans. Advertisements for the colony in the community newspaper, *Western Comrade*, described an idyllic California locale with a stunning mixture of snow-covered peaks and radiant deserts. In fact, winters in the Antelope Valley were cold and summers hot, and it was arid and flat. Yet, what began with five families and their livestock grew rapidly to one hundred colonists—many of whom lived in tents and makeshift adobe structures during the first year. Within weeks of starting, Llanoites put up barns and workshops, and they framed small family houses. They gathered stones from cleared fields to construct a dormitory; began work on a hotel; and planted alfalfa, corn, and grain.[28] Because the land was arid, the communitarians at Llano del Rio dug miles of irrigation ditches to channel water into dusty fields, and they planted orchards on hundreds of barren acres. Community industries rapidly developed, including such diverse enterprises as a fish hatchery, a quarry and lime kiln, rug works, a paint shop, a brickyard, and a laundry. The community soon owned trucks, several automobiles, wagons, plows, and buggies, and they operated a dairy, a rabbitry, an apiary, a cannery, leatherworks, and shoe shops.[29]

Like Kaweah Colony, the residents of Llano del Rio Cooperative Colony tended to be labor unionists and socialists, and community publications advertising membership and extolling the virtues of the society used the terms "colonist" and "socialist" almost synonymously.[30] One advertisement for Llano del Rio printed in *Western Comrade* promised "the opportunity of a lifetime to solve the problem of unemployment and provide for the future of yourself and children."[31] Although such announcements encouraged men and women practicing useful occupations to join, families and individuals generally paid a base fee that went into the common fund, and they contributed labor to the community. By 1915, the colony's second year, some 150 residents called Llano del Rio home; two years later, membership topped 1,100 people, many of them lured by the promise of paradise for a few hundred dollars.[32] Those arrivals swelled the ranks of the community, but their presence meant more mouths to feed out of a limited store of provisions.

In addition to emphasizing the formation of revenue-generating industries, Harriman made education a central focus of colonists' lives. The community established a comprehensive school system featuring three distinct elements (a public school, a Montessori school, and an industrial school), and it enrolled 125 students by 1917. The Llano Montessori School was among the first in California, and the industrial school (known as Junior Colony) taught high school students a trade through experiential learning. All three schools committed to state and county curricula, received tax funds, and abided by county regulations.[33] Adults at Llano attended night classes and read freely from a library of several thousand volumes. A small community brass band and orchestra performed regularly, dances took place two nights a week, and Sunday evening programs offered additional cultured entertainment. The colonists built warehouses, a post office, a dairy, a laundry, a dining hall, and a hotel.[34] Their homes had electricity—and some of them running water.

Despite those impressive accomplishments, several years passed without the joint stock company turning a profit, and the wage agreement (that theoretically ensured everyone the same pay) broke down. To entice potential residents, the colony had promised $4 per day, but it deducted $1 off the top for shares of unpurchased labor stock, and charges were made against the balance for food, clothing, and shelter at prices near to cost. Whatever positive balances accrued over time, the colony paid them only after realizing a profit. Llano residents, many of whom were more conscious of their ideals than their wages, came to call the ersatz credits "dobey money," after the adobe walls of their homes that melted away when roofs leaked.[35] Even if colonists had managed to produce a marketable excess through production, the fact that Llano lay 20 miles from the nearest railroad depot, and the colony owned just two trucks, presented further obstacles to profitability. Governing the community proved difficult as well, since the directors of the Llano del Rio Com-

FIGURE 24. Ruins of Hotel Llano

pany held little political power. Real control rested with stockholders—that is, the members of the community who elected officers and members of the board, formulated policies, and dictated to the superintendent.[36] The Llanoites practiced a belligerent form of democracy, where passionate voices vied to be heard amid the din of assembly.

Unruffled by these and other challenges at Llano, Harriman planned a model city of the future that would accommodate 10,000 residents. In his blueprints, schools, stores, hotels, clubhouses, garages, and industrial buildings radiated outward from a civic center situated at the heart of the city. He envisioned each family living comfortably in a five-room house. Before commencing construction on the City of Llano, Harriman felt the need to first purify the Llanoites in Antelope Valley to make their minds "as sweet and gentle and loving as in babyhood."[37] That task proved futile when conflicts of interest among residents resulted in attacks upon his leadership by people Harriman remembered as "the malingerers, who criticized but refused to work," the "greedy, with their clamor for special privileges," and the "power lovers who envied him and were ambitious to take his place."[38] Looking backward in 1924 on that short-lived colony, Harriman fumed that some residents "were selfish, arrogant, and egotistical and shirked their duties, quit early, went to work late, rested often, talked much, criticized everything and everybody, wanted the lion's share at the commissary, wanted the best houses, with extra furniture, neglected the animals, were careless with tools, and did everything that might be thought of by those who were seeking the advantage of those about them."[39] His is a sad, yet familiar, refrain in the song of intentional living.

Although Harriman's memories of Llano were not entirely fond, that colony might have survived internecine feuding had not the impossibility of sustaining a growing membership on barren land ultimately doomed it. At first, residents attempted to secure additional water from Big Rock Creek by digging more irrigation ditches, but that approach proved insufficient.[40] They considered constructing a dam to form a reservoir, but the underground flow from Big Rock Creek washed small due to a fault that diverted much of the water. Local ranchers also challenged the colony's water rights in a series of lawsuits.[41] Seeing that no amount of hard work or enthusiasm could overcome the problem of an inadequate water supply, the colonists considered moving. When they heard of 20,000 acres of land in Louisiana put on the market by a defunct lumber company for $120,000—a bargain price since the property included the buildings of an old mill town—Harriman and associates arranged for its purchase.[42] At the close of 1917, about one hundred colonists moved to the Pelican State and named their settlement Newllano. Llano Del Rio survived in California for another year or so before succumbing to bankruptcy.

By January, three hundred socialists lived communally at Newllano in abandoned lumber shacks, a few large homes, and an eighteen-room hotel. They operated a store, several warehouses, and a small school.[43] Sadly, drought devastated their first crop, though residents muddled through by selling cord wood processed at the lumber mill. During those first few years at Newllano, Harriman largely remained in California beset by legal problems surrounding the dissolution of Llano del Rio. George Pickett (and for a time Ernest Wooster) assumed the duties of director in Harriman's absence. Pickett established new industries, including a brick kiln, a printing operation, a rice farm, and a power plant. After he returned to Newllano in 1920, disillusioned and sick with tuberculosis, Harriman's health continued to decline. He retired from active leadership and moved to Los Angeles in 1925. Soon thereafter, Harriman collapsed and died (virtually penniless) while visiting a former colleague from Llano del Rio.[44]

Over the next decade, Newllano consolidated its gains. Membership fluctuated, rising rapidly in the 1920s and then leveling off. Pickett managed to attract a socialist newspaper, *American Vanguard*, to Newllano in 1923, and he provided a rich social life to residents that included dancing, concerts, silent movies, educational forums, May Day parades, and sports activities. Residents also enjoyed a park, a swimming pool, and a library with thousands of books. Every home included electricity, most had running water, and all families received daily deliveries of ice. For a time, colonists even took free courses at Commonwealth College in Newllano. In addition, the community operated a general store, a bath house, a hospital, a private telephone system, and an open-air theater.[45] Yet those impressive developments could not overcome a series of woes that beleaguered the Louisiana settlement: the prospect of discovering oil on the property proved illusory; fire claimed several communal buildings; and Pickett's efforts to secure federal financial support, by having Newllano designated as one of the Farm Security Administration's cooperative farms, failed.[46]

The agonies of the Great Depression boosted the population of Newllano to about four hundred people, all of whom worked in the community, or on three auxiliary sites, to provide members with rice, citrus fruit, and beef. Pickett repeatedly suspended membership fees during the 1930s to accommodate the destitute, but those acts of charity only exacerbated Newllano's economic travails.[47] Open revolt against Pickett's leadership broke out on May Day 1935, and a new group of directors took control of Newllano. That development did little to appease warring factions—and on at least one occasion shots were fired. A court-appointed receiver selected new leaders and kept the colony operating until it was formally dissolved in 1938.[48] Pickett died in his Newllano home in 1962. Today, the Museum of the New Llano Colony keeps Harriman's dream alive—and it marked the hundredth anniversary of the Llano del Rio Cooperative Colony's move to Louisiana in 2017.

*   *   *

In the early part of the twentieth century communitarianism remained an essential part of the American cultural landscape, but finding opportunities for groups of like-minded people to march into the wilderness and carve out a community on cheap land meant venturing ever farther from large commercial centers. Meanwhile, government propaganda during World War I stoked patriotic and nationalistic sentiments, which slowed the spread of socialism. When the fighting ended in 1918, unemployment rose (as wartime demand for goods and services shrank), manufacturing and industry slowed, and commodity prices that had ballooned during the conflict fell precipitously.

Consequently, the early years of the 1920s were lean ones for many Americans. Members of the working and middle classes struggled to make ends meet. Farmers, who had borrowed heavily at high rates of interest to increase output during the war took the hardest hit (along with millions of marginalized individuals—women and minorities, immigrants, and the disabled—who suffered disproportionately during the prolonged economic crisis). The economy gathered steam as the decade ended, but economic prosperity only dampened public enthusiasm for socialist cooperatives that challenged the perceived ills of industrialization.[49]

By the time that Republican Herbert Hoover defeated Democrat Al Smith and won the presidency in 1928, the postwar economy had gained momentum. Real gross national product rose 38 percent, and the value of common stock tripled over 1922 levels. Unemployment stood at 3.2 percent.[50] Their pockets full again, Americans grew increasingly optimistic as the stock market peaked in early September 1929 (with values tripling in just three years). Automobile sales surged (led by Henry Ford's legendary Model T), refrigerators replaced iceboxes, women "bobbed" their hair and raised their hemlines, and radios invited the world into every home.[51] The skillful evasion of Prohibition became sport, powerful images graced the silver screen, Babe Ruth "knocked 'em out of the park," and Charles Lindbergh made transcontinental flight a viable possibility. That tremendous affluence, students of history know, proved fragile and fleeting. On October 29, 1929, "Black Tuesday," the stock market plummeted. By year's end, it had given up one-third of its peak value, and the nation entered a prolonged economic depression that cast millions out of work and forever challenged suppositions about the role of the federal government in the lives of its citizens. Nationwide, unemployment doubled just five months following the crash. Seemingly oblivious to the staggering scale of job losses, President Hoover declared in March 1930: "All the facts indicate that the worst effects of the crash on employment will have been passed during the next 30 to 60 days."[52]

The Great Depression of the 1930s shattered American confidence in laissez-faire capitalism, and it called forth a multitude of utopian schemes aimed at addressing widespread unemployment, hunger, and destitution. Until his resounding electoral defeat by Franklin Roosevelt in 1932, Hoover stubbornly insisted that the economic crisis was merely a brief setback when more than 1,300 banks failed in 1930, taking with them $853 million in deposits, and in excess of twenty-six thousand businesses folded. Almost 2,300 banks, representing almost $1.7 billion in deposits, closed in 1931, and more than twenty-eight thousand businesses shuttered.[53] Unemployment skyrocketed from about 1.5 million before the stock market crash to nearly 12 million by the beginning of 1932. Having lost everything, the homeless slept in doorways, panhandlers filled street corners, and furniture belonging to the evicted appeared overnight on sidewalks. One wandering reporter, Edmund Wilson, discovered an old, tottering seven-story building with a broken heating system on Chicago's South Side "jam-crammed" with African Americans too impoverished to pay for lights. In Appalachia, a sickly child was told to go home to get something to eat: "I can't," she replied, "It's my sister's turn to eat."[54] Some Appalachian families survived on dandelions and blackberries.

Makeshift communities for the homeless, known as Hoovervilles, sprawling shanty towns constructed from scrap wood and metal patched haphazardly together to form rudimentary shelters, appeared in and around every major city. Many unemployed people opted to hop on freight trains and drift aimlessly around the nation. The Southern Pacific Railroad estimated that it threw 683,000 transients off its box cars in a single year alone—at least 200,000 of them adolescents.[55] The vast extent of economic hardship challenged cherished American notions of self-reliance, liberty, and upward mobility through hard work regardless of social station. Before the Great Depression, most Americans felt that the national government should not intrude into the personal lives of its citizens. For that reason, when the proportions of the crisis could no longer be ignored, President Hoover appealed to the charitable sensibilities of the general public and pressed local governments to adopt paternalism. Neither of those calls to action proved adequate, and subsequent efforts to jumpstart the stalled economy by investing in public works projects failed. No matter how desperate the measures taken by private and public agencies to ameliorate the economic crisis, nothing proved effective enough to get the economy going again.[56]

In July 1932, Hoover authorized the Reconstruction Finance Corporation to lend money directly to states for relief and public works projects, but deflation continued. As prices spiraled downward (eroding wages and earnings), Hoover lost control of the crisis and retreated in defeat to the seclusion of the White House.[57] In desperation, millions of Americans turned to labor unions and threw their support behind the Communist Party. The economic depression enhanced the appeal of radical politics by mid-decade, and the profession of communist sympathies "would become almost respectable" in the country.[58] In response to passionate pleas for assistance from the unemployed, organizations such as the American Red Cross and Veterans of Foreign Wars operated soup kitchens, and private relief groups offered employment, food, and shelter to the indigent. Barter systems appeared across the nation to facilitate exchange in the absence of cash.[59] Franklin Delano Roosevelt, the wealthy and partially paralyzed Democratic governor of New York, challenged an exhausted Hoover for the presidency in 1932.

In his acceptance speech for the Democratic nomination, Roosevelt extolled Jeffersonian values, called for a new era of cooperation in place of cut-throat competition, and promised the electorate a "New Deal," premised upon "a fundamental belief that the American farmer, living on his own land, remains our ideal of self-reliance and spiritual balance—the source from which the reservoirs of the nation's strength are constantly renewed."[60] Roosevelt won a landslide victory that swept Democrats into both houses of Congress, and he took the oath of office on March 4, 1933, just as the economy bottomed out. He moved swiftly in the first one hundred days of his administration to address the crisis by declaring a bank holiday (during which financial institutions were audited and reopened if determined solvent), and he took the country off the gold standard to raise the prices of commodities. He answered growing pleas for public assistance with economic experimentation, optimism, and a set of New Deal policies that emphasized relief, recovery, and reform.[61]

New Dealers, like many religious leaders, blamed the Great Depression on selfish individualism stemming from the relentless pursuit of profit over the interests of the common weal. Honestly believing the future would look nothing like the roaring 1920s, they hoped to construct a virtuous society out of the ruins of a wrecked economy. At Roosevelt's prompting, Congress directed federal government resources to a variety of programs designed to provide employment and to "introduce a socialist esprit to a land where every man still fiercely guarded his castle."[62] The most popular New Deal program, the Civilian Conservation Corps, moved unemployed men from urban to rural areas and paid recruits $1 per day (and an additional $25 per month for their families) in return for their help building bridges and roads, planting trees, and maintaining parks. Within two years of the program's founding in 1933, half a million young men lived in camps run by the Civilian Conservation Corps. By the time it ended in 1940, more than two million men had participated in projects organized by the Corps.[63]

With the assistance of Congress, Roosevelt and the New Dealers speedily established government agencies to restore fair prices for farm goods (the Agricultural Adjustment Administration), to provide flood control and electricity in the South (the Tennessee Valley Authority), to put young men to work (in the Civilian Conservation Corp), and to raise wages for industrial workers (the National Recovery Administration).[64] Although the economy rebounded in the closing months of 1933, unemployment stood at 20 percent, and gross national product remained far below 1929 levels. The slow pace of recovery stirred social and political unrest, and widespread labor strikes erupted in 1934 as wages stagnated.[65] The sheer scale of poverty and destitution caused by the Great Depression opened the way for a variety of demagogues, including Senator Huey Long, who advocated confiscatory taxation on the wealthy; Father Charles Coughlin, who wanted the banks nationalized; and Dr. Francis Townsend, who proposed generous old-age pension plans.

In response to lingering public discontent with recovery efforts, Roosevelt and the Democratic Congress unveiled a series of radical reformist programs, known as the "Second New Deal," that abandoned the regulation of industrial production following an unfavorable Supreme Court ruling in 1936 and instead stressed direct improvement of income and security for blue-collar workers, the unemployed, the elderly, and their dependents.[66] The Works Progress Administration employed nearly seven million people in "pick and shovel" projects (such as LaGuardia Airport in New York City). The Wagner Act protected the right of workers to collectively bargain, and the Social Security Act established old-age pension and unemployment insurance. For these and other efforts, Roosevelt handily won reelection in 1936 by one of the widest margins in presidential electoral history. The economy appeared to be improving, but believing that recovery to be self-sustaining, Roosevelt mistakenly cut back on work relief and other New Deal programs in 1937. A return to 19 percent unemployment and stock market volatility followed. Real economic prosperity did not return until 1941, when government spending on defense rose to make the nation into an "arsenal for democracy" in a world increasingly at war.[67]

*   *   *

New Deal programs funded many historically unique community building projects between 1933 and 1937. "We are definitely in an era of building, the best kind of building," Roosevelt assured the public in August 1934, "the building of great public projects for the benefit of the public and with the definite objective of building human happiness."[68] Although decentralized colonies founded by individuals continued to appear, and a combination of governmental and private agencies directed assistance to people in the greatest need, the most ambitious Depression-era communities were connected to the federal government and to the New Deal. With a budget of over $100 million, a variety of agencies (including the Division of Subsistence Homesteads, the Federal Emergency Relief Fund, and the Resettlement Administration) worked to establish hundreds of agricultural and industrial settlements, garden cities, and other innovative nonindividualistic approaches to the economic crisis whose cooperative organization reflected the new reality of widespread underemployment.[69]

Interior Secretary Harold Ickes, the head of the Division of Subsistence Homesteads, oversaw a $25 million allotment of funds from the National Recovery Act to build self-sufficient communities. Ickes and others drafted prospectuses for rural settlements typically involving twenty-five to one hundred families working toward cooperative self-sufficiency on 1 to 5 acres each.[70] The first loan went to writer and back-to-the-lander Ralph Borsodi for the Liberty Homesteads project in Dayton, Ohio. In 1933, with a third of the city's workforce unemployed, the Council of Social Agencies of Dayton invited Borsodi to help them revamp a series of "Cooperative Production Units," urban buildings for 350 to 500 families who cooperated to produce food, clothing, and other basics, who bartered their excess with other units, and who exchanged their products for raw materials.[71] After council members discovered that production units did not effectively solve the unemployment crisis, they started to consider moving unemployed families into the surrounding countryside and onto homestead farms.[72]

The city purchased a 160-acre farm near Bear Creek with an impressive brick house and a few outbuildings. Borsodi became an official adviser to that project and used it as a platform to advance his ideas and demonstrate their viability on a large scale. The families who moved to Liberty Homesteads planted small gardens and broke ground on new housing, but at the end of the first summer, many still lived in huts, sheds, and tents.[73] Three other homestead projects faltered, and when Borsodi failed to raise funds selling "Independence Bonds," local newspapers criticized him for ineffective leadership, possible fraud, and the promotion of racial integration. Undaunted, Borsodi petitioned Roosevelt's Reconstruction Finance Corporation for $2.5

FIGURE 25. View from Arthurdale Center Hall

million to expand those projects to accommodate two thousand homesteading families on leased 3-acre tracts.[74] Scaling back those plans considerably
when he received only $50,000, Borsodi protested the federal strings attached
to that money, and Ickes essentially forced Borsodi out by federalizing all
homestead projects.[75] Borsodi went on to found several other cooperative
intentional communities, including the School of Living in Suffern, New
York—a private colony with workshops and studios that emphasized pragmatic
experiential learning.[76]

The second disbursement of funds issued by Harold Ickes established the
Arthurdale community near Morgantown, West Virginia, for "stranded" coal
miners left jobless as mines closed. President Roosevelt had campaigned on
a political platform that laid blame for the Great Depression on selfishness
and greed, and he championed equal opportunity and a more equitable distribution of wealth. Subsistence projects like Arthurdale appealed to Roosevelt because they were spread across the nation and designed so that homesteaders could generate sufficient income to make house payments and
cover expenses (instead of engaging in agricultural production of commodities to create a profit or surplus).[77] Homesteaders lived in modest houses
financed at low interest rates, grew their own food, worked part-time to

supply unmet needs, and established local educational facilities and constructed community centers.

First Lady Eleanor Roosevelt developed a keen interest in federal homestead communities after visiting a poverty-stricken Appalachian coal camp at Scotts Run with her friend and confidant journalist Lorena Hickok in August 1933. The squalid living conditions she observed firsthand galvanized her determination to improve the lives of mine workers and their families. Scotts Run, a product of late nineteenth-century industrial development and one of the most intensively developed coal districts in the country, occupied a 5-mile hollow near the Monongahela River.[78] The mine became synonymous with grinding poverty during the Great Depression, since its residents suffered, in the estimation of one historian, more than most Americans "from the maladies of unemployment, ignorance, ethnic and racial prejudice, and the other corollaries of abject poverty."[79] When Hickok traveled through north central West Virginia to visit Scotts Run as part of a tour to survey the effects of the Depression, she called it the worst place she had ever seen. She described, for instance, houses that "most Americans would not have considered fit for pigs."[80]

Period photos show a congested makeshift town consisting of white clapboard industrial buildings precariously situated on the lower reaches of the valley floor between two ridges. Rickety homes and cabins rose up in tiers along the steep slopes of the gulch, and their sewers and privies drained into the stream from which drinking water was drawn.[81] Like everything else in Scotts Run, children were covered in coal dust and grime—and they frequently went to bed hungry. Entire families suffered malnourishment, and illnesses such as dysentery spread quickly in unsanitary conditions. Simmering tensions between the United Mine Workers and the Communist-backed National Miners Union turned Scotts Run into a hotbed of violence. When Hickok and the first lady toured the coal community, Eleanor Roosevelt quizzed the miners about their lives and took careful notes. Upon her return to Washington, she provided detailed reports to Ickes and the president about the area's potential as "an agricultural experimental station" run by "local corporations but with the advice of the federal planners."[82] She imagined a community where two hundred long-term unemployed coal miners and their families could live cooperatively and sustainably.

In large part due to Mrs. Roosevelt's petitioning, Arthurdale became the nation's first New Deal Homestead Community in October 1933, when Ickes announced the purchase of the Arthur family farm. Years earlier, the hotelier and engineer Richard Arthur had retired to that Preston County farm, where he grew wheat, oats, and buckwheat and raised Bourbon-Wilkes horses, pedigreed Jersey cows, Irish white chickens, and Japanese gamecocks.[83] Arthur built an elegantly appointed Victorian mansion with a wraparound porch, flared roof, large windows, and two turrets. Although later demolished to make way for the twenty-room Arthurdale Inn, the mansion provided early homesteaders with lodging, along with the Red Onion boarding house in Reedsville. The $1 per month that settlers paid for accommodations included meals, but lights went out at 10:30 P.M. At the two-story clapboard Red Onion, boarders had to shave once a week, take a midweek bath, and make their own beds.[84] With martial-like discipline, Arthurdaleans cleared trees, drained portions of property, dug foundations for prefab houses, and constructed 13 miles of roads following a design by renowned city planner John Nolen.

Ickes and the first lady planned Arthurdale as a model of cooperative living, and they hoped that it would enthuse the general public about other homestead projects. Therefore they created a self-governing entity with an administration "patterned after the New England town meeting plan," and selected families participated in cooperative enterprises, such as farming, processing, and light commercial industries.[85] In the official press release for the federal "demonstration project," Ickes promised that Arthurdale (initially called the Reedsville Experimental Project) would measure "the possibilities of decentralizing industry in this country where the evils of over-urbanization have become all too evident in this depression." Eleanor Roosevelt called it a "place where new types of rural schools might be tried," one that "could serve as an object lesson to communities of a similar kind throughout the country."[86]

Because subsistence projects were highly politicized, and the Roosevelt administration needed them to succeed, the selection of Arthurdale residents became of critical importance. An advisory committee of West Virginia University faculty members designed and implemented a complex screening process intended to identify homesteaders with "intelligence, perseverance, and foresight," and those dons scrutinized the eight-page questionnaires that petitioners completed (with questions such as "Would you quit farming if the mines opened up full time?" and "How much education would you like your children to get?").[87] Committee members also conducted long personal interviews with potential Arthurdaleans. Selection criteria mandated good mental and physical health, knowledge of farming and animal husbandry, evidence of previous manual labor, and some formal education.

On account of the limited number of homes planned, the advisory committee selected only fifty-five families out of six or seven hundred applicants. Although roughly 25 percent of bids for admission came from African Americans, selected Arthurdale homesteaders were entirely Caucasian (due to protests in Reedsville against blacks moving into local neighborhoods and to a West Virginia law segregating schools).[88] Half of the first cohort of residents came from the mines, while the other half brought much needed experience in farming, woodworking, and sawmill operation. The 5-acre lots awarded to the homesteading families included prefabricated homes hastily ordered in the summer of 1934. Designed as summer cottages by the E. F. Hodgson Company, they arrived in sections and were assembled on site. However, they proved ill-suited to the West Virginia climate, too small to accommodate many families, and a poor fit for foundations already in place.[89] The homes underwent considerable renovation at significant expense, but once workers enlarged them and reinstalled plumbing and sewer after the foundation fiasco, quaint one-story, T-shaped structures dotted the landscape.

The cost overruns that resulted proved the first of many targets for New Deal detractors who called Arthurdale administrators financially irresponsible, but actually the first fifty Arthurdale homes represented a considerable improvement in living conditions for selected families. The heated homes included two bedrooms, a bath, a kitchen, a living room, a porch, and running water. Eleanor Roosevelt developed interior designs with her business partner Nancy Cook, and the Civil Works Administration paid Arthurdale women to make curtains and bed sheets for homes.[90] The Mountaineer Craftsmen's Cooperative Association produced the handcrafted furniture (much sought after today) that completed decors. The first homesteaders paid monthly fees for their homes (although in 1941 they were permitted to purchase them outright from the federal government). A second building phase of 75 two-story houses with cinder-block foundations, wood frames and siding, and gabled roofs followed in 1935. A final group of 40 stone houses in two basic designs (a one-and-a-half-story bungalow and a two-story English Tudor) meant that Arthurdale included 165 homes by 1937.[91]

FIGURE 26. Wagner-style home at Arthurdale

Representatives of the West Virginia University Department of Agriculture taught Arthurdaleans the best methods for planting crops, and the homesteaders learned to supply meat, produce, and fruit for their families (sometimes with excess to sell in the market). Even during a difficult first year, eighty-one homesteaders managed to produce tons of fruit, squash, potatoes, pumpkins, cabbage, and root vegetables valued at over $14,000.[92] Many recruits felt they had escaped the bleak sootiness of mine towns such as Scotts Run and entered a new world of green meadows and blue skies. A community center, a federal office building, a general store, a steam power plant, a weaving room, a barbershop, and a forge (which gained a national reputation for its metalwork) rounded out the little town. Homesteaders demonstrated an interest in cooperative enterprise as early as summer 1934, and the Arthurdale Association of the Mountaineer Craftsmen's Cooperative took out loans funneled through the Resettlement Administration to start an inn, an industrial factory, a farm, a service station, and a dairy. Although the low profits generated from such cooperative enterprises failed to cover the high costs required to sustain them, they provided residents with skillsets after the craft industries folded.[93] So that labor would not consume the lives of

FIGURE 27. Arthurdale Forge

residents, a men's club and a women's club organized leisure activities ranging from square dancing and athletics to a singing group and an adult drama club.

For a time, the Arthurdale Community School became an epicenter of progressive education. The first lady recognized the need for a school oriented toward the specific needs of a growing population of children in rural Depression-era Appalachia. She appointed Elsie Ripley Clapp as the founding principal. Clapp supervised a group of teachers expected "to be residents of the community from the beginning and to assume economic responsibilities similar to the homesteaders."[94] Her instructors resided throughout the community to understand residents' problems and to engage families with neighborliness. Well regarded in progressive education circles, Clapp graduated with an undergraduate degree in English from Barnard College and a master's degree in philosophy at Columbia University. She began doctoral work in English and philosophy at Columbia and completed all degree requirements but the dissertation. She studied with famed educator John Dewey and worked under him as a teaching assistant.[95] Clapp wanted the Arthurdale School to "revive the cooperative, democratic spirit" that she believed the industrial revolution had displaced, and she insisted that "no distinction" between school life and the world outside should persist.[96] She felt that learning should entail the "acquisition of moral and spiritual values"; therefore Clapp grouped children according to inclination (rather than age) and sent them off to "learn by doing."[97] Her decision to eschew traditional courses of study, to reject standardized grading schemes, and to group children by interest led to a failure to secure accreditation from West Virginia. While not everyone thought negatively of her school, the homesteaders expressed open displeasure with Clapp's education methods in 1936, and thereafter the school drifted away from its founding progressive principles.

New Dealers, anxious to hype a self-sufficient community based on subsistence agriculture and light industry as a model for cooperative living, infused Arthurdale with an idealistic promise it could never live up to. In fact, Arthurdale and other subsistence homesteading communities, such as Phoenix Homesteads in Arizona and Aberdeen Gardens in Virginia, struggled to demonstrate economic viability over the long term. The considerable cost of resettlement, the logistical difficulties associated with cooperative community building, and the controversy surrounding federal homesteads more generally meant that these experiments failed to slow population growth in urban centers during the 1930s.[98] Out of the thirty-four projects initiated by the Division of Subsistence Homesteads, twenty-four were industrial homesteads, four were stranded communities (like Arthurdale), three were farm communities, one a resettlement community, one a cooperative industrial community, and one a "garden city" built by blacks for blacks.[99]

The subsistence homestead project in Phoenix provided the Arizona urban poor with safe residences and small plots of land in rural areas close to the city. Such an arrangement permitted residents to dedicate time to farming small plots attached to their homes, while still managing part-time wage employment in the city. In the early 1930s, Arizona, having gained statehood only in 1912, remained a remote outpost in the desert Southwest with a diverse population composed of Anglos, Hispanics, and Native Americans. The Great Depression devastated the state economy when the price of copper plummeted (from 18.1 to 5.6 cents per pound), cotton production slipped (from 152,000 to 69,000 bales), and the per-head cost of cattle dropped (from $40 to just over $10) between 1929 and 1933.[100] The Phoenix Homesteads provided assistance to middle-class people unable to secure loans for housing from private sources, thus making the project "a middle-class movement for selected people."[101]

Due to Arizona's almost year-round growing season, the size of each homestead in Phoenix could be smaller than in other parts of the country: an acre or less for the part-time farmers. Thus a 74-acre plot of land located less than 3 miles northeast of Phoenix—a substantial population center with shopping, schools, churches, and recreational facilities—sufficed.[102] Landscape and building architect R. T. Evans designed modest yet noteworthy adobe houses for the community in a distinct Pueblo Revival style. Evans used tile or slabstone for low-pitched roofs, and he included a wide veranda on the shady side of the homes for shelter from the desert heat and intense sunlight.[103] A forty-year mortgage on one of these homes, valued at $2,500, cost about $125 per year. Construction began in March 1935 on twenty-five units situated on 20 acres (with 54 acres dedicated to common pasturage). As word spread about the planned community, applications flooded in. All but eight of the twenty-five families selected earned less than $100 per month. Only eight residents claimed birth in Arizona, but every adult selected had completed grammar school, fifteen had attended college, and five had graduated.[104]

When the Resettlement Administration took over operations at Phoenix Homesteads, the first twelve families had to wait until October 1935 to take possession of their homes; but by the end of January, settlers occupied every available unit. The Resettlement Administration built and managed four additional cooperative settlement communities in Arizona over the next several years, all geared toward assisting agricultural workers.[105] When the Resettlement Administration granted permission for Phoenix Homesteaders to fully repay the purchase price of their homes in 1944, the Homestead Association in just four years eliminated its indebtedness to the federal government (which thereafter relinquished legal interest in the properties). Today, the Phoenix Homesteads Historic District stands out in the sprawling Southwestern city for its tall Washington Palms and Aleppo Pines that grace pleasant streets and provide merciful shade over small, but stylish, adobe homes.

In Virginia, the first of several subsistence homestead programs for African Americans, Aberdeen Gardens, featured 158 brick houses completed by black Works Progress Administration workers at a total cost of $1.4 million.[106] Located 3½ miles outside of Newport News, and surrounded by a "greenbelt" of farms and gardens, Aberdeen Gardens provided homesteaders an opportunity to use their free time to produce some of their own food and lift themselves "to a higher social and health level."[107] In pursuit of that goal,

FIGURE 28. Adobe house in Phoenix Homesteads

program administrators assigned each homesteader a house, ranging in cost from $2,000 to $2,600, including a garden, a chicken coop, and fruit trees on 1-, 2-, or 3-acre lots. Twelve homesteaders tended mules to work their own gardens and those of neighbors; and another twelve minded the cows. Everyone in the cooperative community enjoyed access to the poultry houses, pig pens, and stables.[108] A cooperative store also opened in 1938.

The design for the community by architect Hilyard Robinson at Hampton Institute (now Hampton University) grew out of concerns among the faculty and administration over substandard housing for low-income black families in the South. Robinson supervised a team of students from Hampton Institute in the construction of five- to seven-room Colonial Revival homes on streets named after prominent African Americans.[109] Every house came furnished and included electricity, indoor plumbing, a furnace, a bathroom, a living room, closets, a spacious front and back yard for growing food, and an attached garage. Once completed in 1937, Aberdeen Gardens featured a one-story white commercial building that doubled as a management office, a large brick school with spacious classrooms, and a church. The only homestead community designed by a black architect and built by black workers under the supervision of a black construction superintendent, Aberdeen Gardens became a national historic landmark in 1994. Two residents, as late as 2000, remained "grandfathered in" for raising chickens and pigs.[110]

Franklin Roosevelt, under the presidential executive order that authorized resettlement of "destitute and low-income families from rural areas," established a greenbelt town program in 1935 to relieve unemployment and homelessness.[111] Rexford Tugwell, economist and director of the Resettlement Administration, believed in cooperative enterprise. He oversaw government assistance for cooperative farms, cooperative industries, and greenbelt cities. Although later absorbed by the Farm Security Administration, the Resettlement Administration had already opened thirty-eight communities, and had eighty-four more under construction, in 1937.[112] Tugwell hoped to build three thousand greenbelt towns based on the garden city method of urban planning championed by Ebenezer Howard. "My idea," Tugwell explained, "is to go just outside centers of population, pick up cheap land, build a whole community and entice people into it. Then go back into the city and tear down whole slums and make parks of them."[113] Conveniently located near urban centers for employment opportunities, Tugwell's garden cities provided low-cost housing, relieved slum congestion, and fostered a sense of social cohesion amid pleasant natural surroundings.

Tugwell planned for twenty-five towns of ten thousand residents each, but the government built just three greenbelt communities: Greendale, Wisconsin, 3½ miles southeast of Milwaukee; Greenhills, Ohio, 4½ miles from Cincinnati; and Greenbelt, Maryland, 12 miles outside of Washington, D.C. Tugwell insisted that the greenbelt communities include coherent economic and cultural centers accessible to all residents. In Greenbelt, Maryland, footpaths and bicycle lanes passed under major street intersections to ease access to the Art Deco community center, the supermarket, the movie theater, the recreational center, and the elementary school.[114] Filled with parks, and surrounded by a greenbelt, Greenbelt included more than 8,000 acres. When the government put those holdings up for sale in the early 1950s, residents collectively purchased a majority of the houses and turned the community into a cooperative. About 20 percent of the homes in Greenbelt still belong to the cooperative—as do the supermarket and café.

As a result of its proximity to Milwaukee, the federal government paid almost $100 more per acre for the 3,400-acre tract at Greendale than at Greenhill—and $200 per-acre more than at Greenbelt.[115] Its construction provided much needed work for between twenty and thirty thousand people. Greendale stood out among the three greenbelt towns for its architectural design and layout inspired by a fusion of styles (the European Renaissance marketplace, midwestern county seats, and colonial Williamsburg in Virginia), also conspicuous for its seventeen dairy farms, twenty-three poultry farms, and excellent agricultural land.[116] As it developed, Greendale became increasingly reminiscent of a European village, with tidy houses and matching chimneys and roofs that suggested simplicity and functionality, promoted a sense of community, and lent the town a gracefulness enhanced by the natural beauty of the setting. In this respect, Greendale, as one observer noted, "looked back to a time in America before cities were a way of life, and before governments, corporations, and collusions took away the prerogatives of average citizens."[117]

Selection officers screened more than two thousand families for admission to Greendale in an effort to find residents who would take care of their properties and get along well with their neighbors. Greendale opened on May 1, 1938, and it was filled the following year with young families headed mostly by blue-collar wage earners. The Greendale Cooperative Association leased a grocery store, a service station, and a barbershop from the federal government.[118] In subsequent years, those enterprises achieved moderate financial success. Their public library contained three thousand volumes, some graduates of the University of Chicago taught at the local school, and residents attended a wide array of social events. Tourists also poured into town—some of them from as far away as the Soviet Union. An astonishing 650,000 people reportedly visited Greendale and its model home from September 1936 to August 1937.[119] Collectively, early residents of Greendale, Greenbelt, and Greenhill cultivated attitudes of self-help and interdependence, and they came to view themselves as "pioneers" of a new form of community, a perception enhanced by managerial rhetoric and local newspaper coverage.[120]

* * *

Without question, New Deal subsistence homestead and greenbelt communities permitted residents to escape dire economic situations, to buy land and houses on attractive terms, and to create better lives for themselves and their families. As President Roosevelt observed, subsistence "is not [merely] a question of keeping people from starvation. It is a matter that affects education, social contacts, and a chance to live. It is the thing that we have called the 'more abundant life,' and even if it costs a little more money to see that these communities have American facilities in them, this government is rich enough to provide the additional funds."[121] With the onset of World War II, however, there were wartime priorities, and the vaulting idealism that inspired the federal government to build cooperative communities began to wane. Conservative opponents of the New Deal gained ground by championing individualism and deriding the Farm Security Administration for promoting a type of cooperation that amounted to communism (at the time the most devastating epithet in the American lexicon).[122] A resurgence of older, more established American social values of individualism and self-reliance doomed the experimentations under way in many New Deal communities—and most of them were liquidated by 1943 or shortly thereafter. Government financial support of the citizenry again became "un-American," and between the Second World War, the Cold War, and McCarthyism, the altruistic impulse to build a better society remained dormant until the mid-1960s, when it reemerged in startling new ways.

Before turning to that wave of community building during the counter-culture revolution, other nongovernmental efforts provided direct assistance to the needy during the agonizing years of the Great Depression. The cooperative Celo land trust established in western North Carolina by Arthur Ernest Morgan in 1937 still provides "an opportunity for its members to enjoy a life that includes personal expression, neighborly friendship and coopera-tion, and appreciative care of the natural environment."[123] Morgan, at the age of sixteen, first conceived an intentional community during a spiritual vision so intense that he could provide a detailed account of it at the age of ninety. Morgan foresaw clusters of modest four- to eight-room houses of natural building materials nestled among rich farmlands. Its citizens lived simply, sus-tained light industries and agriculture, learned the practical matters of com-munity experientially, practiced free inquiry, valued self-discipline, and com-mitted to intellectual and spiritual growth.[124] Instead of penning a utopian novel detailing his social vision, as did Edward Bellamy, Morgan determined to make it a living reality.

Morgan's first wife died shortly after their marriage in 1904, leaving him an infant son to raise alone. Seven years later, he married a faculty member at Wellesley College, a Quaker who shared his interests in social reform and likewise dreamed of starting an intentional community. Morgan, an engineer who ran a company involved in flood control, joined the board of trustees at Antioch College in Ohio in 1919. Appointed to serve as that institution's pres-ident one year later, he restructured the curriculum at the financially strapped college by extending the cooperative concept embedded in the college to include a requirement that all students work—whether they needed money or not.[125] Within a year, enrollment at Antioch quadrupled, and the revitalized college, with its "work-study" program, received good press. But by 1931–1933, Morgan's moralistic and authoritarian leadership stirred disgruntlement among faculty and staff. Franklin Roosevelt tapped Morgan, on the point of resigning from Antioch, to be chairman of the Tennessee Valley Authority—a huge project. In that capacity, Morgan oversaw the construction of a planned community containing three hundred electrified family homes, each on a 4-acre plot of land, in Norris, Tennessee. Businesses in Norris operated according to a nonprofit, cooperative model, and Morgan attempted a number of other innovations in the area, such as integrating black and white workers and equalizing pay scales, but public disputes with his fellow directors—and with Roosevelt—led to his dismissal in 1938.[126]

With the nation still mired in economic depression, Morgan sought other opportunities to build communities. He managed to convince wealthy Chicago manufacturer William H. Regnery to fund one populated by "young men wanting to get a foothold for themselves" on a 1,250-acre tract in the Toe River Valley of western North Carolina.[127] A long-time advocate of small towns and traditional family life, Morgan incorporated the tract as the Celo Community, a nonprofit enterprise. He thought of it as a model for a series of linked communities that would cooperate to recruit members and coordinate mutually beneficial economic exchange. Several managers came and went before cooperative farming and a cooperative store took hold, but pacifist sentiments in Celo aroused the ire of the local populous. Their scanty clothing, vegetarian diets, and wooly beards encouraged rumors about the "freaks" and "misfits."[128]

After the cessation of hostilities in 1945, the population of Celo increased, and members put in place a method of consensus decision making that persisted for decades. In signing the cooperative agreement, residents agreed to "forgo some elements of private control" in order to promote the welfare of everyone.[129] They instituted a provision that allowed compensation to departing members in return for their contributions to community improvement projects, and they established a tax system (essentially a household and income tax payable in cash or labor) designed to promote equality. Members owned their own homes and worked collectively or individually at nonexploitative jobs (from farming to various forms of manual labor), and cottage industries ranging from a woodworking shop to a hand-knitting business were tried.[130] The Celo Health Center opened in 1948, and the Arthur Morgan School began boarding students by 1962. Renewed interest in communal living and Celo's pacifism drove people opposed to the war in Vietnam to join, and by 1973 every home was occupied. That vibrant and progressive rural intentional community in the rolling hills of western North Carolina remains at maximum occupancy.

Dorothy Day's Catholic Worker Movement endures as well, though most communities founded in the Depression era proved shorter lived than her Hospitality Houses. Day, a journalist and Catholic convert, chronicled the plight of the unemployed, reported on rent strikes organized to fight forced evictions, and wrote to counter the increasing popularity of the Communist Party. In 1933, she and French radical Peter Maurin collaborated as editors of a monthly newspaper for the unemployed, the *Catholic Worker*, and they dedicated themselves to distributing food to the poor, establishing communal farms, and operating Houses of Hospitality.[131] St. Joseph's, the first Hospitality House, opened later the same year in Manhattan, and it provided food (and frequently sleeping quarters) to the most destitute. By the end of the decade, thirty-two autonomous Houses of Hospitality of various sizes operated in cities from coast to coast. Whereas St. Joseph's House fed about 1,200 people per day and hosted 150 overnight, the St. Louis location fed 2,600 per day and sheltered 300 per night.[132] None of the houses adopted a constitution, but they found their own reasons for existing, including organizing labor and rent strikes, conducting charity operations, and hosting Christian discussion groups. Residents of Houses of Hospitality took a pledge of voluntary poverty, and they devoted themselves to feeding the poor and collecting and distributing clothing to the needy.[133]

Because Hospitality Houses generally excluded couples with children, the movement acquired its first farm on then rural Staten Island. It attracted several members who worked diligently enough to make the commune sustainable. The donation of a farm near Easton, Pennsylvania provided another venue for teaching the urban poor to become productive small-scale farmers. In total, the Catholic Worker Movement established about a dozen subsistence farm projects, though most of them closed by the mid-1940s.[134] The new burst of American communalism in the 1960s, the subject of the next chapter, breathed new life into Catholic Worker farms, and some of them remain in operation today (along with faith-based Houses of Hospitality and the *Catholic Worker*). Dorothy Day died in 1980, holding her daughter's hand, at Maryhouse—a Hospitality House in New York City where she resided for many years. As a testament to her vow of poverty, Day's entire wardrobe consisted of secondhand clothes from the Catholic Worker's free clothing store. Hundreds attended her memorial service at a local parish church to say their final goodbyes—among them, "Jews, Catholics, Protestants, the rich and the shabby, the well known and the unknown."[135]

Like Arthur Morgan, who penned a book on Edward Bellamy, the Russian-born Jewish immigrant and anarchist Joseph Cohen carefully studied utopian literature and intentional communities before starting a "Collectivist Co-operative Colony" in rural Michigan called Sunrise Cooperative Farm. The Great Depression focused Cohen's attention on finding employment and housing for evicted skilled workers: he imagined a self-sufficient community of farmers, millers, bakers, butchers, carpenters, masons, teachers, tailors, and doctors who would own "the means of production in common" and therefore would be provided "with all they needed."[136] After Cohen and a friend located a large farm 95 miles outside Detroit purchasable for back taxes of $40,000, Cohen's *Voice of the Free Worker* newspaper announced a $500 admission fee to raise a down payment for property. Only those under forty-five years of age and without large numbers of children—they were not to be conservatives, religiously minded, or professed Communists—could apply.[137] Even with those restrictions on membership, thousands of applications arrived, and the Sunrise Cooperative Farm sprang to life in July 1933.

Operations began smoothly, partly because the property included 5,000 acres of pasture, 3,500 acres of tillable land, and 500 acres of timberland. Already there were some eighty buildings, among other structures, including a gas station, a school, a central kitchen, a dining hall, and a bakery.[138] Cohen oversaw an elected executive committee to manage daily affairs at Sunrise. Residents ate three meals together each day, operated a community school subsidized by the county with six teachers and 65 children, and erected a line of toilets and showers to accommodate a rapidly growing population.[139] Cohen worked eighteen hours a day to coordinate community activities; to oversee hired workers; and to attend to a constant stream of visitors, journalists, and politicians interested in Sunrise. By the fall of 1934, 80 families (some 260 people) lived on site, and their first harvest was successful. The absence of formal rules cooled initial enthusiasm when dissension arose that winter, and members split into warring factions of anarchists, socialists, unionist, and "Yiddishists."[140] Cohen offered exit packages to the dissenters, but with the departure of so many rank-and-file members, cash reserves quickly dwindled, and a subsequent labor shortage hampered farming efforts.

Compounding those difficulties, fires destroyed one home, several barns, stockpiles of hay, and truckloads of stored furniture. When remaining families began to depart, Cohen negotiated with Rexford Tugwell for the purchase of Sunrise Cooperative Farm by the federal government. Under the terms of the agreement, residents who wanted to leave received compensation, while those who stayed gained an opportunity to apply for individual land deeds. The federal government bought the property for $286,000 in 1936. Cohen attempted to establish another community in Virginia, but he eventually accepted the "plain fact" that "when a number of people—strangers to each other—are thrown together in such a way that their interests are intertwined, there is bound to be trouble and misunderstanding."[141] It would be another thirty years before political and economic forces of social transformation pushed Americans "back to the land" again in search of more sustainable ways of living, but the mania for community building that swept through the nation from the mid-1960s to the mid-1970s supports Joseph Cohen's observations about human nature.

4 ▸ HIPPIES, ARCOLOGY, AND ECOVILLAGES

O N AN UNUSUALLY warm, early December day in 1948, in the picturesque Southern Tier region of New York state, more than forty thousand mourners gathered to remember the life and legacy of the ninety-one-year-old shoe magnate, welfare capitalist, and humanitarian George F. Johnson. They assembled in a spacious public park in Endicott (donated by Johnson) for one of the largest funeral services ever held for a private citizen. Businesses and schools in the triple cities of Binghamton, Johnson City, and Endicott closed out of respect for the humble cobbler turned industry leader who spent millions on the construction of parks, schools, and churches for the communities that surrounded his factories.[1] Such genuine outpouring of affection for a businessman, while not unprecedented in American history, speaks to Johnson's "Square Deal Policy" that provisioned nearly twenty thousand employees with generous benefits, including full medical care, profit sharing, and a home-building program. From the vantage point of the twenty-first century, we understand that his passing heralded more than the end of industrial paternalism; it marked the

FIGURE 29. Endicott–Johnson Square Deal Arch

beginning of a twenty-year lull in communitarianism (from the mid-1940s to the mid-1960s).

The Second World War vanquished the Great Depression as a boom in industrial production pushed unemployment rates below 2 percent, raised wages, and kept inflation low (because of rationing, price, and production controls).[2] That economic growth ushered in a period of unparalleled American prosperity that lasted into the Reagan presidency. Widespread affluence of the postwar era diminished the American enthusiasm for intentional living, though when it reemerged in the 1960s and 1970s, it took forms unimaginable to the conservative, business-minded Johnson. On his eighty-fifth birthday in 1942, George F. (as he was known to his employees) inspected all twenty-seven factories belonging to his shoemaking organization, and then he celebrated with twenty-three thousand employees. "If I felt any better," he mused, "I'd be drafted."[3] The affable George F. stood tall, shoulders back, the buttons of his gray suit fastened, white collar buttoned, necktie high and centered. His silver hair, thinning but parted to the side, covered a wide forehead, and bright eyes flashed from behind round, wire-rimmed glasses. In one of his leathery hands, a simple wooden walking cane—in the other, a worn tweed cap.

Born from a long line of hardy sailors who lived in and around Plymouth, Massachusetts, the husky, red-haired lad started work in the shoe trade at thirteen years of age, cutting boot soles in one of the Seaver Brother factories in Ashland.[4] At sixteen, Johnson took a position as a boot treer in Worcester, then moved from town to town plying that trade before entering the employ of Henry B. Endicott. Along the way, Johnson recognized that most employers kept wages low and profits high, and he found such commonplace business logic shortsighted. If business owners looked farther ahead, Johnson mused, "they'd see that they would be better off paying good wages and helping their workers to lead normal, happy lives, owning their own homes and being a real part of the community."[5] By contrast, most employers only want to make quick money and think "they can get it by paying as little as possible, exploiting their workers and the people who buy their product."[6] This compelling insight remained with Johnson throughout his life, and it led to sustained community-building efforts unique in the history of American business.

When he arrived in Binghamton, New York, in 1881, Johnson had just 8 cents in his pocket and an invitation to take charge of a treeing room in the Lester Brothers factory. A self-made tycoon, Henry Endicott subsequently bought the Lester enterprises, and he made Johnson assistant superintendent in 1887—and superintendent the following year—after George F. promised to produce more goods, cut unnecessary costs, save on materials, and sell shoes for less without taking a raise for himself. When Endicott returned to the area in the fall of 1889, he took pride in the solid growth of the company and its reputation for high wages and good treatment of workers. Endicott tried to give Johnson a salary increase for that outstanding work, but he refused it. Johnson did, however, offer to buy half of the business for $150,000—on credit from Endicott—at 6 percent interest.[7] It was a bold move, but Endicott wisely lent his honest and efficient superintendent the money.

Now in his early forties, Johnson became a powerful force in the shoe industry by keeping wages high, establishing cooperation and harmony among his employees, and following the Golden Rule. "It is putting yourself in the worker's place and doing by him as you would have him do by you," Johnson explained to a professor at Hamilton College. People talk a lot about "the machinery of industrial democracy," he observed, but it is "the human factor that makes the machinery worth while."[8] Johnson rapidly paid off his debt to Endicott, continued to live simply, and began generously contributing to local churches and hospitals. He opened new workshops in the triple cities, and because he had always imagined a factory in the open countryside with the homes of employees around it, the Endicott–Johnson Shoe Company started building houses for its workers.

In 1904, on 15 acres overlooking the Susquehanna River, the Endicott–Johnson ("E-J") Corporation constructed seventy-five six- to seven-room homes on large lots with lawns and gardens that ranged in price from $3,000 to $3,500.[9] Demand for that housing far outstripped supply, and so the company purchased an additional 1,350 acres in 1922 (two years after the death of Henry Endicott). Johnson named the property West Endicott, and he built two tanneries and a couple welt factories at one end, and a village of attractive homes and gardens on lighted streets on the other. Workers contributed a few hundred dollars as down payment and paid $6 a week out of their paychecks until the price of their home was repaid. The company initially charged 5 percent interest on mortgage balances, but that rate fell to 3 percent in 1930. The company paid for a hospital, a community center, a public school, playgrounds, and the En-Joie Health Golf Club for workers.[10] In 1940, workers voted overwhelmingly not to unionize as an upsurge of strikes in manufacturing and nonmanufacturing industries swept across the nation.

A 1948 pamphlet published in memory of Johnson by the Endicott–Johnson Shoe Company highlighted his achievements, some of which recall attempts by business owners such as Robert Owen and George Pullman to find a balance between the well-being of employees and shareholder profit. The booklet touted the pension plan for E-J workers who completed twenty years of service, the comprehensive medical program that served "the general welfare of workers and their families," and the company-built houses sold at cost.[11] Community schools, colleges, and religious institutions underscored "the spirit of human kindness" that guided the company ethos, and workers and their families benefited further from access to modern theaters, dance pavilions, clubhouses for veterans, and parks for summer and winter sports. At the time of Johnson's death, Endicott–Johnson employed 18,000 workers and operated twenty-eight shoe factories, six tanneries, and three rubber mills with a capacity of forty-five million pairs per year.[12] Family members continued to manage the company until the mid-1950s, but slow decline set in once they hired profit-minded administrators from outside. Increasing globalization in subsequent decades made cheap foreign labor available to American businesses, and Endicott–Johnson was sold in the mid-1990s.

George F. Johnson lived long enough to see the GI Bill help millions of veterans returning from World War II pay for vocational training, college, and graduate school. By the early 1950s, many recipients of those funds had moved from the working class into the middle class, and from cramped city apartments into suburban homes. The modest houses they bought on neatly laid out streets lined with sidewalks in the suburbs exemplified a strong impulse toward social conformity. During the 1950s media personalities projected consensus, and television fostered images of conspicuous consumption and emphasized the necessity of "keeping up with the Joneses." Gender expectations kept women in the home (despite their essential role in wartime industry), while the unconscious censorship of television and radio programming created an optimistic, but ultimately unrealistic, image of a white middle-class America (from which Hispanics, Jews, Asians, and African Americans were largely excluded).[13] Lurking behind that projection of conformity, confidence, and prosperity, cultural anxiety and rebellion, forces of dissonance and change, generated a counterculture revolution grounded in recognizable American traditions of communalism, bohemianism, back-to-the-land romanticism, and Depression-era socialism.[14]

As the economy shifted from an industrial to a service base, American teenagers took part-time jobs in retail stores, restaurants, and gas stations. They spent their money on clothes, on nights out at the movies and dances, on used automobiles to "trick out," and on music. They danced the Jitterbug, did the Twist, and clapped to the Hand Jive. In short, they wanted to rock 'n' roll. The walls of segregation crumbled as Elvis Presley electrified youngsters with pelvic gyrations and renditions of black rhythm and blues. Chuck Berry duckwalked across the stage with distorted chords ringing from his electric guitar amplifier. The hipsters of the interwar era—outsiders and unrooted delinquents whose jive language was inherently aggressive and sexual—were reimagined by a small group of hipster-like friends who first raised the counterculture banner in the 1950s. Among them, the writers Allen Ginsberg, Jack Kerouac, William Burroughs, Gary Snyder, Michael McClure, and Lawrence Ferlinghetti who proclaimed themselves members of the Beat Generation. They challenged conventional mores, transgressed literary norms, questioned the sanctity of the nuclear family, and explored Eastern thought.

Like their hipster predecessors, the Beats smoked copious amounts of cannabis—but they also accessed a variety of consciousness-expanding psychedelics that encouraged creative thinking and perceiving. In the late 1930s, the Swiss research chemist Albert Hoffman first synthesized LSD (lysergic acid diethylamide) in an effort to stimulate the body's respiratory and circulatory systems. Five years would pass before he inadvertently ingested a small amount of LSD in the laboratory (perhaps by touching a "contaminated" finger to his mouth). Forced to interrupt his work due to the effects of the drug, Hoffman went home, lay down, and sunk into what he described as a "not unpleasant intoxicated-like condition, characterized by an extremely stimulated imagination." The next day at work, he deliberately dissolved a quarter milligram of LSD (a massive dose) in water and drank it. He experienced dizziness, anxiety, visual distortions, but also an irrepressible desire to laugh. He endured a "dreadful fear of going insane" and underwent "the dissolution of the ego," but he emerged from those experiences with "a feeling of good will and fortune."[15]

In order to develop a "truth serum" that would elicit information from foreign spies and prisoners of war, the United States Office of Strategic Affairs (the precursor to the CIA) tested peyote and several barbiturates before settling on a potent cannabis extract.[16] When LSD became legally available after World War II, the CIA began experimenting with it, most infamously in Project MKUltra (during which sometimes unknowing subjects were administered that psychedelic). As interest in consciousness-altering substances like LSD grew, research clinical psychologists became interested in peyote and mescaline as a means to better understand mental illness—particularly the hallucinations associated with schizophrenia. In 1951, the New York Times reported on LSD and mescaline research at the Psychiatric Institute of New York, and Time did a story on the use of peyote among Navajos to induce visions and "dreams in Technicolor."[17] Other such exposés followed, but acclaimed novelist Aldous Huxley popularized the use of entheogens in Doors of Perception (1954) and Heaven and Hell (1956).

The widespread use of psychedelics among young Americans contributed significantly to the development of a counterculture—as well as to the formation of thousands of communes. LSD, mescaline, and psilocybin, along with the milder and gentler cannabis plant, broke down social and intellectual conditioning, heightened disaffection for the status quo, and created a camaraderie among those willing to explore consciousness.[18] In a society that valued growth, speed, and overconsumption, proponents of the hippie movement called for a nonviolent way of living in tune with the ecosystem. Hippies paradoxically valued communal life and individualism while simultaneously rejecting the order, bureaucracy, manipulation, conspicuous consumption, racial segregation, and social conformity of the existing order.[19] Undoubtedly unique in the history of American intentional living, the communes and collectives founded by denizens of the counterculture movement nevertheless evoke perennial themes encountered throughout our journey: a condemnation of private ownership, a passion for spiritual development and personal growth, a concern with natural foods and wholesome diets, an embrace of noncoercive cooperation, and back-to-the-land romanticism.

Trenchant criticisms of American capitalism, capable of initiating revolutions culminating in the realization of an ideal society, flourished long before the rise of the counterculture movement and its demands for free speech, gender equality, civil rights, and world peace. The transcendentalists railed against the damaging effects of industrialization and proclaimed the need for an integrative vision of nature and the cosmos during the nineteenth century. They also experimented with intentional living at Fruitlands and Brook Farm, and deemphasized formal learning in favor of life experience and practicability. The back-to-the-land movement of the 1930s (partly inspired by transcendentalists) anticipated expanded ecological consciousness during the 1960s and 1970s, but the contours of a more expansive future informed by psychedelics took shape at Harvard University in 1960 when psychology professors Richard Alpert (Ram Dass) and Timothy Leary administered psilocybin to graduate students and to inmates at the Concord state prison.[20] According to their findings, an astounding 85 percent of Harvard graduate students reported that "trip" as the most educational experience of their lives, and many inmates at Concord experienced what Leary called satori, or spiritual awakening.[21] In 1963, when Harvard fired Alpert for giving psilocybin to an undergraduate, and Leary for breaking an agreement to exclude undergraduates from psilocybin research, both men became famous—and some would say infamous.[22]

Later that year, the novelist and arch-prankster Ken Kesey met the two advocates for the consciousness-expanding potential of entheogens at Millbrook, New York, on a sprawling estate arranged for them by an heiress to the Mellon fortune. There they continued experimenting with psychedelics with a large cadre of seekers who lived a bohemian existence in an improvised community and searched for a permanent route to higher consciousness. Kesey, an accomplished athlete and communications major at the University of Oregon, studied creative writing at Stanford University on a Woodrow Wilson Fellowship. Kesey still hoped to make the 1960 U.S. Olympic Team when he agreed to participate in the CIA's Project MKUltra Mind Control Program at Menlo Park Veterans Hospital, because it paid $20 to $75 per session. Those government-run studies introduced Kesey to psilocybin, mescaline, LSD, morning glory seeds, and Ditran.[23]

In part to secure access to those and other perception-altering substances, Kesey took a job as a nurse's aide at Menlo Park Veterans Hospital. That experience inspired him to write *One Flew Over the Cuckoo's Nest* (1962), the novel that catapulted Kesey to national fame. After suffering arrest for possession of cannabis in 1964, he outfitted an old International Harvester school bus with refrigeration, bunks, and a sound system, and he painted it in psychedelic colors. He then purchased video equipment to shoot a film and set off on a road trip from California to New York—and back again—with a motley crew of acquaintances known as the Merry Pranksters. When they returned to Kesey's 3-acre California residence at La Honda, they formed a "party" community that in the estimation of one participant "pioneered what have since become the hallmarks of hippie culture: LSD and other psychedelics too numerous to mention, body painting, light shows and mixed-media presentations, total aestheticism, be-ins, exotic costumes, strobe lights, sexual mayhem, freakouts and the deification of psychoticism, Eastern mysticism, and the rebirth of hair."[24]

*   *   *

Drop City, founded a year after Kesey's bus odyssey, may sound like an acid-inspired community of hipsters following Leary's injunction to "turn on, tune in, drop out," but the young artists who started that prototype of hip communalism perched in the high deserts of southeastern Colorado in May 1965 were recreational cannabis users, not acid freaks. "At Drop City," cofounder Gene Bernofsky remembered, "we didn't want the hype to get out that we smoked dope. We didn't want a bunch of people lying around taking drugs and experiencing eternal insights. We were outside everyday making things. There wasn't any place for heavy drugs."[25] Bernofsky, with his wife Jo Ann and their friends Richard Kallweit and Clark Richert, worked indefatigably to create a live-in work of "drop art" in the desert inspired by Buckminster Fuller's geodesic domes. As art students at the University of Kansas, they had developed a unique brand of impromptu performances called happenings, which included "droppings" of objects, such as painted rocks, from the rooftops of buildings in downtown Lawrence. They also once placed a complete breakfast tray on the sidewalk of the city's main hotel just to gauge people's reaction to it. "We were kinda hoping someone would eat it," Richert remembered, but most people just walked around it, trying not to get close to us."[26] By bringing conceptual performance art out of the gallery and into the streets, Droppers tested staid artistic conventions and challenged social values.

Drop City took shape after the Bernofskys were unable to start their own civilization in an isolated locale on the African continent—having not made it passed Morocco. Disappointed but not discouraged, the performance artists turned community builders returned to the United States, where Gene knew they "wouldn't have a problem with language and good, solid capitalistic goods were available instantaneously everywhere."[27] The couple visited Richert in Boulder, where he was a graduate student, and with Gene's life savings, they bought 6 acres of goat pasture near the New Mexico border. Short of funds after that purchase, the Bernofskys slept on the property in their car. To create more permanent shelters, Richert scavenged around the railhead and mining town of Trinidad for wooden beams, which he joined together into two dome-shaped frames. He covered those frames with painted steel panels hacked from junkyard automobiles with a felling axe. One Dropper, named Peter Rabbit, remembered that the first swing of the axe into a car roof was the most difficult, and dangerous, due to the potential for bounceback. However, once the axe penetrated the sheet metal, "you just work in the previous cut—sort of like a can-opener."[28] Richert attached the cut metal panels to the wooden house frames and sealed them with tar to keep the rain out. The domes, living works of scavenged art, cost less than $200 each to build. When inventor, designer, and professor of architecture Steve Baer visited Drop City during its first year, the commune's population had reached fifteen to twenty adults who had put into practice a lived-manifesto of cooperative labor, resource sharing, and scrounging.[29] Baer exchanged designs for his "zomes" (dome-like structures involving fewer parts than Fuller's geodesics) in return for Dropper labor to build them. After Baer published the *Dome Cookbook* in 1968, Drop City became a counterculture pilgrimage site, as tourists in the Southwest came to witness hippies in action on as many as twenty communes (including Libre, New Buffalo, Morning Star East, and the Lama Foundation).[30]

Those who made Drop City home used wire, bottle caps, scrap metal, salvaged glass, and disassembled bridges to erect shelters—and they survived on expired food products from the local Safeway.[31] They built a total of fifteen multicolored domes with open polygonal rooms that evoked indigenous structures (such as the tipi and the yurt) and became collective dwelling spaces. Drop City founders formulated no rules, nor did they devise any standards for membership. Rather, they welcomed all newcomers and offered them the use of community resources. Gene Bernofsky recalls that when new folks showed up, everyone pitched in to build domes for them. In the spirit of cooperative ownership, residents pushed Bernofsky to sign over the deed to the property, and Drop City was transformed into a nonprofit corporation with all current Droppers on the board of directors.[32] That generous transfer of assets failed to mollify some residents, and personality conflicts erupted. Community chronicler Mark Matthews argues that Bernofsky might have benefited from studying the history of Ephrata Cloister, at one point the largest artist colony in the country, since its members also cobuilt houses, practiced austerity, put little structured governance in place, and nearly succumbed to schism.[33]

Even before Drop City hosted the Joy Festival in June 1967, life grew increasingly chaotic as wandering hippies passed through on the way to join the Summer of Love in San Francisco or to attend the Monterey Pop Festival. As the Joy Festival, which booked big name artists and musicians, approached, disorder prevailed in the triple-dome complex, and long queues formed for bathrooms and showers. During the weeklong event, hundreds of people "partied hard" as Bernofsky seethed in his private dome. "Everything you can imagine at the height of the psychedelic period of the mid-60s," Bernofsky remembered, "happened the whole week."[34] When it was finally over, beer cans littered the grounds, latrines overflowed, forgotten clothing blew in the wind, and vomit and dried macaroni and cheese (a staple food) festered. When no one made a move to clean up, Bernofsky, broke and saddened at the demise of his refuge for creative people, packed his family into an old station wagon and settled into a job in San Francisco with the U.S. Postal Service.[35] As the Haight-Ashbury neighborhood emptied following the Summer of Love, Drop City became an outpost for indigent transients. A motorcycle gang of speed freaks took it over, then local scavengers descended on the domes and gutted many of them. Arson claimed several other Drop City structures, and surviving domes, sans maintenance, began to crumble in just a few years.

Religious studies scholar and writer Timothy Miller estimates that "probably tens of thousands" of secular and religious intentional communities sprung into being between 1960 and 1975, and their members "collectively thumbed their noses at conventional American society."[36] The great majority of them proved short-lived affairs like Drop City, but hundreds endured, often with much of the original membership intact. Libre, for instance, took shape when disaffected Droppers departed to start another intentional community with artists Dean and Linda Fleming in the Huerfano valley of southern Colorado. Libre succeeded in part because of what members learned from the demise of Drop City (often regarded as the first hippie commune in the United States). Miller calls Libre "a refinement of Drop City," which, like its predecessor embodied a good measure of anarchy, a devotion to the arts, an interest in unconventional architecture, and a healthy skepticism concerning the materialistic values of mainstream American culture.[37]

The Flemings left behind a successful artist co-op in New York and moved to southern Colorado, by chance settling near Drop City. Their proximity to the Droppers enchanted the couple with organizing life around art, and they began to imagine a similar but less frenetic community. Dean understood that by not turning anyone away at Drop City, the most capable people (including its founders) were "driven out by pure criminals and misfits that had no place else to hide."[38] Determined, but lacking funds, the couple turned for assistance to Peter Rabbit, the most visible member of the Droppers and the force behind the Joy Festival. Peter introduced the Flemings to Rick Klein, a wealthy benefactor who financed the New Buffalo commune in Taos, New Mexico. Klein gave them money to purchase 360 acres near the Sangre de Cristo range in Colorado—and Libre was born.[39]

Together with Peter Rabbit and his wife, the Flemings wrote a set of bylaws for the community that has stood, with only slight revision, to this day. They nixed the open-door policy adopted at Drop City and to safeguard privacy constructed houses out of sight of each other. In making no provision for communal facilities, they deprived outsiders of a place to crash. They agreed on important matters by consensus and instituted annual community dues.[40] Potential members underwent an intimidating admission process wherein petitioners had to persuade Libre residents that they were capable of constructing their own homes. Successful candidacy also required unanimous approval at a council meeting. The Flemings imitated the early Droppers and built a geodesic dome with salvaged or scavenged materials following a Buckminster Fuller design. Peter Rabbit adopted a more flexible "zome" design by Steve Baer featured in the *Dome Cookbook* for do-it-yourselfers.[41] To attract interest in Libre and to raise money for building materials, the couples embarked on a twenty-stop, six-week lecture tour around the nation. When their geodesic architecture began to seem outdated, clichéd, and impractical, those who joined Libre during the early to mid-1970s constructed artistic homes that reflected personal aesthetic sensibilities. The subsequent mix of architectural designs and countercultural lifestyles made Libre different from many intentional communities of the period, and, save for one major bust for cannabis cultivation in 1979 and two battles with neighbors over water and road access, Libre has coexisted peacefully with other residents of the valley for decades.[42]

Counterculture communities such as Drop City and Libre grew in the public imagination as the Civil Rights Movement challenged the ideological foundations of racism and inequality, protests against the Vietnam War intensified, and Asian spiritual teachers introduced more Americans to Eastern religious traditions. Millions of people adopted counterculture lifestyles, and before long a vast wave of commune-building was under way.[43] During the late 1960s and early 1970s, the center of the counterculture moved north from San Francisco and Berkeley to Marin County, Sonoma County, Mendocino County, and Humboldt County, and on to Oregon. Along that route, communards found welcoming outposts: Morning Star Ranch and Wheeler's Ranch near Occidental, Olompali in Sonoma, Rainbow near Philo, Table Mountain and Big Foot on the Noyo, and Black Bear in Humboldt.[44] Many of these communes emerged from a desire to escape the noise and pollution of the city; to evade agents of social repression (police, health inspectors, complaining neighbors); and to cast off consumer-driven, media-saturated, stress-filled life styles. In brief, many Americans sought out communal alternatives to advanced industrial society and wanted to live more authentic, connected, and spiritual lives.[45]

When he purchased Morning Star Ranch in Northern California, Lou Gottlieb, the charismatic bassist for the eclectic folk trio The Limeliters, was already in his early forties. Having earned a doctorate in musicology from UC Berkeley before forming the group in 1959, Gottlieb devised a unique choral

FIGURE 30. Bohemian Highway in Occidental

effect formed by three voices that made The Limeliters very popular. He also served, according to liner notes for the album "Cheek in Our Tongue," as "comic-arranger-musicologist" for the band.[46] Behind the bass, the telegenic Gottlieb wore a bow tie, dark slacks, and a buttoned V-neck sweater that accentuated black-framed glasses and a clean-shaven face. After surviving a plane crash in Colorado in 1962, and already well wearied of life on the road, Gottlieb left The Limeliters. A brief stint as a classical music critic for the *San Francisco Chronicle* followed before he established Morning Star Ranch in 1966. The now heavily bearded Gottlieb played piano in a modestly renovated one-room egg shed situated on acreage near Occidental, which once constituted an apple orchard and chicken farm. He referred to himself as the "resident piano player."[47]

An ex-communist, Gottlieb ascribed to a philosophy of open land, believed in "voluntary primitivism" (spiritual awakening through harmonious coexistence with nature), and he welcomed anyone to live at Morning Star for free. Rather than stipulating criteria for admission, Gottlieb let "the land choose its inhabitants thereby forming a tribe."[48] In that way, the ranch, which started out as a weekend and holiday retreat spot for friends, soon attracted a small band of spiritual seekers who practiced yoga and meditation and read scripture from a wide variety of traditions. In November 1966, seven young people arrived from Haight-Ashbury, but the Summer of Love six months later turned that trickle into a deluge. Gottlieb attributed that unexpected influx to several Diggers who came to the ranch in hopes of harvesting free apples for their food program in San Francisco. Although Gottlieb gave them the apples, unbeknownst to him, the Diggers posted directions to Morning Star Ranch in their Haight-Ashbury store. Much to the chagrin of local law enforcement officials, Gottlieb accepted homeless drifters who streamed in. After one year, two hundred people lived primitively on his property.

In a nation teeming with stunningly beautiful landscapes, the scenery around Occidental must rank among the loveliest. Warm reds and yellows of the California sun filter through stands of tall redwoods as the hills underneath turn golden and fill with colorful flowers. In that paradisiacal setting, the folk artist turned communitarian, who believed "the communal endeavor an important thing in America," made "voluntary poverty, or life for minimal cost, and a life of sharing" defining communal principles.[49] The temperate Northern California climate, the ample sunshine, and the absence of formal rules at Morning Star encouraged residents to go about their daily routines completely or partially naked. Their nakedness, their practice of free love, and their use of psychedelics notwithstanding, Morning Star communitarians during the early years remained focused on spiritual development.

The *Morning Star Scrapbook*—attributed to Unohoo, Coyote, Rick, and the Mighty Avengers—chronicled the community from 1966 until its dissolution in 1973. That work preserves photos, press reports, commentaries, and the central tenets of the community. Residents vowed to live a "primitive life in harmony with revealed Divine Law," and they adopted as their central mission the "opening of lands as sanctuaries for the One, naked, nameless and homeless. The purification of the land by replenishment of the soil, invisible land use, and Voluntary Primitivism."[50] Gottlieb regarded private ownership of land as an original sin out of which a myriad of social ills arose. His "pilot study" in voluntary primitivism at Morning Star meant living according to Divine Law (which "supervenes both statutory and judicial law") by embracing "a voluntary return to the ancient tested ways—living close to God's nature and in harmony with the elements." In the Founder's

Message, Gottlieb recognized that all human beings were born divine, but as children most traded that "birthright for an inherited mess of conditioned attitudes and imprints that create a 'dis-eased' lifestyle."[51]

Although Gottlieb positioned Morning Star Ranch in a long and vibrant "tradition of the intentional community—Brook Farm, Oneida, New Harmony, etc.," and he endeavored to make it a shelter for the "first wave of technologically unemployed," the rural and conservative communities surrounding Occidental wanted nothing to do with the anarcho-primitivists.[52] In the wake of a *Time* cover story on hippies in July 1967, which included a photograph of resident Pam Read in the nude, Morning Star received regular visits from Sonoma County health officials and building regulators (who were frequently greeted by a host of naked women).[53] Unrelenting complaints from locals unleashed a series of injunctions aimed at shutting down the improvised community on the grounds that it was a public health and safety nuisance. Gottlieb initially prevailed against efforts to prevent him or his friends from operating and maintaining an organized encampment, but then hepatitis struck in August.

Injunctions to clear the community followed in September, and by October Gottlieb was held in contempt for refusing to prohibit entry to the ranch while sanitary and building improvements were undertaken. Arrests followed, and as fines and legal fees accrued, Gottlieb became his own lawyer. When penalties reached $14,000, the former Limeliters bassist offered to give Morning Star Ranch to Sonoma County, on the condition that officials allow his experiment in open-access living to continue for five years, after which it would be converted into a museum of "folk architecture." His offer declined, Gottlieb deeded Morning Star to God and took off. Three years later, in 1972, the First Appellate Court of Appeal of the State of California ruled that according to the Civil Code a "deity does not qualify as a grantee," and that consequently "the trial court properly ruled that appellant's purported deed of the property to God was a nullity."[54] Before county and state officials forcibly cleared the premises, most residents had already departed Morning Star Ranch, though sometimes only after repeated arrest. Many of those individuals made their way to Wheeler's Ranch a few miles to the west.

As he watched the saga at Gottlieb's place unfold, Bill Wheeler became, in his own words, "deeply sensitive to the fact that I had more land than I needed. I began to feel it was my duty to share it. The Morning Star family was being hassled and arrested daily. It was a heartbreaking drama. They desperately needed a home."[55] Wheeler, like his friend Gottlieb, believed in a doctrine of open land, and so he encouraged the communards to join him on a beautiful 360-acre parcel of land that nearly touched the Pacific Ocean and to express themselves through art and music.[56] To guarantee order, Wheeler formulated a few basic rules, but before long the authorities showed up—ostensibly to search for draft dodgers among the two hundred residents. Building inspectors ordered the destruction of improvised shacks and primitive lean-tos on the property. Faced with a legal battle they could not afford, along with a huge bill for bulldozing condemned structures, Wheeler and settlers burned fifty or so buildings one by one, watching with a "strange pleasure, a morbid fascination" as the flash of nature's energies consumed a house in just five minutes.[57] Abandoning all hope of establishing another open land counterculture commune, Wheeler built a cottage out of hand-milled timber that just met code, and with a land mate or two, he turned his energies to painting.

*   *   *

Well-heeled communitarians financially supported Morning Star Ranch and Wheeler's Ranch—a practical advantage also enjoyed by members of the Chosen Family at Rancho Olompali. Native Californian Don McCoy and his brother operated a property investment and construction company that developed the first houseboat marina at the Sausalito heliport on Richardson Bay.[58] McCoy separated from his wife in 1966, and worn out by business pursuits, he leased the 690-acre estate at Rancho Olompali (now Olompali State Historic Park) and invited twenty-six of his closest friends and their children to join him. In the months before McCoy and the Chosen Family moved in, the psychedelic rock band the Grateful Dead had lived communally in the twenty-two-room mansion house. Members of the band hosted parties that attracted musical icons such as Janis Joplin and Grace Slick. Even after McCoy leased the property, members of the Grateful Dead regularly visited and occasionally performed at Rancho Olompali.

Because no one had to work, members of McCoy's Chosen Family lived contented lives. Nude socializing around the swimming pool and copious marijuana smoking occupied a good part of everyone's day. McCoy paid the bills, bought gifts for his friends (including motorcycles, horses, television sets, musical instruments, and clothes), and he provided almost anything else family members wanted. McCoy invested in equipment for a commercial-sized baking operation, and twice a week family members sent hundreds of free loaves of mushroom-shaped bread to San Francisco communes.[59] McCoy also started a community school (nicknamed by students the Not School) that provided instruction following the progressive, democratic model of education at the experimental Summerhill School in England.[60] Spiritual but not formally religious, the Rancho Olompali community attracted actors, spiritualists, astrologers, numerologists, and musicians. Had the money lasted, it might have remained a hippie paradise, but when refugees from Morning Star Ranch took shelter in the woods at Rancho Olompali, strife emerged between Gottlieb's anarcho-primitivists and the high-living Olompalians. Before that dissension could be resolved, the McCoy family imposed a conservatorship on the former businessman that stemmed the flow of money. A series of unfortunate incidents brought McCoy's experiment to a close: the police conducted two cannabis raids on the property, the mansion house caught on fire, and two children drowned in the pool while playing unattended.[61]

Some Olompalians blamed those calamitous events on the spirits of disgruntled Native Americans. The Miwok people had inhabited the region from about 500 C.E., though Olompali State Historic Park literature suggests human habitation in the area as early as 6,000 B.C.E. The territory remained in Miwok possession after the arrival of Spanish conquistadores, and the indigenous leader Camilo Ynitia constructed a sizable adobe home there in the mid-nineteenth century. Its walls became part of the foundation for the Victorian-style Burdell Mansion built in 1911. That structure fell into disrepair during the Great Depression, but in 1948 the University of San Francisco purchased it as a Jesuit retreat center and added the swimming pool. By the time the Grateful Dead rented the house and grounds for $1,100 a week in 1966, bassist Phil Lesh reported that he regularly "made contact with the spirits of what I thought were the Olompali Indians. They asked, 'What are you doing here, white boy?'"[62] Drummer Bill Kreutzmann noted the burial grounds scattered around the Olompali estate and recalled that he and his compatriots "could feel the presence of the Indian spirits," and "not all of them were so friendly." Kreutzmann writes: "We'd get high on acid and see spirits and things" come out of a window into the ancient part of the house, and "they just flooded the whole house with all this weird energy. Jerry, Bear, and Phil all saw horrible stuff coming out from the old bricks. They saw fire

FIGURE 31. Ruins of the Burdell Mansion (center) at Rancho Olompali

and saw that the house was eventually going to burn down, which I think ended up happening. The bricks from the original house may have actually survived."[63] Despite such haunting experiences, out of the many places the band stayed, Olompali remained Kreutzmann's favorite.

The Grateful Dead became a pivotal center of San Francisco's counterculture movement from their shared home in the heart of Haight-Ashbury. They cultivated an image of themselves as anticommercial artists unmotivated by economic success, and to foster it, they frequently gave free performances in the Panhandle of Golden Gate Park. They collaborated with the Diggers, who handed out free food and supplies to those in need and served more generally as Haight-Ashbury's social workers and welfare providers. Inspired by their seventeenth-century namesakes, the farming radicals who defended the commons, the Diggers staged elaborate street happenings, distributed leaflets, and transformed the Haight-Ashbury district into a "free city" with several stores that gave away clothing, household items, and food.[64] These urban communards and champions of the dispossessed combined avant-garde theater with radical politics, operated thirty-five communal houses, and practiced "garbage Yoga" (collecting leftover food products and distributing them free of charge). Physicians sympathetic to their cause began to offer no-cost medical care at a Digger store, which became the Haight-Ashbury Free Medical Clinic.

To signal the end of the Summer of Love and to protest the commercialization of the counterculture revolution by the popular media, in October 1967, the Diggers staged a mock funeral, known as Death of Hippie. They burned hippie clothing and newspapers, and they carried a coffin down Haight Street to dramatize the end of that social experiment. Thereafter, it fell to Wavy Gravy (Hugh Romney) and the Hog Farmers' "Please Force" to staff a free kitchen and a bad trip tent, and on the East Coast to provide medical care to the multitudes at the Woodstock Music Festival in 1969. Those three mud-filled days of rock and roll, psychedelic exploration, and peace and love went down in American lore as one rollicking time that singularly captured the virtues and excesses of the counterculture movement in its waning years.[65] After Woodstock, Wavy Gravy and the Hog Farmers continued their social and political activism. For example, Gravy and Ram Dass set up the Seva Foundation, a nonprofit organization dedicated to providing eye care to "underserved communities, especially women, children, and indigenous peoples."[66] Since then, the focus of the Hog Farm has shifted to sponsoring performing arts camps for children and hosting several music festivals per year.

Consider also native Coloradoan Stephen Gaskin, founder of The Farm in Tennessee, who grew up following his father, a cowboy and construction worker, from job to job. He dropped out of high school to join the Marines in 1952 and saw combat in Korea. Subsequently drawn to the Bay Area, Gaskin earned bachelor's and master's degrees in English at San Francisco State University.[67] When his graduate teaching assistantship ended, Gaskin rose to prominence as a spiritual teacher by offering an experimental class on Monday evenings, beginning in 1967. Entitled "Group Experiments in Unified Field Theory," course readings explored quantum physics through a series of discussions on topics ranging from the Book of Changes, Yoga, and Zen to extrasensory perception, psychedelics, and Tarot cards. Within two years, the course drew audiences of two thousand people, sometimes more. Gaskin taught that enlightenment, which he called a permanent "high," resulted in an exquisite sensitivity to the beauty of nature, and produced joy and contentment. Enlightenment also unleashed creative energies to accomplish meaningful tasks and ultimately to help transform the world through the power of love. Awakened people, he posited, are "actually able to do things," because they are friendly, sane, and functional.[68]

Gaskin abruptly suspended the Monday night course midsemester in 1970 and embarked on a nationwide speaking tour—accompanied by a caravan of followers in fifty school buses that doubled as mobile homes. When he returned to the Bay Area, interest in his course had faded, and so Gaskin turned his energies to establishing a rural commune on 1,700 wooded acres in Summertown, Tennessee. He referred to the community as a "family monastery," but his followers simply called it The Farm.[69] Like intentional religious communities founded centuries earlier, Farmers cited the Book of Acts to justify setting up a Community of Goods: "And all that believed were together, and had all things common; And sold their possessions and goods, and parted them to all men, as every man had need."[70] In accordance with that apostolic example, they pooled resources and fed, clothed, sheltered, healed, and cared for anyone who came to The Farm. Community rules remained unwritten, but a basic understanding existed regarding acceptable behavior, as did agreement upon key principles, such as nonviolence, equality, agricultural self-sufficiency, respect for the earth, and the essential oneness of humanity with the cosmos.[71] As spiritual leader of the community, Gaskin held Sunday services (that included an hour of meditation) and conducted counseling sessions, while a board of directors managed day-to-day affairs. At its height, The Farm boasted an estimated 1,500 permanent residents, and it received over 10,000 visitors per year.[72]

Initially, however, Farmers lived quite primitively as compared with other communitarians of the day. Approximately three hundred people cleared 150 acres of the 1,700-acre tract, dug wells, and began constructing houses. Many of the settlers lived in tents or school buses for years until completing more permanent structures. They took lessons in simple living from their Amish neighbors and washed their clothes by beating them on rocks near the creek. Farmers sometimes referred to themselves as the "technicolor Amish."[73] Their reverence for the sanctity of life meant practicing veganism by avoiding meat, eggs, milk, honey, leather, and other products of animal origin. They invested in a huge soy operation to make tofu and soymilk decades before those health foods became part of the nation's dietary landscape. Unlike many back-to-the-landers, the Farmers embraced technology. They used reel-to-reel video recorders to tape Gaskin's talks, pioneered the use of solar energy, experimented with crude computers for tracking inventory and customer orders, and built a small recording studio.[74]

Gaskin discouraged jewelry and personal ornamentation, and he banned alcohol and prohibited guns and violence on The Farm. Like other counter-

FIGURE 32. The Farm Store

culture gurus of the time (including Timothy Leary, Ram Dass, and Alan Watts), Gaskin endorsed psychedelic mysticism and professed that LSD could guide some to mystical states of consciousness. In later years, Gaskin refused to endorse LSD as a spiritual tool due to its potency and unpredictability, but he continued "being a psychedelic-type teacher on the basis of doing it with organics," or "what grew in the woods."[75] Natural entheogens such as psilocybin revealed unitive truth and made possible a reorganization of life according to the values of care and responsibility (rather than competition and consumption). Gaskin believed the arising of compassion in the heart, which coincided with spiritual awakening, encouraged the mystic to descend from the ecstatic peaks of religious experience to help other people. When the sage perceives the world as a dynamically interconnected and coevolving process, then the only reasonable response to suffering is altruism. The force of direct and unmediated spiritual insight clarified a commitment among the Farmers to communal expressions of philanthropy and unstinting support of its charity branch, Plenty International. Founded in 1974 to undertake local and international relief and development work,

Plenty International marshaled volunteers to build 1,200 prefab homes in Guatemala after an earthquake in 1976, and it established an ambulance service in the impoverished South Bronx and on an Indian reservation in upstate New York.[76]

The "spiritual midwifery" pioneered on The Farm represents another expression of the community's commitment to serving others. While traveling around the country in a caravan of 250 seekers searching for a good place to buy land and start a new community, Ina May Gaskin (Stephen's wife) unexpectedly helped to deliver a baby in a camper-converted school bus in the parking lot of Northwestern University. After that birth, she felt called to practice midwifery. On The Farm, she developed a method of natural childbirth premised on the notion that the body's innate intelligence could, in most cases, direct the birthing process with a minimum of interference from midwives or attendant physicians.[77] She sought training from a Tennessee doctor who had worked among the Amish and attended home births. A condemnation of birth control on The Farm evolved out of a more general preference for the organic and natural over the artificial and synthetic, and as a consequence, many more children were born to community members. Ina May's experience assisting with that "baby boom" led to the publication of Spiritual Midwifery (1978), an influential work now in its fourth edition. She called it a "spiritual book," since it expressed a profound belief that the sacrament of birth "belongs to the people and that it should not be usurped by a profit-oriented hospital system."[78]

As part of their community outreach efforts, Farmers built a modest public primary health clinic that included examining rooms, essential equipment, a dispensary, and a Midwifery Center. Hundreds of babies entered the world on The Farm every year, many of them born to parents from outside of the community drawn by Gaskin's at-home, no-drugs birthing method. Ina May outfitted the Tower Road birth house with oxygen tanks and bilirubin lights, and it could provide around-the-clock nursing care when necessary.[79] Gaskin emphasized giving birth as an opportunity for women (and those present at the delivery) to experience what Abraham Maslow called peak-experiences—that is, spiritual moments of expanded unitive perception. The Farmers, due to their opposition to abortion, made a remarkable offer that many women found irresistible: "Don't have an abortion, come to The Farm and we'll deliver your baby and take care of it, and if you ever decide you want it back, you can have it."[80] A pregnant woman could receive prenatal care at the Midwifery Center, deliver her baby there, and stay at The Farm with her child or return later to claim it—all at no charge.

In the late 1970s, The Farm expanded into a self-sustaining community able to purchase a 2,300-acre greenbelt surrounding the original tract of land. To generate income, Farmers worked for construction and farm crews, grew crops organically on site, operated a certified school with several hundred students, developed soy grocery products, and printed books (including *Spiritual Midwifery*). Through these and other enterprises, Gaskin and the Farmers devised a method of resource allocation that provided complete support to residents for life.[81] Salaries for workers tended to be low, but the nonprofits The Farm operated provided a number of job opportunities for residents, and the community generated additional revenue through donations from individuals, businesses, and foundations.

As Farm membership in the community expanded from less than 300 to approximately 1,500, the organization became financially overextended.[82] Matters grew so dire that residents took vows of poverty and renewed their dedication to austere lifestyles. Even after adopting those drastic measures, a shortage of supplies soon impacted their children. In fact, the open-door policy at The Farm meant that more people came needing than giving—and conflicts necessarily arose among members. Moreover, Plenty International and other organization charity projects too often provided money and labor to others that The Farm could ill spare. When a disastrous agricultural recession hit rural America in the late 1970s and early 1980s, the Farmers found themselves over $1 million in debt.[83] They voted to decollectivize in 1983 and institute monthly dues. Those changes reduced the population to less than 400 within three years, easing considerably the community's financial difficulties.

In the early 1990s, Gaskin opened a 100-acre retirement community adjacent to The Farm as a place where aging hippies could build retirement homes. He called it Rocinante: "It's the name of Don Quixote's horse and John Steinbeck's pickup truck," Gaskin explained, "so it's a vehicle for an incurable idealist."[84] Under Gaskin's direction, The Farm set up an Ecovillage Training Center—a whole-systems immersion experience of ecological living that offered information, tools, and resources to thousands of visitors interested in working models of organic farming, biological waste treatment, hybrid vehicles, alternative building styles, and solar power.[85] These and other activities on The Farm and at Plenty International affirmed collective

FIGURE 33. Painted grain silo at The Farm

adherence to a "moral imperative toward altruism" built upon a "belief in Spirit, nonviolence, collectivity, and social activism."[86] The vibrant paintings of entheogenic mushrooms on a community grain silo suggest continued psychedelic mysticism on The Farm.

*   *   *

The emergence of communities accepting of same-sex relationships and inclusive of nonconforming expressions of sexuality marks another distinctive contribution of the counterculture revolution to the history of American intentional living. Lesbian groups led the way with the Womanshare Collective and Oregon Women's Land Trust (OWL Farm) located in the Pacific Northwest. Womanshare took shape in 1974 when three women purchased two houses on 23 acres in southwest Oregon with the purpose of living self-sufficiently, which meant mastering traditionally male skills, such as automotive repair.[87] The Oregon Women's Land Trust purchased acreage to hold in trust, and the organization encouraged self-redefinition as environmentally conscious feminists and lesbians through collective living. Because these communities (and their male homosexual counterparts) generally practiced gender segregation, few of them during the 1960s and early 1970s correspond with LGBT (lesbian, gay, bisexual, transgender) communities today. Stephen Lenton's Mulberry Family commune in Richmond, Virginia, stood against that trend.

A graduate of the political science program at UC Berkeley and an early Peace Corps volunteer in the Philippines, Lenton moved to Richmond in 1970 to become assistant dean of Student Affairs (later Student Services) at Virginia Commonwealth University. He moved quickly at that large public institution in the heart of the city's historic Fan District to establish an Awareness Series featuring retreats, mini-classes, and workshops on topics such as human sexuality, personal growth, leadership, women's studies, and cross-cultural communication.[88] Lenton lectured for the Series, taught courses as an instructor of education, and earned a master's degree in education from the university in 1973. Three years later, he completed a doctoral dissertation in applied behavioral sciences at Union Graduate School (a consortium of thirty-four experimenting colleges and universities) on Mulberry Family, a residential urban commune that he founded.

While completing his doctoral coursework, Lenton helped to organize the Gay Alliance of Students at Virginia Commonwealth University in 1974. At that time, Richmond, a conservative city in the Upper South, the capital of the Confederacy, did not value inclusivity. When the vice president of Student Affairs and the Board of Visitors denied students in the Gay Alliance official registration on campus (which would allow them to apply for funding), Lenton joined their lawsuit against the administration.[89] The students won, but the ruling exemplified the state's backward attitude toward homosexuality. It stated that Virginia law prohibited "the practice of certain forms of homosexuality," though that did not "make it a crime to be a homosexual." No matter how "abhorrent, even sickening" the values of any group to other citizens, the opinion read, the "stifling of advocacy is even more abhorrent, even more sickening."[90] Virginia's "Crimes Against Nature" anti-sodomy provision in the state constitution was not overturned until 2013.

Unlike "free-love" communities on the West Coast where sexual promiscuity sometimes seemed obligatory, Mulberry Family formed to provide a safe space where residents could live openly and in harmony with a diverse group of tolerant and inspiring individuals, such as Gloria Norgang, an activist involved with the Richmond Lesbian-Feminists and the WomensBooks store on East Main Street.[91] Lenton's dissertation, "Mulberry Family Scrapbook: An Intentional Community Presented as an Experiment in Creative Recordation," remains the single most comprehensive source of information on the commune. Lenton and his friends founded Mulberry Family as a sanctuary in a "world which is increasingly complex and ambiguous, wherein people are closer together geographically and territorially, yet in which individuals and groups are more frequently experiencing loneliness, depersonalization, alienation, isolation, detachment and a lack of significant relationships with other people."[92]

Rather than penning a dissertation on academic program design or his duties as assistant dean at Virginia Commonwealth, Lenton chose to focus on the experiment at Mulberry "so that there would be some recordation of our existence in a world which desperately needs new explorations and experiments in establishing human community."[93] He described the search for an apartment in a quiet neighborhood of the Fan, a district that took its name from the streets radiating outward west of downtown starting at Monroe Park. The tidy tree-lined avenues that grace the Fan, a large walkable inner-city neighborhood developed between 1890 and 1930, include restaurants, shops, and elegantly appointed townhomes painted in a variety of muted shades: blues, beiges, light greens, and grays. Lenton wanted to find living quarters that were close enough to the university to bike to work, yet far from the rowdy undergraduates who filled the flats around campus. That quest led to the discovery of a first-floor unit in a duplex at the intersection of Mulberry and Grace Streets.

One week after he moved in, the second-floor unit became available to rent. Lenton alerted several long-time friends, who secured it on good terms. Their decision to establish a commune took place unexpectedly in Septem-

FIGURE 34. Mulberry Family townhouses

ber 1972 when roommates Stephen, Karyn, Kenny, Albert, Betsy, and Martin weighed the economic advantages of living collectively. Rent and food, for starters, would cost less if they fully pooled their resources. Enthused with an egalitarian spirit, the group decided that all members would pay the same rent, regardless of the size of their bedrooms. Thus, after an hour-and-a-half discussion, they became "a commune of six in a rented Richmond duplex townhouse."[94] The following spring, the owners of the property put the townhouse up for sale. Concerned that they might not find a more suitable location, the group bought it, and one year later, they purchased the brick home next door and Mulberry Family expanded. The original house on the corner of Grace and Mulberry featured twin entry doors protected from the elements by a small porch, which doubled as a walkout balcony for residents of the upper unit. The new brick townhome had a single front door, a large covered portico, and ample room for new community members.

The roommates set out to create more than an LGBT boardinghouse; they wanted to form a communal association based on the family model. Karyn explained that they intended to "share more things" than ordinary roommates, including groceries and vehicles, and they planned to hold regular meetings too. Betsy expressed a "need to feel loved" and challenged in a "unique living environment."[95] The openly gay, lesbian, bisexual, and hetero-sexual individuals who joined the hopeful band on Mulberry affirmed a commitment to protecting the well-being of everyone, and a shared vision gradually emerged out of the diverse views of its members. Steve Fuhrmann, for instance, aspired to live with a "democratically socialistic" group of indi-viduals "moving toward authentically expressing themselves in direct I–thou encounters, being aware of themselves and their environment in the here and now."[96] Many of the forty or so portraits in Lenton's doctoral dissertation on "the Mulberries," as Fuhrmann called them, depict people determined to cre-ate an open and supportive environment that encouraged personal and spiritual growth at a time when most gay and lesbian people in Richmond were still closeted.

To explain why people joined the Mulberry Family, and how their motiva-tions impacted the formation of the community's guiding principles, Lenton cited the hierarchy of needs formulated by Abraham Maslow. He observed that Mulberry Family provided food and shelter for just $120 per month; pro-tected physical and psychological safety; satisfied love and belongingness needs; and increased self-esteem in members through expressions of "confi-dence, competence, mastery, adequacy, achievement, independence and free-dom, and respect from others."[97] In this way, the community encouraged Maslow's self-actualization, the realization of one's full potential, in an envi-ronment where chores rotated with no distinction by gender, where bath-rooms were shared, and where bedrooms were typically kept private. Mem-bers ate together as often as possible, and they expected discretion in regard to cannabis and alcohol use. Lenton called it a "private, middle-class" commune in "two long-term financed townhouses, with partial economic sharing" among eighteen to twenty-four mostly white peers "of all sexes and affectional preferences" (with no children).[98] Anyone who came to Mulberry Family, submitted Lenton, "with the express purpose of talking about living with us has been accepted."[99] The diverse occupations among members of the group, which varied from wait staff to professors, lent credence to that assertion.

In summing up the experiment, Lenton recognized the financial and per-sonal benefits of communal living, but acknowledged that they often came at the cost of some personal freedom.[100] Because the average stay at Mulberry was sixteen months, after four years it proved necessary to levy a modest $100 admission fee to raise money and to measure commitment. Although members paid monthly dues, Lenton never aimed to make Mulberry Family economically self-sufficient, nor did he attempt to set up business enterprises that would generate revenue. Departing residents received no money for the property donated to the community, and no payments were made in return for labor. Guests paid $2 per day for food and could stay up to one week.[101] The Mulberry experiment, which lasted nearly fifteen years, came to a close when one of the townhouses was sold in 1986 and the other in 1987. Years later, Lenton asserted that Mulberry Family was but one facet of a sustained effort to build an "intentional family," and the many LGBT rights organizations to which he contributed time and energy suggest other important ways of forming a "family of choice."[102]

A devout Catholic, Lenton advocated for the LGBT community beyond the Fan neighborhood and the Virginia Commonwealth campus by serving on many parish committees, including the diocese's Sexual Minorities Commission. He helped to arrange the inaugural meeting of the Gay Awareness in Perspective group in April 1974 (the first formal gay rights organization in Richmond) and guided its activities until 1978.[103] Lenton left Virginia Commonwealth in June 1980 to become a therapist at the Psychiatric Institute of Richmond and Commonwealth Professional Services, and he volunteered with the Richmond AIDS ministry. He received the Greater Richmond Community Foundation Award for Outstanding Humanitarian Service in the field of AIDS in 1992.[104] Before his death in 2002 from complications related to that disease, Lenton continued to live purposefully by studying for ordination as a permanent Catholic deacon in 2001. Although Mulberry Family remains one of the best examples of gay and straight people living and interacting socially in a counterculture commune during the 1970s, it is little known and less written about. However, the sea change in local and national views about sexuality over the last two decades is traceable to the efforts of community builders and activists such as Stephen Lenton.

* * *

Two years before Lenton and friends bought the first house on Mulberry Street in 1972, Italian architect and urban designer Paolo Soleri broke ground at Arcosanti—a bold experiment in "arcology" rising above the Arizona desert canyon like a futuristic cathedral to a new God. Soleri, horrified by inequity and unnecessary suffering in the world, designed dense ecologically sustainable cities meant as "instruments for the acceleration of the evolution of human culture."[105] Arcosanti, Soleri's prototype for "arcology" (a portmanteau of "architecture" and "ecology"), weaves home, community, and landscape into an interconnected whole that for more than fifty years has stood as a powerful rebuke to the sprawling cities of Scottsdale to the north and Phoenix to the south. A consummate designer, Soleri left war-torn Italy after earning a doctorate in architecture from Torino Politechnico in 1947 to study with renowned architect Frank Lloyd Wright at his school in Arizona on the Taliesin Fellowship. Soleri bristled under the dictatorial apprentice program, and Wright dismissed the Italian visionary after one and a half years, perhaps angry that the Museum of Modern Art published a Soleri design for a bridge next to one by Wright.[106]

Unruffled by his dismissal, Soleri moved to nearby Paradise Valley, sketched designs for domelike structures in the desert, and won a commission to build a subterranean home with a rotating glass-dome roof made from recycled and salvaged materials and stones gathered on-site. Dome House, as it came to be known, received wide acclaim for its architectural innovations, and in 1952 Soleri secured another commission to design and build a ceramics factory in the hillside town of Vietri sul Mare in Italy that combined production, commercial, and residential spaces in one building—a concept that profoundly influenced the artist's later work.[107] When he returned to the United States two years later, Soleri assumed control over the production of distinctive ceramic bells for a manufacturer in Santa Fe, New Mexico. With the profits, he purchased 5 acres in Paradise Valley and began to build an ecologically sensitive home nestled in the cool of the earth (rather than rising above it). Drawing upon his experience casting ceramics, Soleri poured concrete into a structural network made of earth and silt, let it dry, and then excavated under it to create basement-like interior living spaces for Earth House. Well adapted to the desert climate, Earth House, and subsequent earth-form structures, stayed cool during the day but retained solar warmth on chilly evenings.[108] A complex of buildings, which Soleri called Cosanti (from the Italian terms "anti" and "cosa," meaning "against things") took shape as a small army of apprentice architects, artists, and artisans joined him to experiment with new architectural shapes, structures, and concepts.

Soleri broke ground on Arcosanti in the high Arizona desert 70 miles north of Phoenix as a positive response to "the many problems of urban civilization, those of population, pollution, energy, natural resource depletion, food scarcity, and quality of life."[109] He regarded Arcosanti as an urban laboratory, a place where he and fellow artists and environmentalists could design, construct, and operate a functional prototype of arcology (his theory of compact city design) as a lean alternative to urban sprawl. By reorganizing urban communities into dense three-dimensional cities, Soleri sought to eliminate the waste of "enormous amounts of time and energy transporting people, goods, and services over their expanses."[110] He envisioned six to seven thousand people living, working, and engaging in activities that could sustain human culture on just 16 of 860 acres. By living closely together and restricting polluting automobiles to the periphery of the community, the remainder of the property could be set aside for agricultural use and recreational activities.

Soleri believed that people would thrive in dense urban environments with lots of natural light and panoramic views of the landscape. By emphasizing compactness, and building upward rather than outward, Soleri also made walking between any two points—such as work and home—a breeze. The first phase of Arcosanti, known as Old Town, includes living quarters in complex houses for one hundred people. Two massive apses (designs representing a quarter of a sphere) house a ceramics facility and a bronze foundry to forge bells that support the nonprofit Cosanti Foundation dedicated to Soleri's humanistic ideals.[111] Upon completion, at some unknown future date, Arcosanti will include three or more massive twenty-five-story curved buildings interconnected by an apron of solar greenhouses to grow food year-round.[112] The use of passive solar architectural techniques, such as the apse effect and greenhouse architecture, in addition to solar power generators and channeled ventilation, greatly reduces energy usage related to heating, cooling, and lighting.

Soleri felt that single-family home ownership, a pillar of the American Dream, would prove catastrophic to the planet if adopted as an aspiration by six to ten billion people worldwide. "Consider," Soleri wrote, "the asphalt, the concrete, the garages, the basements, the attics, the storerooms, the back porches," the backyards, and the alleyways required to build those private dwellings. For that reason, Soleri designed Arcosanti as an alternative to the automobile-centric urban planning and hyperconsumptive lifestyles in vogue as an invitation for Americans to adopt frugality as a virtue and to redefine the pursuit of happiness along less-materialistic lines. Suburbia, argued Soleri, represents a supreme overconsumption of resources, which leads to an "unraveling of the living into dissolution and death."[113] He demanded recognition of a shared "nonfuture" created by our complacency and indifference to the

FIGURE 35. Apse at Arcosanti

ecological impact of so-called modern life. "I am a realist," asserted Soleri flatly, "realistic about a reality that is not the one fantasied by the do-gooders of the 'New Age,' steered by Deep Ecologists and Eco-theologians, the 'Mother Nature' lovers."[114]

To become a persuasive instrument of change, Soleri knew that Arcosanti (whose population generally remains under one hundred people) required a critical mass of at least a thousand residents "interested in building and experiencing a habitat that might produce answers to some of the problems *Homo sapiens* is facing: hyperconsumption, environmental collapse, sprawl, waste, pollution, physical and cultural segregation, materialism, violence, mediocrity, despair, intolerance, xenophobia."[115] A critical mass of like-minded people would turn Arcosanti into an effective testing ground for a lean society with a lean economy. The lean credo, an antidote to greed, simply means doing more with less. The lean linear cities that Soleri designed linked economic needs with cultural interests via pedestrian walkways, cycling paths, light rail, and vertical-transport systems that addressed the problems of energy inefficiency and pollution caused by conventional transport systems.[116] In June 2017, a large blackboard in a red wooden frame wel-

FIGURE 36. Arcosanti home interior

comed visitors with a reminder, attributed to Soleri, of the community's mission: "We are engaged in the betterment of man's condition and in the conservation of nature, inasmuch as they both depend on the creation of efficient and humane cities."

The long gravel road leading to Arcosanti reduces traffic around the complex, and delivery and construction vehicles rarely move beyond parking lots. Most visitors follow a paved walkway of sand-colored stones to the complex's entrance. On the left, a stand of tall, narrow cypress trees rises adjacent to the multiuse Crafts III building (a welcome center that includes housing on the first level, a café on the second, a bakery on the third-floor mezzanine, and an art gallery on the fourth floor). Tourists may only venture passed Crafts III on guided tours that include the Vaults, the Ceramics Apse, East and West Housing, and the Foundry Apse where residents cast bronze bells. In the winter, the foundry furnace provides heat to campus buildings via ducts and concrete heatsinks. Most residents of Arcosanti are young adults, who pay to complete a five-week workshop required for living on-site and who stay afterward for varying lengths of time. Wages only amount to a few hundred dollars per month, but no charge is levied for room and board.

Soleri's intention for "what is in essence a company town" run by the Cosanti Foundation may remind readers of Robert Owen's New Lanark, but as one cultural anthropologist observes, Arcosanti more closely resembles an updated version of the preindustrial Italian village.[117] Today, about two-thirds of community income comes from the sale of patinated wind bells, with tourism and charitable contributions making up the remainder of revenues. While he was alive, Soleri traveled to Arcosanti from Cosanti every week to lead discussions as part of a "School of Thought" forum. Six years before his death in 2013, he ventured to hope that his "neomonastic" internship program might develop similarities with the monastery and university in the creation of a "faculty" consisting of Arcosanti residents and students who stayed for one or more years and lived alongside "the construction and maintenance people, the cooks, the bakers, the gardeners, etc."[118] At the moment, in absence of the critical mass of one thousand people that Soleri envisioned, Arcosanti struggles for continuity of enterprise, since many enter the community and leave it after several months of training. Our guide, a young woman who had lived on-site less than one year, noted that around thirty core individuals trained newcomers in the vital aspects of the community, such as bronze casting and ceramics, but the constant turnover makes it difficult to complete construction on the remaining 95 percent of Arcosanti.

Despite that fact, Soleri's emphasis on moving away from equating hyper-consumption with the good life, and his embrace of dense and dynamic "miniaturized" urban centers in harmony with the landscape, makes more sense now than ever, given that the average size of a new American single-family home grew from 983 square feet in 1950 to 2,479 square feet in 2007, an increase of 152 percent![119] At Arcosanti, Soleri proposed a "modest, limited" alternative to the existing order in most Western societies where "the 'haves' seem bent on monopolizing land, resources, and culture at the expense of a more just and less materialist inclination."[120] Leanness, miniaturization, compactness, conservation, and community—these principles of arcology help to create sustainable environments in which inhabitants interact cooperatively (as do organs, tissues, and cells in highly evolved organisms). According to this model, multiple systems act in coordination "to minimize waste while maximizing efficient circulation of people and resources, employing multi-use structures, and exploiting solar orientation for lighting, heating, cooling, food production, and esthetic impact."[121] It is a philosophy of architecture and life that recognizes the need for good stewardship of the earth and respect for its immense gifts.

*   *   *

Out of the communalism and environmentalism of the counterculture move-ment emerged a new awareness of the integration of all living beings with nature and a better understanding of the landscapes, seascapes, and airspaces that form the biosphere of the planet. A surge in the formation of cohousing communities and ecovillages during the mid-1980s and 1990s contributed to a greening of the intentional community movement. The Farm, for instance, started as a religious commune dedicated to psychedelic mysticism but later self-identified as an ecovillage using solar cookers and showers, composting toilets, and gray water for irrigation. Ecovillages—comprising individuals attempting to maintain sustainable low-impact lifestyles in harmony with each other, the creatures of the earth, and the biosphere—employ sustain-able technologies and materials, and they foster economies based on equity and fairness.[122] Ecovillages provide a measure of ideological coherence around principles of shared and sustainable living, formulate ways of deal-ing with conflict resolution, and address community needs into an indefinite future.

The cohousing movement, from which many ecovillages sprung, repre-sents a postcounterculture approach to intentional living modeled on coop-erative preindustrial villages, tightly knit urban neighborhoods, and small towns where residents lived above street-level shops and cottage industries flourished.[123] In such communities, people knew one another's families over generations and developed a sense of security and belonging often absent in modern cities and towns strictly zoned into residential, commercial, and industrial sectors. To break down those artificial barriers that compartmen-talize life and separate people, cohousing communities permit diverse groups to live together based on values of choice and tolerance—and residents choose when and how to participate in communal activities.[124] While planned communities conceived during the nineteenth and early twentieth centuries to improve the housing, working, and living conditions for work-ers (such as those in New Lanark, Pullman, and the "Triple Cities" of the Southern Tier) may be regarded as precursors of the modern cohousing movement, they depended more upon the engagement of philanthropic indi-viduals than on the self-organization of community members.[125]

Cohousing developed to meet the needs of people who desired more interaction and cooperation with their neighbors, but who did not want to share finances, or a specific ideology, as in other intentional communities. Cohousing projects usually included a planning process in which future residents participated, a neighborhood design that fostered community interaction, common facilities for daily use, resident management, nonhierarchical decision making, and the absence of a shared economy.[126] Danish architect Jan Gudmand-Høyer established the first cohousing community in 1974. He and his wife, eager to raise a family, could not locate an apartment complex or a single-family home in Denmark that offered the mix of privacy and community that they desired. Inspired in part by Renaissance philosopher and statesman Thomas More's novel *Utopia* (1516), which features groups of thirty families on a fictional island using common facilities and partaking in communal meals, Gudmand-Høyer conceived a housing complex that would combine the cooperative interaction of a rural village with proximity to the city.[127] He and a group of friends gathered to discuss constructing a housing complex pleasant enough to sustain the level of social interaction necessary to encourage residents to use the common house as an extension of their own homes. They purchased land outside of Copenhagen and developed plans for twelve terraced houses with private yards set around an inconspicuous common house and swimming pool.

Despite Gudmand-Høyer's careful planning, and avoidance of the term "collective," when locals heard about their plans, they only saw "red" (communism).[128] Forced to sell the property, many participating families settled for traditional forms of housing. Gudmand-Høyer wrote about that experience for a national newspaper, and his article, "The Missing Link between Utopia and the Dated One-Family House," generated enormous interest in cohousing. Encouraged by that reception, Gudmand-Høyer regrouped and purchased two properties with several families who had joined his first attempt at community building. During the fall of 1972, twenty-seven families moved into Hillerød, and one year later, another thirty-three families opened a cohousing community in Jonstrup.[129] Most of these two-income families could have afforded larger houses, but they chose cohousing as an alternative to the single-family homes owned by 65 percent of Danes. They wanted smaller living spaces, believing them conducive to a more meaningful way of life. Most of the twenty-two cohousing projects completed in Denmark by 1982 were structured as limited equity cooperatives financed with government-sponsored loans.[130]

Muir Commons in Davis, California, brought cohousing to the United States in 1991, and before long an American version of intergenerational community took shape. Muir residents worked together to design the layout of the complex and its houses (which ranged in size from 800 square feet to 1,400 square feet).[131] They built a pedestrian path through a colorful landscape of native California plants, vegetable gardens, and young fruit trees. Many residents at Muir Commons purchased homes with the assistance of subsidies offered by the developer and the City of Davis. In their first year, Muir Commoners welcomed dozens of curious journalists, photographers, and people from around the world who wanted to learn more about the country's first cohousing community.[132] Other cohousing experiments followed, including EcoVillage Ithaca nestled in the stunning Finger Lakes region of upstate New York.

Established the same year that Muir Commons reached completion, Eco-Village Ithaca began with a vision for a socially and ecologically sustainable community designed and governed through a participatory process. The brainchild of two single mothers, Joan Bokaer and Liz Walker, EcoVillage Ithaca was conceived during the Global Walk for a Livable World in 1990. Participants in that epic journey walked from Los Angeles to New York City to raise awareness of environmental crises and solutions, and they visited a few intentional communities (including Arcosanti) along the way. Inspired by those visits, Bokaer returned to her progressive hometown of Ithaca and delivered an "EcoVillage vision" presentation in May 1991 to an excited audience of about one hundred people at the local Unitarian church.[133] A five-day "envisioning" retreat for interested families from across the nation took place in June. Walker flew in from San Francisco to help facilitate the retreat. Group leaders set up white tents in a field outside the city; hired cooks, made presentations; and held discussions about purchasing land, crafting a mission statement, building green, and farming organically.

In the weeks following the retreat, a formal organization coalesced with Bokaer and Walker as codirectors. The pair organized fifteen committees, raised money, and purchased a 175-acre site for $400,000 that included open rolling meadows, rich farmland, a small pond, and hilltop views of the city with Cornell University and Ithaca College visible in the distance.[134] Many founding and current members of Ecovillage Ithaca enjoy affiliations with those respected centers of higher learning, and some joint educational ventures have emerged among the three institutions. Set up as a not-for-profit educational organization, the bylaws of EcoVillage Ithaca define the purpose of the community as: "1) the preservation and conservation of open space; 2) the development of scientific methods to implement ecologically and socially sustainable high density community living; and 3) the teaching of these successful methods to the broader public."[135] Community members adopted a permaculture (permanent agriculture) model of sustainability that emphasized the harmonious integration of human beings with land in the provision of local needs such as food, shelter, and energy.

The first of three distinct neighborhoods in EcoVillage Ithaca, FROG (an acronym for First Residents Group), opened in 1996. It consists of thirty duplex homes (ranging from about 900 square feet to 1,600 square feet) set facing each other along a winding gravel footpath lined by young shade trees and a proliferation of colorful flowers during the spring, summer, and fall. On the south side of FROG sits a 1-acre pond teeming with birds and wildlife. Residents hired a cohousing architect and design team to build contemporary duplexes with long, steeply pitched roofs (to prevent snow and ice accumulation) and wood siding stained in natural browns, grays, and greens. South-facing windows 14 feet in height provide light and warmth during long winters—and well-insulated walls help to retain it.[136] An array of solar panels delivers electric power to neighborhood homes. The FROG Common House includes a large communal kitchen, a spacious eating area, and a lounge, and it provides a comfortable venue for a variety of community events.

Completed in 2006, the SONG (Second Neighborhood Group) contains thirty large, unpainted clapboard duplexes that diverge from the standardization employed in the FROG neighborhood to keep costs down by limiting possibilities for customization. In addition, SONG residents built using locally sourced woods, permitted a good deal of architectural variation, and integrated newer green technologies, such as rooftop solar electric power and composting toilets. SONG homeowners also spaced buildings farther apart than in FROG resulting in a level of privacy unavailable elsewhere in EcoVillage Ithaca. Although often larger, the heavily insulated SONG homes significantly lowered heating costs compared to FROG. A centrally located SONG common house draws residents together in ways not possible in more

FIGURE 37. FROG common house (right) and SONG duplexes (left)

conventional neighborhoods.[137] As the landscaping matures, SONG increasingly resembles American frontier homesteads in the eighteenth and nineteenth centuries, whereas FROG conjures preindustrial European villages.
The decision to limit automobiles to the edges of EcoVillage Ithaca height-
ens that effect.

The TREE (Third Residential Ecovillage Experience) neighborhood dif-
fers considerably from FROG and SONG. Built to the highest standards for
energy efficiency, TREE became the first Passivhaus cohousing neighborhood in the United States in 2015.[138] Its large, blue, four-story common house
and Sustainable Living Center, which looms over the EcoVillage complex,
contains fifteen units designed for aging in place. A series of smaller blue and
gray duplexes stretch out beside the Living Center and face each other along a
series of pedestrian paths. A grassy courtyard, outlined by newly planted trees,
provides TREE folk with ample space for outdoor gatherings. Their sharp
angular roofs are fitted with solar panels that, along with an additional ground-
mounted array, provide hot water and electric heat. TREE duplexes and apartments use 80 to 90 percent less energy than typical homes in the Northeast.[139]
The layout of EcoVillage Ithaca, based around pedestrian rather than vehicular

FIGURE 38. Four-story common house (left), duplex (center), and homes (right) in TREE

traffic, increases face-to-face interaction and promotes communication among members of the community. Cofounder Liz Walker recounts one summer afternoon when taking out the compost meant engaging a couple of friends about their children, helping someone move a ladder, having a cup of coffee with a new neighbor, and viewing a freshly painted kitchen along the way.[140] Living in such a community also means honoring the cycle of birth and death, and EcoVillage residents share their accomplishments and failures, their hopes and fears for the future, in sincere and intimate ways absent in many American communities today.

EcoVillage Ithaca began as an educational project designed to demonstrate social and ecological alternatives to the existing order through a whole-systems approach to interactions between human beings and the natural world. Founded under the auspices of the Center for Religion, Ethics, and Social Policy at Cornell University, EcoVillage Ithaca works with interns, graduate students, and independent scholars; conducts workshops for planners, architects, and green builders; and hosts tours year round.[141] Many residents make a living through on-site employment (from childcare providers to software engineers), and many goods and services are exchanged.[142] Everyone living in the community pays monthly dues and contributes two to four hours of labor per week on tasks ranging from dishwashing to service on administrative committees.

As for shortcomings, the consensus model of governance can be slow and tedious, residents tend to be white and middle-class (despite attempts to foster diversity), and housing prices continue to rise, eroding affordability—though a "flip-tax" on sales supports affordability initiatives.[143] On the other hand, residents paid off the mortgage on the property long ago—and the ecological footprint of the village is considerably smaller than that of typical American neighborhoods. Muir Commons, EcoVillage Ithaca, and other ecologically minded cohousing experiments continue to inspire new ways of addressing the social and architectural demands of cooperative sustainable communities. Although a comprehensive treatment of them is beyond the scope of this book, multigenerational housing, integrative housing for the physically and intellectually challenged, grouped housing for families adopting children from foster care, innovative assisted living for seniors, housing that promotes inclusion and well-being, and neighborhood development are just some of the ways that cohousing communities are being adapted to the needs of local populations.

AFTERWORD
The Next Wave

MY DECISION TO entitle this book *American Community* stems from a desire to highlight an essential feature of the nation's historical landscape obscured during the previous century. Government propaganda stoked patriotism as the American military engaged in conflicts around the world (from the Border War with Mexico to the Persian Gulf War). Red Scares followed World War I and II, and intermittent periods of economic prosperity intensified individualism and eclipsed alternate ways of organizing society and community. As a teenager in the 1980s, a time of conspicuous consumption and oblivious disregard for the welfare of others, I understood "communism" and "socialism" as pejorative terms associated with authoritarian regimes in the Soviet Union, China, and Vietnam, or with Cold War governments in East Germany and Poland (and only rarely with successful political parties in Switzerland, France, and elsewhere in Western Europe). The widely held presupposition that American capitalism generates greater prosperity, guarantees more individual freedom, and encourages people to work harder than in socialist or communist economic systems has gone largely unchallenged.

Not surprisingly, similar views endure today despite nearly forty years of misguided economic policy. The Reagan era produced wealth inequality comparable to the Gilded Age and amplified fissures in the social fabric of the nation around issues of race, economics, and politics. These and other failures of American capitalism starkly impact the lives of millions of lower and middle class people currently experiencing diminishing educational levels in a knowledge economy, declining social mobility as wages stagnate, and decreasing life spans due to poverty.[1] These palpable shortcomings of the American economic system have also made many people susceptible to the rants of phony conservatives, such as Ann Coulter and Rush Limbaugh, and to the regressive nationalisms of demagogues, such as Donald Trump and Steve Bannon. As a result, a widespread presupposition persists among the general public that capitalism is fundamentally an American economic system—when actually it was formed in Europe, and thus socialism (though it has a distinguished history in this country) is a subversive foreign import best barred at the border.

Misguided views such as these tend to reinforce a conviction that the tangible benefits of competitive individualism, free enterprise, and entrepreneurial capitalism are evidenced in American prosperity, while western European socialist governments demonstrate the shortcomings of public ownership of utilities, collectivism, social welfare programs, and high taxes (though they ensure health care, good wages, and subsidized education). Thus trade unions are bad for American business, progressive taxation is inherently evil, and any kind of "sharing the wealth" is necessarily "antithetical to the nation's founding."[2] I hope that our wide-ranging journey through four centuries of intentional living challenges these and other such assumptions and reminds readers that many early American communitarians were Christians who lived collectively and shared resources in imitation of the apostles, that cooperation and community played an essential role in settling the American frontier, and that the term "socialism" carried positive connotations from its coining in the early decades of the nineteenth century until the Great War.

Perhaps no individual has done more to rehabilitate the socialist label in recent years than Senator Bernie Sanders, who ran for the 2016 Democratic Party nomination for president as a "Democratic Socialist" on a progressive platform reminiscent of Franklin Roosevelt's New Deal. The American political scientist W. J. Conroy grew up during the Cold War, and therefore he always "believed that a socialist label of any sort could apply to only a fringe candidate running an informational campaign with no hope of winning any states at all."[3] Sanders defied such suppositions, and in the process, rekindled interest in socialism as a viable political and economic vehicle for social amelioration. He began his run for the party nomination in 2016 with a 3 percent approval rating, but buoyed by an outpouring of support by young people, he went on to win twenty-two primaries and caucuses.

The historian and former editor of the *Catholic Worker* Michael Harrington observes that the purpose of Democratic Socialism is to salvage the values of progressive Judaism and Christianity (only "not in religious form"), to democratize the workplace and create new forms of community, and to empower ordinary people to preserve and extend democratic freedom.[4] Following his primary defeat by Hillary Clinton and the improbable rise of Donald Trump, Bernie Sanders issued a twelve-step "Agenda for America" that included plans for instituting progressive taxation, providing universal health care, raising the minimum wage, growing the trade union movement, creating worker co-ops, and establishing pay equity for women.[5] Much more than a system of government championed by labor parties and advocates of social democracy, socialism is a method of organization that enables people to rely on a society or a community for maintenance, rather than on individual effort alone, and thereby prevents exploitation through the democratic socialization of wealth.[6]

In casting off associations that socialism acquired with authoritarianism and fascism during the last century, and jettisoning the term's grounding in theories promulgated by Marx and Engels, or by the so-called Utopian Socialists (Henri de Saint-Simon, Charles Fourier, Étienne Cabet, and Robert Owen), we recover a long tradition of American "socialism" in the form of intentional community building and cooperative enterprise from the colonial era to the present day. We remember the early European settlers to North America who braved perilous voyages in search of religious freedom, equal opportunity, and material prosperity. They drew inspiration from the promise of a new social order based on divine justice implicit in Millennialism; from a form of religious socialism based on the teachings of Jesus; and from New Testament injunctions to care for the poor, the sick, and the dispossessed. The "astounding idea of a total transformation of society," asserts political theorist Bernard Crick, "was invented by the Hebrew prophets and popularized by early Christians, not Rousseau or Marx."[7]

Long-time social activist and Occupy protestor Frances Goldin finds ignorance "about what socialism really is and how it could be realized here in our own country" appalling—and she attributes that lack of understanding to the mainstream media, and to "the powers that be," which have "made the word 'socialism' frightening, foreign, unpatriotic, and menacing."[8] With most of the world caught in the grip of hypercapitalism, better known as neoliberalism, the global economy suffers from increasingly frequent cycles of instability, the ecological crisis continues to worsen, and record levels of wealth inequality have returned. The time, therefore, has come to weigh alternative methods of organization that sharply reduce social, political, and economic inequity.[9] Such a move seems more urgent than ever when the American Dream, the classic post–World War II middle-class life, now costs an estimated $130,000 per year for a family of four—*as household income hovers at about $57,000.*[10]

Admittedly, the prospect of recovering the American Dream may seem a faint beacon in the midst of a stormy Trump presidency, but as the historian Jon Meacham notes (citing St. Augustine), the ideal of nationhood is "as a multitude of rational beings united by the common objects of our love."[11] If we love liberty under the law and cherish equality of opportunity, then we must rediscover a capacity for moving forward together in a nation more divided than since the 1850s. As these pages attest, periods of tremendous social upheaval, such as the Civil War and the Great Depression, proved tremendously transformative. In world history too, surges in social amelioration coincide with rejuvenation of the utopian spirit during troubled times, for instance, in the Israel of the prophets, in the Athens of the Peloponnesian wars, in the Roman Empire at the time of Jesus, in the breakdown of European feudalism, and in the transformations of work life brought about by the Industrial Revolution.[12]

If by socialism we simply mean the belief that everyone should benefit from participation in the economy, instead of a few owners of capital reaping large returns as others go hungry, then there exists a venerable tradition of intentional communities with a socialist orientation in American history. People belonging to such communities labored collectively to create living models of societies where the well-being of all members served as an important measure of success. Consider, for example, the thousands of American communitarians who practiced a Community of Goods (Pilgrims in Massachusetts, Ephratans in Pennsylvania, Zoarites in Ohio, Icarians in Iowa, New Harmonists in Indiana, and hippie Farmers in Tennessee) and the multitude of secular intentional communities formed on the basis of economic cooperation (Ruskin, Kaweah, Llano del Rio, Mound Bayou, and Mulberry Family).

Detractors, no doubt, will jeer at the brevity of many intentional communities chronicled herein—though the longest-lived of them endured decades longer than Chinese or Soviet communes. Even those societies that disbanded after a short time did not fail in their efforts to create a better world, since they left a record of what worked—and what did not—for those who followed. The communities that collapsed were bedeviled by a common set of problems ranging from conflict and division sown by disgruntled individuals and the lack of formal admission criteria to the waning of early enthusiasm after years of backbreaking work and the deaths of charismatic leaders. Other communities ceased to exist when they failed to become self-supporting, when technology displaced cottage industries, and when misunderstandings and simmering hostilities toward communitarians from local populations broke into dispute. In too many intentional communities that professed social equality, women fell into traditional gender roles (particularly around the home and housework). The history of intentional living in America is also very white. Even associations that valued interracialism and practiced inclusion, such as Koinonia Farm in Georgia, failed to attract minorities.[13] In addition, as founding members aged and died, many intentional communities found it difficult to keep young people from the material lures of the outside world. Success sometimes proved equally ruinous, since it created covetousness among members anxious to live more comfortable lives by means of shared assets.

However, it is equally true that many of these social experimentations anticipated paradigm shifts in social consciousness (including emancipation, gender equality under the law, the establishment of social welfare programs for the indigent, and the protection of the environment), and they provided models for alternate forms of social organization that do not foster injustice and exploitation as a consequence of an economic system based on capital accumulation. Most of the communities explored in this book rejected capitalism as a vehicle for the transformation of consciousness because it produces inequality, subverts democracy, remains prone to crisis, and is fundamentally at odds with the planet's ecology. Although absolute ideal

communism has eluded most intentional communities, in the most successful of them, living was certainly superior to that found in the industrial and
agricultural societies outside their walls.[14] When communitarians held fast
to a commonly accepted ideology, be it religious or secular, they were more
likely to succeed. Clear standards for admission also improved the chances
of success, as did a means to expel individuals who, for whatever reason, did
not prove a good fit with the community. Moreover, everyone must work—
there is no utopia for shirkers!

Acute dissatisfaction with the status quo and a refusal to accept the world
as they found it unites American communitarians across the centuries. The
people who founded intentional communities—like those who joined
them—believed that their manner of communal association offered tangible advantages over the existing order, and they tended to demand from life
"more fellowship, more pleasure, more learning, more time, more dignity, and
more equality."[15] That Walt Whitman, the most American of poets, spent his
final years in a working-class neighborhood attended by bohemian radicals
(despite being one of the world's most recognizable literary figures) speaks
to a simplicity and pragmatism once regarded as integral to the "American
character." Born into a moment when former presidents Thomas Jefferson
and James Madison were active citizens, Whitman died after the births of
future presidents Franklin Roosevelt and Harry Truman. He therefore lived
at a time when the nation was still defining itself.

Asked by a reporter for the radical British journal *Today* (a periodical to
which the American bard contributed) if he accepted the piece entitled "Walt
Whitman Is a Socialist Poet," Old Walt, as he was known, acknowledged that
he read it carefully. "I find," Whitman replied, "that I'm a good deal more of
a socialist than I thought I was: maybe not technically, politically, so, but
intrinsically, in my meanings."[16] That admission of his true sympathies, shared
by many at the time, led Ralph Waldo Emerson to deem Whitman's *Leaves
of Grass* "indisputably American," John Burroughs to hail him as "our poet
of democracy," and artists from Carl Sandburg to Woodie Guthrie to Allen
Ginsberg to find inspiration in his expression of progressive spiritual and
democratic values.[17]

I also hope that *American Community* reveals something important about
the way in which secular and religious societies of intention organized life
and managed the sharing of resources. The religious settlers at Plymouth,
Zwaanendael, and Bohemia Manor eschewed private property, and the

Ephratans developed the most advanced comprehensive economic-industrial system in the colonies. Democratic-minded Zoarites achieved self-sufficiency by sharing profits from collective industries, and Practical Christians at Hopedale insisted on absolute social equality for all members—irrespective of sex, color, occupation, wealth, or rank. The Sanctificationists sheltered battered women and provided them with meaningful work, and Equity Stores priced goods and services at cost based on a time-labor system that alleviated income inequality and protected individual sovereignty along with the interests of the consumer.

At Mound Bayou, residents made bold assertions of African American autonomy and entrepreneurialism after emancipation, and they created a self-governing community of like-minded individuals. New Deal subsistence homesteads and greenbelt communities, such as Arthurdale and Greendale, raised Americans out of poverty by providing them with affordable housing and dignified work at a living wage. Lomaland and Rugby contributed to the common good by developing superior educational systems for children and adults, and The Farm created international, privately funded, relief efforts for victims of natural disaster. The primitivism and open land ethos practiced at Morning Star Ranch harkened back to efforts by seventeenth-century English Diggers to farm common land and gave voice to a new generation of back-to-the-landers, while the Mulberry Family modeled tolerance for many expressions of love and anticipated the LGBT rights movement.

These and other experiments in intentional living, founded by visionary men and women over the last four hundred years, attempted to put into practice ideas increasingly embraced by mainstream culture (including multiculturalism, sexual liberation, alternative medicine, home birthing and free clinics, whole foods and organic farming, Eastern religions, progressive politics, and a rediscovery of the importance of community).[18] Although *American Community* examined many past attempts at building a better world, the dense sustainable urban habitat at Arcosanti designed to blend into the landscape, and the green cohousing community at EcoVillage Ithaca, provide glimpses into a future premised upon the responsible use of natural resources, sensitivity to the beauty of the earth, and recognition of a complex web of sustaining relationships between human beings and the environment.

Millions of people now live in ecovillages, cohousing neighborhoods, communes, worker and student cooperatives, and other intentional communities in the United States and around the world. That steady growth in

intentional living suggests that we are on the cusp of a new wave in community building, in part due to the moment of moral crisis in which we find ourselves, one that includes reckoning with the cascading consequences of
human-caused climate change, the mass extinction of species on a scale
unparalleled since the dinosaurs perished from the earth, the overconsumption of dwindling natural resources, and the lingering effects of polluting the
environment. For the remainder of the twenty-first century, individuals will
start intentional communities that offer solutions to these and other pressing problems facing humanity, including poverty and food insecurity; sense-
less violence and warfare; and the displacement of jobs by robotics, auto-
mation, and artificial intelligence looming on the horizon. Indeed, human
survival may depend on our ability to find better ways of living with each
other and on becoming better stewards of the earth.

Fortunately, if America has a particular genius, it is reinvention. The community builders whose stories fill these pages were not wild eccentrics full
of quixotic idealism, but inventors who in response to oppression and social
injustice forged a better future. The next wave of leaders in intentional living
will foster the growth of socialist communities that provide stark alternatives
to American capitalism with its for-profit production, mind-boggling con-
centrations of wealth, relentless competition for resources, and egregious
exploitation of labor. Tomorrow's communitarians will construct cooperative societies of ecological sanity, shared material abundance, and equality
where social relations are premised on solidarity and production for public
use.[19] They will sever the chains of wage slavery, institute democratic reforms,
eliminate terror and oppression, and create inclusive cultures. Such claims
might strike some as fanciful, but the fight for freedom and equality—for a
more perfect union—is a perennial theme in American history.

As Frederick Douglass observed, "If there is no struggle, there is no progress. Those who profess to favor freedom and yet deprecate agitation are
men who want crops without plowing up the ground; they want rain without thunder and lightning. They want the ocean without the awful roar of its
mighty waters."[20] If the history of socialist intentional communities in the
United States teaches us anything, it is to believe that we will awaken from
the slumber of complacency and discover what the poet-painter William
Blake called "Divine Vision," the expanded perception that results from deepening spiritual awareness, and from that understanding build a new society
based upon "Mercy, Pity, Peace, and Love."[21]

ACKNOWLEDGMENTS

With gratitude, I remember the support of my parents and the guidance of former professors Walter Coppedge, Cliff Edwards, Marcel Cornis-Pope, and W. Scott Howard. In choosing to research intentional communities, conversations with friends and colleagues—Darryl Wood, Roger Hecht, Arnaud Brichon, Wesley Graves, and Alice Cudlipp—sparked interest in a group, a region, or an arresting aspect of American history. I began reading for this project with students in a capstone course at State University of New York and thank them for their willingness to plow through thousands of pages and hundreds of years of American history together. Walter Coppedge, J. Jeremy Wisnewski, William Simons, and Nancy Cannon reviewed the manuscript and provided invaluable feedback. I am thankful for the assistance of the librarians and student-staff at the Cornell Libraries in Ithaca and Milne Library in Oneonta, and for the small patio with a splendid view of the hills around Ithaca, belonging to Richard and Denise Coyle, where I wrote during the summer and fall of 2017. How fortunate also to meet Nicole Solano at Rutgers University Press who recommended printing *American Community* with color images.

Liangmei Bao, to whom this work is dedicated, shared my enthusiasm for experiments in intentional living and traveled to visit the sites of many communities featured in these pages. Those excursions meant making accommodations along the way—many thanks to Roger and Corinne Bouchard (and Alice) at Pillsbury House Bed and Breakfast in Woonsocket, Rhode Island; Rich and Bert at Hurst House Bed and Breakfast in Lancaster, Pennsylvania; Trellis Smith and Lucas Tatham at Modern Homestead in Reedsville, West Virginia; Teresa Bowman at Newbury House in Historic Rugby; the Clines at Garver House in Strasburg, Ohio; Carlee at Lilla Vita Guest House in Bishop Hill, Illinois; Silas and Bianca in Flagstaff, Arizona; and Michael Mihld in Temecula, California. Our dear friends Joy and Bryce in Salt Lake City, Vinnie in Denver, and Jim and Cory in the San Francisco Bay Area hosted us graciously. Nor do we forget the fine folks at Old Town Tire and Service in Temecula who replaced the starter on our 1997 Honda Civic, in just three hours, when it failed after a hot summer run through the Arizona desert!

NOTES

INTRODUCTION

1. From 1618–48, 1672–78, and 1688–1697, respectively.

2. Susan Love Brown, *Intentional Community: An Anthropological Perspective* (Albany: SUNY Press, 2001), 5.

3. Jyotsna Sreenivasan, *Utopias in American History* (Santa Barbara: ABC-CLIO, 2008), 354.

4. Brown, *Intentional* Community, 4–5.

5. Dan Charles, "By Returning to Farming's Roots, He Found His American Dream," *Weekend Edition Saturday*, December 31, 2016, https://www.npr.org/sections/thesalt/2016/12/31/505729436/by-returning-to-farmings-roots-he-found-his-american-dream.

6. William Bradford, *Of Plymouth Plantation*, ed. Caleb Johnson (Bloomington, IN: Xlibris, 2006), 77–78.

7. Bradford, 171–72.

8. Donald E. Pitzer, *America's Communal Utopias* (Chapel Hill: University of North Carolina Press, 1997), 6.

9. Michael P. Winship, *Godly Republicanism: Puritans, Pilgrims, and a City on a Hill* (Cambridge, MA: Harvard University Press, 2012), 172–173.

10. Bernard R. Crick, *Socialism* (Minneapolis: University of Minnesota Press, 1988), 1–2.

11. Donald F. Durnbaugh, "Communitarian Societies in Colonial America," in *America's Communal Utopias*, ed. Donald E. Pitzer (Chapel Hill: University of North Carolina Press, 1997), 15.

12. Pieter Plockhoy, *A Way Propounded to Make the Poor in These and Other Nations Happy: By Bringing Together a Fit, Suitable and Well-qualified People unto One Household-government, or Little Common-wealth* (London: Black Spread-Eagle, 1659), 3.

13. Plockhoy, 5.

14. Durnbaugh, "Communitarian Societies in Colonial America," 15–16.

15. Charles Henry Black Turner, *Some Records of Sussex County, Delaware* (Philadelphia: Allen, Lane & Scott, 1909), 34.

16. Turner, 34.

17. Turner, 286.

18. Foster Stockwell, *Encyclopedia of American Communes, 1663–1963* (Jefferson, NC: McFarland, 1998), 201.

19. Turner, *Some Records of Sussex County*, 287.

20. Turner, 286.

21. Michael Morgan, *Pirates and Patriots, Tales of the Delaware Coast* (New York: Algora, 2005), 13.

22. Arthur Bestor, *Backwoods Utopias: The Sectarian Origins and the Owenite Phase of Communitarian Socialism in America* (Eugene, OR: Wipf & Stock, 2012), 27.

23. Stockwell, *Encyclopedia of American Communes*, 202.

24. Ernest J. Green, "The Labadists of Colonial Maryland, 1683–1722," *Communal Societies* 8 (1988): 105.

25. David Bentley Hart, "Are Christians Supposed to Be Communists?" *New York Times*, November 4, 2017, https://www.nytimes.com/2017/11/04/opinion/sunday/christianity-communism.html.

26. Douglas H. Shantz, *An Introduction to German Pietism: Protestant Renewal at the Dawn of Modern Europe* (Baltimore: Johns Hopkins University Press), 51.

27. Shantz, 51.

28. Shantz, 52.

29. Jasper Danckaerts and Peter Sluyter, *Journal of a Voyage to New York: And a Tour in Several of the American Colonies in 1679–80, Volume 1* (Brooklyn, NY: The Society, 1867), xxv.

30. Danckaerts and Sluyter, xxvii.

31. Shantz, *An Introduction to German Pietism*, 53.

32. Green, "The Labadists of Colonial Maryland," 107.

33. Durnbaugh, "Communitarian Societies in Colonial America," 18.

34. Green, "The Labadists of Colonial Maryland," 109.

35. Green, 110.

36. Green, 114–115.

37. Mark Holloway, *Heavens on Earth: Utopian Communities in America, 1680–1880* (New York: Dover, 2011), 35.

38. Yaacov Oved, *Two Hundred Years of American Communes* (New York: Routledge, 1987), 20.

39. T. J. Saxby, *The Quest for the New Jerusalem: Jean de Labadie and the Labadists, 1610–1744* (Boston: Martinus Nijhoff, 1987), 302–303.

40. Saxby, 306–307.

41. Saxby, 309.

42. E. G. Alderfer, *The Ephrata Commune: An Early American Counterculture* (Pittsburgh: University of Pittsburgh Press, 1985), 16.

43. Alderfer, 16–17.

44. Alderfer, 17–18.

45. Alderfer, 18–19.

46. Alderfer, 22–24.

47. Edwin Wolf, *Germantown and the Germans* (Philadelphia: Library Company of Philadelphia, 1983), 7.

48. Alderfer, *The Ephrata Commune*, 28.

49. Simon J. Bronner and Joshua R. Brown, *Pennsylvania Germans: An Interpretive Encyclopedia* (Baltimore: Johns Hopkins University Press, 2017), 138.

50. Jonathan Strom, Hartmut Lehmann, and James Van Horn Melton, *Pietism in Germany and North America 1680–1820* (New York: Routledge, 2016), 40.

51. Jeff Bach, *Voices of the Turtledoves: The Sacred World of Ephrata* (University Park: Pennsylvania State University Press, 2003), 18.

52. Bach, 17.

53. Alderfer, *The Ephrata Commune*, 46.

54. Alderfer, 44.

55. Alderfer, 47.

56. Alderfer, 49.

57. Sreenivasan, *Utopias in American History*, 115.

58. Bach, *Voices of the Turtledoves*, 134–135.

59. Sreenivasan, *Utopias in American History*, 117.

60. Alderfer, *The Ephrata Commune*, 52.

61. Bronner and Brown, *Pennsylvania Germans*, 140.

62. John Bradley, *Ephrata Cloister: Pennsylvania Trail of History Guide* (Mechanicsburg: Pennsylvania Historical and Museum Commission, 2000), 21.

63. Bronner and Brown, *Pennsylvania Germans*, 140.

64. Bradley, *Ephrata Cloister*, 24.

65. Bradley, 24.

66. Wolf, *Germantown and the Germans*, 74–75.

67. Bradley, *Ephrata Cloister*, 36.

68. Alderfer, *The Ephrata Commune*, 75.

69. Sreenivasan, *Utopias in American History*, 116.

70. Alderfer, *The Ephrata Commune*, 93.

71. Bronner and Brown, *Pennsylvania Germans*, 166.

72. Bronner and Brown, 140.

73. Sreenivasan, *Utopias in American History*, 115.

74. Bradley, *Ephrata Cloister*, 24.

75. Alderfer, *The Ephrata Commune*, 92–93.

76. Alderfer, 93.

77. Alderfer, 98–99.

78. Alderfer, 120.

79. Bach, *Voices of the Turtledoves*, 21.

80. Alderfer, *The Ephrata Commune*, 146.

81. Hiram Erb Steinmetz, "Peter Miller and Michael Witman: A Revolutionary Episode," *Journal of the Lancaster County Historical Society* 6, no. 3–4 (1901–1902), 46.

82. Alderfer, *The Ephrata Commune*, 155.

83. Bach, *Voices of the Turtledoves*, 23.

84. Alderfer, *The Ephrata Commune*, 107.

85. Alderfer, 145.

86. Anthony D. Fredericks, *Historical Trails of Eastern Pennsylvania* (Woodstock, VT: Countryman Press, 2013), 163.

1. REVOLUTION AND SOCIAL REFORMATION

1. William Alfred Hinds, *American Communities: Brief Sketches of Economy, Zoar, Bethel, Aurora, Amana, Icaria, the Shakers, Oneida, Wallingford, and the Brotherhood of the New Life* (Oneida, NY: Office of the American Socialist, 1878), 24–25.

2. Kathleen M. Fernandez, *A Singular People: Images of Zoar* (Kent, OH: Kent State University Press, 2003), 29.

3. Hinds, *American Communities*, 26.

4. Hinds, 26–28.

5. Hinds, 30–31.

6. Hinds, 31–32.

7. Catherine M. Rokicky, *Creating a Perfect World: Religious and Secular Utopias in Nineteenth-Century Ohio* (Athens: Ohio University Press, 2002), 53–54.

8. Rokicky, 55.

9. Rokicky, 55.

10. Carol A. Kolmerten, *Women in Utopia: The Ideology of Gender in the American Owenite Communities* (Syracuse, NY: Syracuse University Press, 1998), 30.

11. Rokicky, *Creating a Perfect World*, 55.

12. Hilda Dischinger Morhart, *The Zoar Story* (Dover, OH: Siebert, 1967), 11.

13. John W. Friesen and Virginia Agnes Lyons Friesen, *The Palgrave Companion to North American Utopias* (New York: Palgrave Macmillan, 2004), 117.

14. An Anglicization of the family name Bäumler.

15. Morhart, *The Zoar Story*, 14.

16. Robert P. Sutton, *Communal Utopias and the American Experience: Religious Communities, 1732–2000* (Westport, CT: Praeger, 2003), 49.

17. Emilius Oviatt Randall, *History of the Zoar Society, from Its Commencement to Its Conclusion: A Sociological Study in Communism* (Columbus, OH: Fred J. Meer Press, 1904), 82.

18. Randall, 82.

19. Sutton, *Communal Utopias and the American Experience*, 49.

20. Rokicky, *Creating a Perfect World*, 59.

21. Rokicky, 60.

22. Sutton, *Communal Utopias and the American Experience*, 50.

23. Rokicky, *Creating a Perfect World*, 74.

24. Sutton, *Communal Utopias and the American Experience*, 51.

25. Morhart, *The Zoar Story*, 55.

26. Morhart, 58.

27. Rokicky, *Creating a Perfect World*, 81.

28. Morhart, *The Zoar Story*, 68–69.

29. Morhart, 71.

30. Randall, *History of the Zoar Society*, 32.

31. Rokicky, *Creating a Perfect World*, 62.

32. Randall, *History of the Zoar Society*, 88.

33. Hinds, *American Communities*, 27–28.

34. Rokicky, *Creating a Perfect World*, 63.

35. Rokicky, 63.

36. Rokicky, 68.

37. Rokicky, 77.

38. Randall, *History of the Zoar Society*, 30.

39. Rokicky, *Creating a Perfect World*, 79.

40. Rokicky, 81.

41. Rokicky, 83–84.

42. Sutton, *Communal Utopias and the American Experience*, 51.

43. Michael Fellman, *The Unbounded Frame: Freedom and Community in Nineteenth Century American Utopianism* (Westport, CT: Greenwood Press, 1973), xvi.

44. Fellman, 4–5.

45. Bowman N. Hall, "The Economic Ideas of Josiah Warren, First American Anarchist," *History of Political Economy* 6, no. 1 (1974): 96.

46. Stockwell, *Encyclopedia of American Communes*, 73.

47. Donald E. Pitzer, "The New Moral World of Robert Owen and New Harmony," in *America's Communal Utopias*, ed. Donald E. Pitzer (Chapel Hill: University of North Carolina Press, 1997), 91.

48. Ophélie Siméon, *Robert Owen's Experiment at New Lanark: From Paternalism to Socialism* (New York: Palgrave Macmillan, 2017), 56–57.

49. Siméon, 59.

50. Pitzer, "The New Moral World," 103.

51. Crispin Sartwell, *The Practical Anarchist: Writings of Josiah Warren* (New York: Fordham University Press, 2011), 21.

52. Pitzer, "The New Moral World," 113.

53. Pitzer, 120.

54. Bowman, "The Economic Ideas of Josiah Warren," 95.

55. Sartwell, *The Practical Anarchist*, 29.

56. Sartwell, 5.

57. Sartwell, 7.

58. Sartwell, 14.

59. Sartwell, 12.

60. Hall, "The Economic Ideas of Josiah Warren," 95.

61. Sartwell, *The Practical Anarchist*, 15–16.

62. Sartwell, 15.

63. Fellman, *The Unbounded Frame*, 8.

64. William Bailie, *Josiah Warren: The First American Anarchist* (Cambridge, MA: Small, Maynard, 1906), 10.

65. Eugene Allen Gilmore, Helen Laura Sumner, and John Bertram Andrews, *A Documentary History of American Industrial Society: Labor Movement, 1820–1840* (Cleveland, OH: Arthur H. Clark, 1910), 124.

66. Gilmore, Sumner, and Andrews, *A Documentary History*, 125.

67. Gilmore, Sumner, and Andrews, 126.

68. Gilmore, Sumner, and Andrews, 128.

69. Bailie, *Josiah Warren*, 11.

70. Gilmore, Sumner, and Andrews, *A Documentary History*, 128.

71. Sartwell, *The Practical Anarchist*, 258.

72. Bailie, *Josiah Warren*, 52.

73. Sartwell, *The Practical Anarchist*, 41.

74. Philip F. Gura, *Man's Better Angels: Romantic Reformers and the Coming of the Civil War* (Cambridge, MA: Belknap Press, 2017), 195.

75. Sartwell, *The Practical Anarchist*, 29.

76. Edward K. Spann, *Brotherly Tomorrows: Movements for a Cooperative Society in America, 1820–1920* (New York: Columbia University Press, 1989), 145.

77. Gura, *Man's Better Angels*, 198.

78. Sartwell, *The Practical Anarchist*, 42–43.

79. Sartwell, 44.

80. Spann, *Brotherly Tomorrows*, 53.

81. Alice Felt Tyler, *Freedoms Ferment* (Minneapolis: University of Minnesota Press, 1944), 169.

82. Tyler, 169.

83. Adin Ballou, *History of the Hopedale Community: From Its Inception to Its Virtual Submergence in the Hopedale Parish* (Lowell, MA: Vox Populi Press, 1897), 24–25.

84. Edward K. Spann, *Hopedale: From Commune to Company Town, 1840–1920* (Columbus: Ohio State University Press, 1992), 15.

85. Ballou, *History of the Hopedale Community*, 50.

86. Ballou, 66.

87. Spann, *Hopedale*, 24–25.

88. Spann, 28–29.

89. Spann, 32.

90. Spann, 32.

91. Spann, 35.

92. Spann, 49.

93. Spann, 54.

94. Spann, 55.

95. Ballou, *History of the Hopedale Community*, 18.

96. Spann, *Hopedale*, 70.

97. Spann, 57.

98. Spann, 64.

99. Spann, 73.

100. Spann, 75.

101. Spann, 114.

102. Spann, 134.

103. Stockwell, *Encyclopedia of American Communes*, 103.

104. Spann, *Hopedale*, 139.

105. Spann, 165.

106. Spann, 168.

107. Spann, 163.

108. Victor Francis Calverton, *Where Angels Dared to Tread: Socialist and Communist Utopian Colonies in the United States* (Indianapolis: Bobbs Merrill, 1941), 225–226.

109. Calverton, 228.

110. Adin Ballou, *Autobiography of Adin Ballou, 1803–1890* (Lowell, MA: Vox Populi Press, 1896), 338.

111. Spann, *Hopedale*, 35.

112. Calverton, *Where Angels Dared to Tread*, 234–235.

113. Michael Barkun, *Crucible of the Millennium: The Burned-Over District of New York in the 1840s* (Syracuse, NY: Syracuse University Press, 1986), 84.

114. Lester Grosvenor Wells, *The Skaneateles Communal Experiment: 1843–1846* (Syracuse, NY: Onondaga Historical Association, 1953), 2.

115. Wells, 2.

116. Wells, 4.

117. Wells, 5.

118. Mark Holloway, *Heavens on Earth: Utopian Communities in America 1680–1880* (Mineola, NY: Dover, 2011), 125.

119. Wells, *The Skaneateles Communal Experiment*, 3.

120. Wells, 6.

121. Wells, 7–8.

122. William Alfred Hinds, *American Communities and Co-operative Colonies* (Chicago: Charles Kerr, 1908), 295.

123. Hinds, *American Communities*, 296.

124. Wells, *The Skaneateles Communal Experiment*, 9.

125. Hal Lieberman, "Cogswells and a Utopian Community," *Cogswell Courier*, April 2000, 6.

126. Wells, *The Skaneateles Communal Experiment*, 9.

127. Holloway, *Heavens on Earth*, 126.

128. Wells, *The Skaneateles Communal Experiment*, 15.

129. Sutton, *Communal Utopias and the American Experience*, 56.

130. George Malcolm Stephenson, *The Religious Aspects of Swedish Immigration: A Study of Immigrant Churches* (Minneapolis: University of Minnesota Press, 1932), 51–52.

131. Stephenson, 58.

132. Jon Wagner, "Eric Jansson and the Bishop Hill Colony," in *America's Communal Utopias*, ed. Donald E. Pitzer (Chapel Hill: University of North Carolina Press, 1997), 301.

133. Hinds, *American Communities*, 345.

134. Jon Wagner, "Eric Jansson and the Bishop Hill Colony," 302.

135. Michael Andrew Mikkelsen, *The Bishop Hill Colony: A Religious Communistic Settlement in Henry County, Illinois* (Baltimore: Johns Hopkins University Press, 1892), 31.

136. Jon Wagner, "Eric Jansson and the Bishop Hill Colony," 305.

137. Holloway, *Heavens on Earth*, 167.

138. Holloway, 168.

139. Sutton, *Communal Utopias and the American Experience*, 59.

140. Paul S. Gauthier, *Quest for Utopia: The Icarians of Adams County: With Colonies in Denton County, Texas, Nauvoo, Illinois, Cheltenham, Missouri, and Cloverdale, California* (Corning, IA: Gauthier Publishing, 1992), 9.

141. Harry W. Laidler, *History of Socialism: An Historical Comparative Study of Socialism* (New York: Routledge, 2000), 48.

142. Holloway, *Heavens on Earth*, 200.

143. Archie Brown, *The Rise and Fall of Communism* (New York: HarperCollins, 2009), 17.

144. Robert P. Sutton, *Les Icariens: The Utopian Dream in Europe and America* (Urbana: University of Illinois Press, 1994), 46.

145. Sutton, 46.

146. Sutton, 58.

147. Sutton, 62.

148. Emile Vallet and H. Roger Grant, *An Icarian Communist in Nauvoo: Commentary* (Springfield: Illinois State Historical Society, 1971), 20.

149. Vallet and Grant, 37.

150. Sutton, *Les Icariens*, 118

151. Sutton, 117.

152. Sutton, 119.

153. Sutton, 119.

154. Sutton, 130.

155. Sutton, *Communal Utopias and the American Experience*, 105.

156. Vallet and Grant, *An Icarian Communist in Nauvoo*, 9.

2. SLEEPING CARS, SPIRITUALISM, AND COOPERATIVES

1. Beth Tompkins Bates, *Pullman Porters and the Rise of Protest Politics in Black America, 1925–1945* (Chapel Hill: University of North Carolina Press, 2001), 17.

2. Margaret Cole, *Robert Owen of New Lanark: 1771–1858* (New York: Augustus M. Kelley, 1969), 45–56.

3. Cole, 48.

4. Cole, 73.

5. Almont Lindsey, *The Pullman Strike: The Story of a Unique Experiment and of a Great Labor Upheaval* (Chicago: University of Chicago Press, 1943), 3.

6. Lindsey, 6.

7. Lindsey, 19–20.

8. Lindsey, 22–23.

9. Susan Eleanor Hirsch, *After the Strike: A Century of Labor Struggle at Pullman* (Urbana: University of Illinois Press, 2003), 17.

10. Hirsch, 17.

11. Frank Beberdick, *Chicago's Historic Pullman District* (Charlestown, SC: Arcadia Publishing, 1998), 41.

12. Donald L. Miller, *City of the Century: The Epic of Chicago and the Making of America* (New York: Simon & Schuster, 1996), 225.

13. Miller, 225.

14. Hirsch, *After the Strike*, 18.

15. Miller, *City of the Century*, 228.

16. Miller, 236–237.

17. Lindsey, *The Pullman Strike*, 94.

18. Hirsch, *After the Strike*, 24.

19. Hirsch, 30.

20. Hirsch, 18.

21. Bates, *Pullman Porters and the Rise of Protest Politics in Black America*, 22.

22. Lindsey, *The Pullman Strike*, 109.

23. Lindsey, 111.

24. Hirsch, *After the Strike*, 33.

25. Hirsch, 39.

26. Hirsch, 40.

27. Herbert Wallace Schneider and George Lawton, *A Prophet and a Pilgrim: Being the Incredible History of Thomas Lake Harris and Laurence Oliphant; Their Sexual Mysticisms and Utopian Communities Amply Documented to Confound the Skeptic* (New York: Columbia University Press, 1942), xiv–xv.

28. Schneider and Lawton, 4.

29. Foster Stockwell, *Encyclopedia of American Communes, 1663–1963* (Jefferson, NC: McFarland, 1998), 137.

30. Gina Misiroglu, *American Countercultures: An Encyclopedia of Nonconformists, Alternative Lifestyles, and Radical Ideas in U.S. History* (New York: M. E. Sharpe, 2009), 361.

31. Thomas Lake Harris, *Brotherhood of the New Life: Its Fact, Law, Method and Purpose* (Santa Rosa, CA: Fountain Grove Press, 1891), 5.

32. Robert P. Sutton, *Communal Utopias and the American Experience: Secular Communities, 1824–2000* (Westport, CT: Praeger, 2004), 124.

33. William Alfred Hinds, *American Communities and Co-operative Colonies* (Chicago: William Kerr, 1908), 425.

34. Sutton, *Communal Utopias and the American Experience*, 124.

35. Hinds, *American Communities and Co-operative Colonies*, 425–426.

36. Hinds, 426.

37. Hinds, 426–427.

38. Sutton, *Communal Utopias and the American Experience*, 124.

39. Hinds, *American Communities and Co-operative Colonies*, 430

40. Sutton, *Communal Utopias and the American Experience*, 124.

41. Robert S. Fogarty, *American Utopianism* (Itasca, IL: Peacock, 1972), 106.

42. Paul Kagan, *New World Utopias: A Photographic History of the Search for Community* (New York: Penguin Books, 1975), 22.

43. Sutton, *Communal Utopias and the American Experience*, 125.

44. Sutton, 125.

45. Sutton, *Communal Utopias and the American Experience*, 126.

46. Arthur Versluis, *The Secret History of Western Sexual Mysticism: Sacred Practices and Spiritual Marriage* (Rochester, VT: Destiny Books, 2008), 117.

47. Kagan, *New World Utopias*, 30.

48. Fogarty, *American Utopianism*, 108.

49. Arthur Versluis, "Sexual Mysticisms in Nineteenth Century America," in *Hidden Intercourse: Eros and Sexuality in the History of Western Esotericism*, ed. Wouter J. Hanegraaff and Jeffrey J. Kripal (New York: Fordham University Press, 2011), 336.

50. John Egerton, *Visions of Utopia: Nashoba, Rugby, Ruskin, and the "New Communities" in Tennessee's Past* (Knoxville: University of Tennessee Press, 1977), 45.

51. Egerton, 45.

52. Gerald Lee Gutek and Patricia Gutek, *Visiting Utopian Communities: A Guide to the Shakers, Moravians, and Others* (Columbia: University of South Carolina Press, 1998), 198.

53. Egerton, *Visions of Utopia*, 46.

54. Gutek and Gutek, *Visiting Utopian Communities*, 199.

55. Egerton, *Visions of Utopia*, 47.

56. Egerton, 51.

57. Gutek and Gutek, *Visiting Utopian Communities*, 199.

58. Gutek and Gutek, 200–201.

59. Egerton, *Visions of Utopia*, 52.

60. "The Typhoid Fever Cases at Rugby Colony," *British Medical Journal* (October 22, 1881): 677.

61. Gutek and Gutek, *Visiting Utopian Communities*, 201.

62. W. Calvin Dickinson, "Whose Sons Settled Rugby? A Study of the Population at Rugby, Tennessee, in the 1880s," *Tennessee Historical Quarterly* 52, no. 3 (1993): 197.

63. Gutek and Gutek, *Visiting Utopian Communities*, 201.

64. Egerton, *Visions of Utopia*, 59.

65. Eleanor James, "Martha White McWhirter," in *Women in Early Texas*, ed. Evelyn M. Carrington (Austin: Texas State Historical Association, 1994), 182–183.

66. Greta Anderson, *More Than Petticoats: Remarkable Texas Women* (Guilford, CT: Globe Pequot Press, 2013), 21–22.

67. Anderson, *More Than Petticoats*, 22.

68. James, "Martha White McWhirter," 184.

69. Anderson, *More Than Petticoats*, 23.

70. Sally L. Kitch, *This Strange Society of Women: Reading the Letters and Lives of the Women's Commonwealth* (Columbus: Ohio State University Press, 1993), 40–41.

71. Anderson, *More Than Petticoats*, 27.

72. Kitch, *This Strange Society of Women*, 10–12.

73. Kitch, 42.

74. Anderson, *More Than Petticoats*, 26.

75. Kitch, *This Strange Society of Women*, 43.

76. Kitch, 48.

77. Kitch, 75.

78. Kitch, 79.

79. Kitch, 111.

80. Janet Sharp Hermann, "Isaiah T. Montgomery's Balancing Act," in *Black Leaders of the Nineteenth Century*, ed. Leon Litwack and August Meier (Urbana: University of Illinois Press, 1988), 293.

81. Joan E. Cashin, *First Lady of the Confederacy: Varina Davis's Civil War* (Cambridge, MA: Belknap Press, 2006), 47.

82. Joel Nathan Rosen, *From New Lanark to Mound Bayou: Owenism in the Mississippi Delta* (Durham, NC: Carolina Academic Press, 2011), 78.

83. Rosen, 80.

84. Rosen, 85–86.

85. Rosen, 82–83.

86. Rosen, 88.

87. Neil R. McMillen, *Dark Journey: Black Mississippians in the Age of Jim Crow* (Urbana: University of Illinois Press, 1990), 186.

88. Kenneth M. Hamilton, *Black Towns and Profit: Promotion and Development in the Trans-Appalachian West, 1877–1915* (Urbana: University of Illinois Press, 1991), 46.

89. Rosen, *From New Lanark to Mound Bayou*, 102.

90. Ted Ownby and Charles Reagan Wilson, *The Mississippi Encyclopedia* (Jackson: University of Mississippi Press, 2017), 873.

91. Ownby and Wilson, 873.

92. Ownby and Wilson, 873.

93. Rosen, *From New Lanark to Mound Bayou*, 111.

94. Ownby and Wilson, *The Mississippi Encyclopedia*, 873.

95. Hamilton, *Black Towns and Profit*, 51.

96. Hamilton, 52.

97. Hamilton, 54.

98. Hamilton, 56.

99. Booker T. Washington, "A Town Owned by Negros," *World's Work* 14 (July 1907): 9125.

100. David Jackson, *Booker T. Washington and the Struggle against White Supremacy: The Southern Educational Tours, 1908–1912* (New York: Palgrave Macmillan, 2008), 73.

101. Rosen, *From New Lanark to Mound Bayou*, 129.

102. Jackson, *Booker T. Washington and the Struggle against White Supremacy*, 73.

103. Hermann, "Isaiah T. Montgomery's Balancing Act," 303.

104. Hamilton, *Black Towns and Profit*, 80.

105. Rosen, *From New Lanark to Mound Bayou*, 148.

106. Fogarty, *American Utopianism*, 101.

107. Robert H. Hine, "California's Socialist Utopias," in *America's Communal Utopias*, ed. Donald E. Pitzer (Chapel Hill: University of North Carolina Press, 1997), 419.

108. Sutton, *Communal Utopias and the American Experience*, 77.

109. Sutton, 79.

110. Sutton, 79.

111. Sutton, 80.

112. Kagan, *New World Utopias*, 85.

113. Stockwell, *Encyclopedia of American Communes*, 115.

114. Kagan, *New World Utopias*, 89.

115. Sutton, *Communal Utopias and the American Experience*, 80.

116. Sutton, 80.

117. Kagan, *New World Utopias*, 93.

118. Sutton, *Communal Utopias and the American Experience*, 81.

119. Sutton, 90.

120. Stockwell, *Encyclopedia of American Communes*, 181.

121. Sutton, *Communal Utopias and the American Experience*, 90.

122. Sutton, 91.

123. W. Fitzhugh Brundage, *A Socialist Utopia in the New South: The Ruskin Colonies in Tennessee and Georgia, 1894–1901* (Urbana: University of Illinois Press, 1996), 33.

124. Brundage, 32.

125. Brundage, 33.

126. Sutton, *Communal Utopias and the American Experience*, 92.

127. Brundage, *A Socialist Utopia in the New South*, 99.

128. Brundage, 100.

129. Brundage, 100–101.

130. Sutton, *Communal Utopias and the American Experience*, 92–93.

131. Sutton, 93.

132. Brundage, *A Socialist Utopia in the New South*, 123.

133. Egerton, *Visions of Utopia*, 73.

134. Jan Bakker and Francelia Butler, *A Study of the Socialist Commune at Ruskin, Tennessee* (New York: Edwin Mellen Press, 2002), 12.

135. Egerton, *Visions of Utopia*, 64.

136. Brundage, *A Socialist Utopia in the New South*, 114–115.

137. Brundage, 132–133.

138. Egerton, *Visions of Utopia*, 82.

139. Brundage, *A Socialist Utopia in the New South*, 145–146.

140. Brundage, 148–149.

141. Brundage, 159.

142. Brundage, 165.

3. THEOSOPHY, DEPRESSION, AND THE NEW DEAL

1. Ruth Levitas, *Utopia as Method: The Imaginary Reconstitution of Society* (New York: Palgrave Macmillan, 2013), 117.

2. Robert P. Sutton, *Communal Utopias and the American Experience: Religious Communities, 1732–2000* (Westport, CT: Praeger, 2003), 129.

3. W. Michael Ashcraft, *Dawn of the New Cycle: Point Loma Theosophists and American Culture* (Knoxville: University of Tennessee Press, 2002), 24.

4. J. Gordon Melton, "The Theosophical Communities and Their Ideal of Brotherhood," in *America's Communal Utopias*, ed. Donald E. Pitzer (Chapel Hill: University of North Carolina Press, 1997), 400.

5. Sutton, *Communal Utopias and the American Experience: Religious Communities*, 129.

6. Sutton, 130–131.

7. Emmett A. Greenwalt, *California Utopia: Point Loma, 1897 to 1942* (San Diego: Point Loma Publications, 1978), 24.

8. Greenwalt, 36.

9. Ashcraft, *Dawn of the New Cycle*, 56.

10. Greenwalt, *California Utopia*, 48–49.

11. Robert V. Hine, *California's Utopian Colonies* (San Marino, CA: Huntington Library, 1953), 45–46.

12. Ashcraft, *Dawn of the New Cycle*, 95.

13. Ashcraft, 101.

14. Melton, "The Theosophical Communities and Their Ideal of Brotherhood," 405.

15. Jyotsna Sreenivasan, *Utopias in American History* (Santa Barbara, CA: ABC-CLIO, 2008), 313.

16. Greenwalt, *California Utopia*, 183.

17. Hine, *California's Utopian Colonies*, 53.

18. Hine, 52.

19. Greenwalt, *California Utopia*, 204.

20. Hine, *California's Utopian Colonies*, 54.

21. Historical Landmarks Designated by the San Diego Historical Resources Board, https://www.sandiego.gov/sites/default/files/legacy/planning/programs/historical/pdf/2013/register130124.pdf.

22. Ashcraft, *Dawn of the New Cycle*, 180.

23. Hine, *California's Utopian Colonies*, 115.

24. Hine, 117.

25. Hine, 116.

26. Robert P. Sutton, *Communal Utopias and the American Experience: Secular Communities, 1824–2000* (Westport, CT: Praeger, 2004), 105.

27. Robert S. Fogarty, *American Utopianism* (Itasca, IL: Peacock, 1972), 130.

28. Sutton, *Communal Utopias and the American Experience: Secular Communities*, 105.

29. Foster Stockwell, *Encyclopedia of American Communes, 1663–1963* (Jefferson, NC: McFarland, 1998), 126.

30. Hine, *California's Utopian Colonies*, 118.

31. Paul Kagan, *New World Utopias: A Photographic History of the Search for Community* (New York: Penguin Books, 1975), 119.

32. Stockwell, *Encyclopedia of American Communes*, 126.

33. Hine, *California's Utopian Colonies*, 126.

34. Sreenivasan, *Utopias in American History*, 248.

35. Hine, *California's Utopian Colonies*, 120.

36. Hine, 122.

37. Kagan, *New World Utopias*, 123.

38. Kagan, 123.

39. Kagan, 123.

40. Sutton, *Communal Utopias and the American Experience: Secular Communities*, 106.

41. Hine, *California's Utopian Colonies*, 128.

42. Errol Wayne Stevens, *Radical L.A.: From Coxey's Army to the Watts Riots, 1894–1965* (Norman: University of Oklahoma Press, 2009), 108.

43. Stockwell, *Encyclopedia of American Communes*, 155.

44. Stevens, *Radical L.A.*, 109.

45. William H. Cobb, *Radical Education in the Rural South: Commonwealth College, 1922–1940* (Detroit: Wayne State University Press, 2000), 32.

46. Stockwell, *Encyclopedia of American Communes*, 156.

47. Hine, *California's Utopian Colonies*, 130.

48. Stockwell, *Encyclopedia of American Communes*, 156.

49. Stockwell, 111.

50. Robert F. Himmelberg, *The Great Depression and the New Deal* (Westport, CT: Greenwood, 2001), xvii.

51. Himmelberg, 5–6.

52. T. H. Watkins, *The Great Depression: America in the 1930s* (Boston: Little, Brown, 1993), 51.

53. Watkins, 55.

54. Watkins, 56–57.

55. Watkins, 60.

56. Watkins, 71.

57. Phillip G. Payne, *Crash!: How the Economic Boom and Bust of the 1920s Worked* (Baltimore, MD: Johns Hopkins University Press, 2015), 91.

58. Watkins, *The Great Depression*, 82.

59. George L. Hicks, *Experimental Americans: Celo and Utopian Community in the Twentieth Century* (Urbana: University of Illinois Press, 2001), 42.

60. Hicks, 43.

61. Payne, *Crash!*, 93–94.

62. Phoebe Cutler, *The Public Landscape of the New Deal* (New Haven, CT: Yale University Press, 1985), 116.

63. Hicks, *Experimental Americans*, 43.

64. Himmelberg, *The Great Depression*, 12–13.

65. Himmelberg, 14.

66. Himmelberg, 15.

67. Himmelberg, 19.

68. Watkins, *The Great Depression*, 141.

69. Timothy Miller, *The Quest for Utopia in Twentieth-Century America* (Syracuse, NY: Syracuse University Press, 1998), 133.

70. Miller, *The Quest for Utopia in Twentieth-Century America*, 134.

71. Miller, 129.

72. Steven Conn, *Americans against the City: Anti-urbanism in the Twentieth Century* (Oxford: Oxford University Press, 2014), 79.

73. Conn, 81.

74. Conn, 83

75. Conn, 83.

76. Miller, *The Quest for Utopia in Twentieth-Century America*, 131.

77. Sam F. Stack, *The Arthurdale Community School: Education and Reform in Depression Era Appalachia* (Lexington: University Press of Kentucky, 2016), 34.

78. Amanda Griffith Penix, *Images of America: Arthurdale* (Charlestown, SC: Arcadia, 2007), 9.

79. Stack, *The Arthurdale Community School*, 35.

80. Penix, *Images of America*, 9.

81. Penix, 16–17.

82. Stack, *The Arthurdale Community School*, 36.

83. Penix, *Images of America*, 26.

84. Penix, 32.

85. Stack, *The Arthurdale Community School*, 36.

86. Stack, 37.

87. Stack, 38.

88. C. J. Maloney, *Back to the Land: Arthurdale, FDR's New Deal, and the Costs of Economic Planning* (Hoboken, NJ: Wiley, 2011), 102.

89. Penix, *Images of America*, 39.

90. Penix, 41.

91. Penix, 46.

92. Penix, 47.

93. Penix, 59.

94. Stack, *The Arthurdale Community School*, 42.

95. Stack, 47.

96. Maloney, *Back to the Land*, 161–162.

97. Maloney, 165.

98. Robert M. Carriker, *Urban Farming in the West: A New Deal Experiment in Subsistence Homesteads* (Tucson: University of Arizona Press, 2010), 159.

99. Carriker, 159.

100. Carriker, 55.

101. Carriker, 60.

102. Carriker, 57.

103. Carriker, 64.

104. Carriker, 70.

105. Carriker, 72.

106. Ronald L. Heinemann, *Depression and New Deal in Virginia: The Enduring Dominion* (Charlottesville: University of Virginia Press, 1983), 123.

107. Paul Carter, Arthur Rothstein, and John Vachon, "'Working on Equality Base' II: Aberdeen Gardens Homesteads Project Photographs," in *Talk about Trouble: A New Deal Portrait of Virginians in the Great Depression*, ed. Nancy J. Martin-Perdue and Charles L. Perdue (Chapel Hill: University of North Carolina Press, 1996), 190.

108. Carter, Rothstein, and Vachon, 190.

109. Colita Nichols Fairfax, *Hampton, Virginia* (Charleston, SC: Arcadia, 2005), 68.

110. Aberdeen Gardens Heritage Committee, *Images of America: Aberdeen Gardens* (Charleston, SC: Arcadia, 2007) 7.

111. Arnold R. Alanen and Joseph A. Eden, *Main Street Ready-Made: The New Deal Community of Greendale, Wisconsin* (Madison: Wisconsin Historical Society Press, 2012), 7.

112. Miller, *The Quest for Utopia in Twentieth-Century America*, 135.

113. Mark Hutter, *Experiencing Cities* (New York: Routledge, 2016), 124.

114. Lisa Benton-Short, *Cities of North America: Contemporary Challenges in U.S. and Canadian Cities* (Lanham, MD: Rowman & Littlefield, 2014), 197.

115. Alanen and Eden, *Main Street Ready-Made*, 18.

116. Alanen and Eden, 40.

117. Alanen and Eden, 45.

118. Alanen and Eden, 61.

119. Alanen and Eden, 84–85.

120. Alanen and Eden, 55.

121. Stack, *The Arthurdale Community School*, 127.

122. Miller, *The Quest for Utopia in Twentieth-Century America*, 136.

123. Hicks, *Experimental Americans*, 226.

124. Hicks, 56.

125. Hicks, 59.

126. Hicks, 67.

127. Hicks, 73.

128. Hicks, 86.

129. Hicks, 93.

130. Hicks, 96.

131. Sutton, *Communal Utopias and the American Experience: Religious Communities*, 155.

132. Sutton, 151–152.

133. Sutton, 152.

134. Miller, *The Quest for Utopia in Twentieth-Century America*, 144.

135. Elaine Murray Stone, *Dorothy Day: Champion of the Poor* (New York: Paulist Press, 2004), 101.

136. Sutton, *Communal Utopias and the American Experience: Secular Communities*, 122.

137. Sutton, 122.

138. Stockwell, *Encyclopedia of American Communes*, 200.

139. Sutton, *Communal Utopias and the American Experience: Secular Communities*, 123.

140. Sutton, 124.

141. Sutton, 126.

4. HIPPIES, ARCOLOGY, AND ECOVILLAGES

1. "40,000 at Service for G. F. Johnson: Shoe Manufacturer's Funeral Conducted on Football Field—Schools, Stores Close," *New York Times*, December 2, 1948, 29.

2. Cornelia J. Strawser, *Business Statistics of the United States 2012: Patterns of Economic Change* (Lanham, MD: Burnan Press, 2013), xxvi.

3. "George F. Johnson Works at 85," *New York Times*, October 15, 1942, 32.

4. William Inglis, *George F. Johnson and His Industrial Democracy* (Endicott, NY: Endicott–Johnson Corporation, 1948), 13.

5. Inglis, 25.

6. Inglis, 25.

7. Inglis, 40.

8. Inglis, 46.

9. Inglis, 50.

10. Inglis, 98.

11. *70 years of Mutual Respect and Confidence* (Endicott, NY: Endicott–Johnson Corporation, 1948), 10.

12. *70 years of Mutual Respect and Confidence*, 16.

13. William H. Young and Nancy K. Young, *The 1950s* (Westport, CT: Greenwood Press, 2004), 21.

14. Timothy Miller, *The 60s Communes: Hippies and Beyond* (Syracuse, NY: Syracuse University Press, 1999), 3.

15. Robert C. Cottrell, *Sex, Drugs, and Rock 'n' Roll: The Rise of America's 1960s Counterculture* (Lanham, MD: Rowman & Littlefield, 2015), 8.

16. Cottrell, 9.

17. Cottrell, 9–10.

18. Miller, *The 60s Communes*, 6.

19. Caroline Maniaque-Benton, *French Encounters with the American Counterculture 1960–1980* (Burlington, VT: Ashgate, 2011), 5.

20. Maniaque-Benton, 18.

21. Cottrell, *Sex, Drugs, and Rock 'n' Roll*, 73.

22. James Penner, *Timothy Leary: The Harvard Years: Early Writings on LSD and Psilocybin with Richard Alpert, Huston Smith, Ralph Metzner, and Others* (Rochester, VT: Park Street Press, 2014), 1.

23. Cottrell, *Sex, Drugs, and Rock 'n' Roll*, 90–91.

24. Cottrell, 93.

25. Mark Matthews, *Droppers: America's First Hippie Commune, Drop City* (Norman: University of Oklahoma Press, 2010), 155.

26. Miller, *The 60s Communes*, 32.

27. Miller, 32.

28. Maniaque-Benton, *French Encounters with the American Counterculture*, 31.

29. Erin Elder, "How to Build a Commune: Drop City's Influence on the Southwestern Commune Movement," in *West of Center: Art and the Counterculture Experiment in*

America, 1965–1977, ed. Elissa Auther and Adam Lerner (Minneapolis: University of Minnesota Press, 2012), 11.

30. Elder, 17.

31. Miller, *The 60s Communes*, 35.

32. Matthews, *Droppers*, 135.

33. Matthews, 137–138.

34. Matthews, 177.

35. Matthews, 178.

36. Miller, *The 60s Communes*, xiii.

37. Miller, 81.

38. Miller, 82.

39. Amy Azzarito, "Libre, Colorado, and the Hand-Built Home," in *West of Center: Art and the Counterculture Experiment in America, 1965–1977*, ed. Elissa Auther and Adam Lerner (Minneapolis: University of Minnesota Press, 2012), 96.

40. Azzarito, 96.

41. Azzarito, 97.

42. Azzarito, 101.

43. Timothy Miller, foreword to *Leaving New Buffalo Commune*, by Arthur Kopecky (Albuquerque: University of New Mexico Press, 2006), xiv.

44. Cal Winslow, "The Albion Nation: Communes on the Mendocino Coast," *Brooklyn Rail: Critical Perspectives on Arts, Politics, and Culture*, April 2, 2012, http://brooklynrail .org/2012/04/express/the-albion-nation-communes-on-the-mendocino-coast.

45. Gilbert Zicklin, *Countercultural Communes: A Sociological Perspective*, Contributions in Political Science, 44 (Westport, CT: Greenwood Press, 1983), 35, 168.

46. William Grimes, "Lou Gottlieb, 72, the Bass Player for 1960's Folk Trio Limeliters," *New York Times*, July 14, 1996.

47. Cottrell, *Sex, Drugs, and Rock 'n' Roll*, 245.

48. Cottrell, 245.

49. Cottrell, 246.

50. Unohoo, Coyote, Rick and the Mighty Avengers, *Morning Star Scrapbook* (Occidental, CA: Morning Star Ranch Tribe, 1973), 7.

51. Unohoo, Coyote, Rick and the Mighty Avengers, 16–17.

52. Unohoo, Coyote, Rick and the Mighty Avengers, 19.

53. Miller, *The 60s Communes*, 48.

54. Unohoo, Coyote, Rick and the Mighty Avengers, *Morning Star Scrapbook*, 184.

55. Miller, *The 60s Communes*, 53.

56. Cottrell, *Sex, Drugs, and Rock 'n' Roll*, 246.

57. Miller, *The 60s Communes*, 56.

58. Peter Fimrite, "Donald McCoy—Marin Developer, '60s Dropout," San Francisco Gate, October 24, 2004, http://www.sfgate.com/bayarea/article/Donald-McCoy-Marin -developer-60s-dropout-2679193.php.

59. Miller, *The 60s Communes*, 71.

60. Dennis McNally, *A Long Strange Trip: The Inside History of the Grateful Dead* (New York: Broadway Books, 2002), 262.

61. Miller, *The 60s Communes*, 72.

62. McNally, *A Long Strange Trip*, 147.

63. Bill Kreutzmann and Benjy Eisen, *Deal: My Three Decades of Drumming, Dreams, and Drugs with the Grateful Dead* (New York: St. Martin's, 2015), 53–54.

64. Nadya Zimmerman, "Performance of an Anti-Commercial Culture," in *Rock Music*, ed. Mark Spicer (London: Routledge, 2011), 81.

65. Miller, *The 60s Communes*, 68.

66. "Seva's Mission," Seva Foundation website, http://www.seva.org.

67. Steve Chawkins, "Stephen Gaskin Dies at 79; Founder of the Farm Commune," *Los Angeles Times*, July 5, 2014, http://www.latimes.com/local/obituaries/la-me-stephen -gaskin-20140706-story.html.

68. Sutton, *Communal Utopias and the American Experience: Secular Communities*, 145.

69. Sutton, 146.

70. Douglas Stevenson, *The Farm Then and Now: A Model for Sustainable Living* (British Columbia: New Society Publishers, 2014), viii.

71. Stevenson, 8–9.

72. Sutton, *Communal Utopias and the American Experience: Secular Communities*, 144.

73. Miller, *The 60s Communes*, 120.

74. Stevenson, *The Farm Then and Now*, 59.

75. Morgan Shipley, *Psychedelic Mysticism: Transforming Consciousness, Religious Experiences, and Voluntary Peasants in Postwar America* (Lanham, MD: Lexington Books, 2015), 230.

76. Steve Chawkins, "Stephen Gaskin Dies at 79."

77. Ina May Gaskin, *Spiritual Midwifery* (Summertown, TN: Book Publishing Company, 2002), 16.

78. Gaskin, 12.

79. Gaskin, 30.

80. Miller, *The 60s Communes*, 121.

81. Miller, 120–121.

82. Stevenson, *The Farm Then and Now*, 64.

83. Miller, *The 60s Communes*, 122.

84. Steve Chawkins, "Stephen Gaskin Dies at 79."

85. Miller, *The 60s Communes*, 124.

86. Shipley, *Psychedelic Mysticism*, 204.

87. Miller, *The 60s Communes*, 138–139.

88. Virginia Historical Society, "A Guide to the Stephen Micheal Lenton Papers, 1941– 2002," http://www.vahistorical.org/collections-and-resources/how-we-can-help-your -research/researcher-resources/finding-aids/lenton.

89. Beth Marschak and Alex Lorch, *Lesbian and Gay Richmond*, (Charleston, SC: Arcadia, 2008), 45.

90. Karin Kapsidelis, "VCU to commemorate Ruling on Gay Rights from Era Before Inclusion," *Richmond Times-Dispatch*, September 25, 2016, http://www.richmond.com /news/vcu-to-commemorate-ruling-on-gay-rights-from-era-before/article_a862951a -e515-5730-9237-9494dcc68483.html.

91. Marschak and Lorch, *Lesbian and Gay Richmond*, 39.

92. Stephen Lenton, "Mulberry Family Scrapbook: An Intentional Community Presented as an Experiment in Creative Recordation" (PhD diss., Union Graduate School, 1976), 11.

93. Lenton, iii.

94. Lenton, 15.

95. Lenton, 25–26.

96. Lenton, 35.

97. Lenton, 201–202.

98. Lenton, 202.

99. Lenton, 210.

100. Lenton, 274.

101. Lenton, 256.

102. "1974: GAP, GAS and the First Women's Festival," Outhistory.org, http://outhistory .org/exhibits/show/rainbow-richmond/the-beginnings-of-pride/1974.

103. Marschak and Lorch, *Lesbian and Gay Richmond*, 46.

104. Virginia Historical Society, "A Guide to the Stephen Micheal Lenton Papers, 1941–2002."

105. Ron Anastasia, introduction to *What If? Collected Writings, 1986–2000*, by Paolo Soleri (Berkeley, CA: Berkeley Hills Books, 2003), xi.

106. Michael Gotkin and Don Freeman, *Artists' Handmade Houses* (NY: Abrams, 2011), 27.

107. Gotkin and Freeman, 28.

108. Gotkin and Freeman, 28.

109. Marie Wilson and Michel Sarda, *Arcosanti Archetype: The Rebirth of Cities by Renaissance Thinker Paolo Soleri* (Fountain Hills, AZ: Freedom Editions, 1999), 8.

110. Wilson and Sarda, 8.

111. Wilson and Sarda, 14.

112. Paolo Soleri and Scott M. Davis, *Paolo Soleri's Earth Casting for Sculpture, Models and Construction* (Salt Lake City, UT: Peregrine Smith, 1984), 106.

113. Paolo Soleri, *What If? Collected Writings, 1986–2000* (Berkeley, CA: Berkeley Hills Books, 2003), 28–29.

114. Soleri, 43.

115. Soleri, 110.

116. Paolo Soleri et al., *Lean Linear City: Arterial Arcology* (Mayer, AZ: Cosanti Press, 2012), 56.

117. Joseph C. Manzella, *Common Purse, Uncommon Future: The Long, Strange Trip of Communes and Other Intentional Communities* (Santa Barbara, CA: Praeger, 2010), 110.

118. Soleri, *What If?*, 100.

119. Soleri et al., *Lean Linear City*, 131.

120. Soleri et al., 118.

121. Soleri et al., 118.

122. Malcolm Miles, *Urban Utopias: The Built and Social Architectures of Alternative Settlements* (London: Routledge, 2007), 120.

123. Kathryn M. McCamant and Charles R. Durrett, *Cohousing: A Contemporary Approach to Housing Ourselves* (Berkeley, CA: Ten Speed Press, 1998), 37.

124. McCamant and Durrett, 38.

125. Michael La Fond, *CoHousing Cultures: Handbook for Self-Organized, Community-Oriented and Sustainable Housing* (Berlin: Jovis, 2013), 27.

126. Sreenivasan, *Utopias in American History*, 91.

127. Sreenivasan, 90.

128. McCamant and Durrett, *Cohousing*, 136.

129. McCamant and Durrett, 139.

130. Sreenivasan, *Utopias in American History*, 91.

131. McCamant and Durrett, *Cohousing*, 212.

132. McCamant and Durrett, 215.

133. Liz Walker, *EcoVillage at Ithaca: Pioneering a Sustainable Culture* (Gabriola Island, BC: New Society, 2005), 10–11.

134. Walker, 17.

135. Corry C. Buckwalter, "The Contribution of Consensus-Building to Participatory Design: A Case Study of Ecovillage at Ithaca" (master's thesis, Cornell University, 1994), 55.

136. "Neighborhoods," EcoVillage Ithaca website, http://ecovillageithaca.org/live /neighborhoods/.

137. Miles, *Urban Utopias*, 215.

138. "Neighborhoods," EcoVillage Ithaca website.

139. "Neighborhoods," EcoVillage Ithaca website.

140. Walker, *EcoVillage at Ithaca*, 79.

141. Walker, 167.

142. Walker, 128, 192.

143. Walker, 211.

AFTERWORD

1. Mark S. Ferrara, *New Seeds of Profit: Business Heroes, Corporate Villains, and the Future of American Capitalism* (Lanham, MD: Lexington Books, 2019), 91.

2. John Nichols, *The S Word: A Short History of an American Tradition . . . Socialism* (London: Verso, 2015), 4.

3. W. J. Conroy, *Bernie Sanders and the Boundaries of Reform: Socialism in Burlington* (Philadelphia: Temple University Press, 2017), ix.

4. Gary Dorrien, "Michael Harrington and the 'Left Wing of the Possible,'" *Cross Currents* 60, no. 2 (2010): 278.

5. Bernie Sanders, "Agenda for America: 12 Steps Forward," https://www.sanders.senate .gov/agenda/.

6. Jessie Wallace Hughan, *American Socialism of the Present Day* (New York: John Lane Company, 1911), 17.

7. Bernard R. Crick, *Socialism* (Minneapolis: University of Minnesota Press, 1988), 5.

8. Frances Goldin, Debby Smith, and Michael Smith, *Imagine Living in a Socialist USA* (New York: Harper Perennial, 2014), xi.

9. Frances Fox Piven, "Welfare in a New Society: An End to Intentional Impoverishment and Degradation," in *Imagine Living in a Socialist USA*, ed. Frances Goldin, Debby Smith, and Michael Smith (New York: Harper Perennial, 2014), 125.

10. Steve Inskeep and Jon Meacham, "What's It Like to Be a Historian at This Political Time? 'Every Day Is Christmas,'" *NPR Morning Edition*, July 4, 2017, http://www.npr.org /2017/07/04/535470981/whats-it-like-to-be-a-historian-at-this-political-time-every -day-is-christmas.

11. Inskeep and Meacham, July 4, 2017.

12. Donald Drew Egbert and Stow Persons, *Socialism and American Life, Volume II* (Princeton: Princeton University Press, 2016), 63.

13. Joseph C. Manzella, *Common Purse, Uncommon Future: The Long, Strange Trip of Communes and Other Intentional Communities* (Santa Barbara, CA: Praeger, 2010), 173.

14. Mark Holloway, *Heavens on Earth: Utopian Communities in America, 1680–1880* (Mineola, NY: Dover, 2011), 223.

15. Chris Jennings, *Paradise Now: The Story of American Utopianism* (New York: Random House, 2016), 381.

16. John Nichols, *The S Word: A Short History of an American Tradition . . . Socialism* (London: Verso, 2015), 3.

17. Nichols, 4.

18. Timothy Miller, *The 60s Communes: Hippies and Beyond* (Syracuse, NY: Syracuse University Press, 1999), 238–239.

19. Michael Steven Smith, "Law in a Socialist USA," in *Imagine Living in a Socialist USA*, ed. Frances Goldin, Debby Smith, and Michael Smith (New York: Harper Perennial, 2014), 53.

20. Paul Le Blanc, "The Third American Revolution: How Socialism Can Come to the United States," in *Imagine Living in a Socialist USA*, ed. Frances Goldin, Debby Smith, and Michael Smith (New York: Harper Perennial, 2014), 256.

21. William Blake, "The Divine Image," in *The Complete Poetry and Prose of William Blake*, ed. David Erdman (Princeton: Princeton UP, 1988), 12.

BIBLIOGRAPHY

Alanen, Arnold R., and Joseph A. Eden. *Main Street Ready-Made: The New Deal Community of Greendale, Wisconsin*. Madison: Wisconsin Historical Society Press, 2012.

Alderfer, E. G. *The Ephrata Commune: An Early American Counterculture*. Pittsburgh: University of Pittsburgh Press, 1985.

Anastasia, Ron. Introduction to *What If? Collected Writings, 1986–2000*, by Paolo Soleri, xi–xxvii. Berkeley, CA: Berkeley Hills Books, 2003.

Anderson, Greta. *More Than Petticoats: Remarkable Texas Women*. Guilford, CT: Globe Pequot Press, 2013.

Ashcraft, Michael. *Dawn of the New Cycle: Point Loma Theosophists and American Culture*. Knoxville: University of Tennessee Press, 2002.

Azzarito, Amy. "Libre, Colorado, and the Hand-Built Home." In *West of Center: Art and the Counterculture Experiment in America, 1965–1977*, edited by Elissa Auther and Adam Lerner, 95–110. Minneapolis: University of Minnesota Press, 2012.

Bach, Jeff. *Voices of the Turtledoves: The Sacred World of Ephrata*. University Park: Pennsylvania State University Press, 2003.

Bailie, William. *Josiah Warren: The First American Anarchist*. Cambridge, MA: Small, Maynard, 1906.

Bakker, Jan, and Francelia Butler. *A Study of the Socialist Commune at Ruskin, Tennessee*. New York: Edwin Mellen Press, 2002.

Ballou, Adin. *Autobiography of Adin Ballou, 1803–1890*. Lowell, MA: Vox Populi Press, 1896.

———. *History of the Hopedale Community: From Its Inception to Its Virtual Submergence in the Hopedale Parish*. Lowell, MA: Vox Populi Press, 1897.

Barkun, Michael. *Crucible of the Millennium: The Burned-Over District of New York in the 1840s*. Syracuse: Syracuse University Press, 1986.

Bates, Beth Tompkins. *Pullman Porters and the Rise of Protest Politics in Black America, 1925–1945*. Chapel Hill: University of North Carolina Press, 2001.

Beberdick, Frank. *Chicago's Historic Pullman District*. Charleston, SC: Arcadia, 1998.

Bellamy, Edward. *Looking Backward: 2000–1887*. Boston: Ticknor, 1888.

Benton-Short, Lisa. *Cities of North America: Contemporary Challenges in U.S. and Canadian Cities*. Lanham, MD: Rowman & Littlefield, 2014.

Bestor, Arthur. *Backwoods Utopias: The Sectarian Origins and the Owenite Phase of Communitarian Socialism in America*. Eugene, OR: Wipf & Stock, 2012.

Blake, William. "The Divine Image." In *The Complete Poetry and Prose of William Blake*, edited by David Erdman, 12–13. Princeton: Princeton University Press, 1988.

Bradford, William. *Of Plymouth Plantation*. Edited by Caleb Johnson. Bloomington, IN: Xlibris, 2006.

Bradley, John. *Ephrata Cloister: Pennsylvania Trail of History Guide*. Mechanicsburg: Pennsylvania Historical and Museum Commission, 2000.

Bronner, Simon J., and Joshua R. Brown. *Pennsylvania Germans: An Interpretive Encyclopedia*. Baltimore, MD: Johns Hopkins University Press, 2017.

Brown, Archie. *The Rise and Fall of Communism*. New York: HarperCollins, 2009.

Brown, Susan Love. *Intentional Community: An Anthropological Perspective*. Albany: SUNY Press, 2001.

Brundage, W. Fitzhugh. *A Socialist Utopia in the New South: The Ruskin Colonies in Tennessee and Georgia, 1894–1901*. Urbana: University of Illinois Press, 1996.

Buckwalter, Corry C. "The Contribution of Consensus-Building to Participatory Design: A Case Study of Ecovillage at Ithaca." Master's thesis, Cornell University, 1994.

Calverton, Victor Francis. *Where Angels Dared to Tread: Socialist & Communist Utopian Colonies in the United States*. Indianapolis: Bobbs Merrill, 1941.

Carriker, Robert M. *Urban Farming in the West: A New Deal Experiment in Subsistence Homesteads*. Tucson: University of Arizona Press, 2010.

Carter, Paul, Arthur Rothstein, and John Vachon. "'Working on Equality Base' II: Aberdeen Gardens Homesteads Project Photographs." In *Talk about Trouble: A New Deal Portrait of Virginians in the Great Depression*, edited by Nancy J. Martin-Perdue and Charles L. Perdue, 190–195. Chapel Hill: University of North Carolina Press, 1996.

Cashin, Joan E. *First Lady of the Confederacy: Varina Davis's Civil War*. Cambridge, MA: Belknap Press, 2006.

Cobb, William H. *Radical Education in the Rural South: Commonwealth College, 1922–1940*. Detroit: Wayne State University Press, 2000.

Cole, Margaret. *Robert Owen of New Lanark: 1771–1858*. New York: Augustus M. Kelley, 1969.

Conn, Steven. *Americans against the City: Anti-urbanism in the Twentieth Century*. Oxford: Oxford University Press, 2014.

Conroy, W. J. *Bernie Sanders and the Boundaries of Reform: Socialism in Burlington*. Philadelphia: Temple University Press, 2017.

Cottrell, Robert C. *Sex, Drugs, and Rock 'n' Roll: The Rise of America's 1960s Counterculture*. Lanham, MD: Rowman & Littlefield, 2015.

Crick, Bernard R. *Socialism*. Minneapolis: University of Minnesota Press, 1988.

Cutler, Phoebe. *The Public Landscape of the New Deal*. New Haven, CT: Yale University Press, 1985.

Danckaerts, Jasper, and Peter Sluyter. *Journal of a Voyage to New York: And a Tour in Several of the American Colonies in 1679–80, Volume 1*. Brooklyn, NY: The Society, 1867.

Dickinson, W. Calvin. "Whose Sons Settled Rugby? A Study of the Population at Rugby, Tennessee, in the 1880s." *Tennessee Historical Quarterly* 52, no. 3 (1993): 192–198.

Dorrien, Gary. "Michael Harrington and the 'Left Wing of the Possible.'" *Cross Currents* 60, no. 2 (2010): 257–282.

Durnbaugh, Donald F. "Communitarian Societies in Colonial America." In *America's Communal Utopias*, edited by Donald E. Pitzer, 14–36. Chapel Hill: University of North Carolina Press, 1997.

Egbert, Donald Drew, and Stow Persons. *Socialism and American Life, Volume II*. Princeton, NJ: Princeton University Press, 2016.

Egerton, John. *Visions of Utopia: Nashoba, Rugby, Ruskin, and the "New Communities" in Tennessee's Past*. Knoxville: University of Tennessee Press, 1977.

Elder, Erin. "How to Build a Commune: Drop City's Influence on the Southwestern Commune Movement." In *West of Center: Art and the Counterculture Experiment in America, 1965–1977*, edited by Elissa Auther and Adam Lerner, 3–21. Minneapolis: University of Minnesota Press, 2012.

Fairfax, Colita Nichols. *Hampton, Virginia*. Charleston, SC: Arcadia, 2005.

Fellman, Michael. *The Unbounded Frame: Freedom and Community in Nineteenth Century American Utopianism*. Westport, CT: Greenwood Press, 1973.

Fernandez, Kathleen M. *A Singular People: Images of Zoar*. Kent, OH: Kent State University Press, 2003.

Ferrara, Mark S. *New Seeds of Profit: Business Heroes, Corporate Villains, and the Future of American Capitalism*. Lanham, MD: Lexington Books, 2019.

Fogarty, Robert S. *American Utopianism*. Itasca, IL: Peacock, 1972.

Fredericks, Anthony D. *Historical Trails of Eastern Pennsylvania*. Woodstock, VT: Countryman Press, 2013.

Friesen, John W., and Virginia Agnes Lyons Friesen. *The Palgrave Companion to North American Utopias*. New York: Palgrave Macmillan, 2004.

Gaskin, Ina May. *Spiritual Midwifery*. Summertown, TN: Book Publishing Company, 2002.

Gauthier, Paul S. *Quest for Utopia: The Icarians of Adams County: With Colonies in Denton County, Texas, Nauvoo, Illinois, Cheltenham, Missouri, and Cloverdale, California*. Corning, IA: Gauthier Publishing, 1992.

Gilmore, Eugene Allen, Helen Laura Sumner, and John Bertram Andrews. *A Documentary History of American Industrial Society: Labor movement, 1820–1840*. Cleveland, OH: Arthur H. Clark, 1910.

Goldin, Frances, Debby Smith, and Michael Smith. *Imagine Living in a Socialist USA*. New York: Harper Perennial, 2014.

Gotkin, Michael, and Don Freeman. *Artists' Handmade Houses*. New York: Abrams, 2011.

Green, Ernest J. "The Labadists of Colonial Maryland, 1683–1722." *Communal Societies* 8 (1988): 104–121.

Greenwalt, Emmett A. *California Utopia: Point Loma, 1897 to 1942*. San Diego: Point Loma Publications, 1978.

Gura, Philip F. *Man's Better Angels: Romantic Reformers and the Coming of the Civil War*. Cambridge, MA: Belknap Press, 2017.

Gutek, Gerald Lee, and Patricia Gutek. *Visiting Utopian Communities: A Guide to the Shakers, Moravians, and Others*. Columbia: University of South Carolina Press, 1998.

Hall, Bowman N. "The Economic Ideas of Josiah Warren, First American Anarchist." *History of Political Economy* 6, no. 1 (1974): 95–108.

Hamilton, Kenneth M. *Black Towns and Profit: Promotion and Development in the Trans-Appalachian West, 1877–1915*. Urbana: University of Illinois Press, 1991.

Harris, Thomas Lake. *Brotherhood of the New Life: Its Fact, Law, Method and Purpose*. Santa Rosa, CA: Fountain Grove Press, 1891.

Heinemann, Ronald L. *Depression and New Deal in Virginia: The Enduring Dominion*. Charlottesville: University of Virginia Press, 1983.

Hermann, Janet Sharp. "Isaiah T. Montgomery's Balancing Act." In *Black Leaders of the Nineteenth Century*, edited by Leon Litwack and August Meier, 291–306. Urbana: University of Illinois Press, 1988.

Hicks, George L. *Experimental Americans: Celo and Utopian Community in the Twentieth Century*. Urbana: University of Illinois Press, 2001.

Himmelberg, Robert F. *The Great Depression and the New Deal*. Westport, CT: Greenwood, 2001.

Hinds, William Alfred. *American Communities and Co-operative Colonies*. Chicago: Charles Kerr, 1908.

———. *American Communities: Brief Sketches of Economy, Zoar, Bethel, Aurora, Amana, Icaria, the Shakers, Oneida, Wallingford, and the Brotherhood of the New Life*. Oneida, NY: Office of the American Socialist, 1878.

Hine, Robert V. "California's Socialist Utopias." In *America's Communal Utopias*, edited by Donald E. Pitzer, 419–431. Chapel Hill: University of North Carolina Press, 1997.

———. *California's Utopian Colonies*. San Marino, CA: Huntington Library, 1953.

Hirsch, Susan Eleanor. *After the Strike: A Century of Labor Struggle at Pullman*. Urbana: University of Illinois Press, 2003.

Holloway, Mark. *Heavens on Earth: Utopian Communities in America, 1680–1880*. Mineola, NY: Dover, 2011.

Hughan, Jessie Wallace. *American Socialism of the Present Day*. New York: John Lane, 1911.

Hutter, Mark. *Experiencing Cities*. New York: Routledge, 2016.

Inglis, William. *George F. Johnson and His Industrial Democracy*. Endicott, NY: Endicott–Johnson, 1948.

Jackson, David. *Booker T. Washington and the Struggle against White Supremacy: The Southern Educational Tours, 1908–1912*. New York: Palgrave Macmillan, 2008.

James, Eleanor. "Martha White McWhirter." In *Women in Early Texas*, edited by Evelyn M. Carrington, 180–190. Austin: Texas State Historical Association, 1994.

Jennings, Chris. *Paradise Now: The Story of American Utopianism*. New York: Random House, 2016.

Kagan, Paul. *New World Utopias: A Photographic History of the Search for Community*. New York: Penguin Books, 1975.

Kitch, Sally L. *This Strange Society of Women: Reading the Letters and Lives of the Women's Commonwealth*. Columbus: Ohio State University Press, 1993.

Kolmerten, Carol A. *Women in Utopia: The Ideology of Gender in the American Owenite Communities*. Syracuse, NY: Syracuse University Press, 1998.

Kreutzmann, Bill, and Benjy Eisen. *Deal: My Three Decades of Drumming, Dreams, and Drugs with the Grateful Dead*. New York: St. Martin's, 2015.

La Fond, Michael. *CoHousing Cultures: Handbook for Self-Organized, Community-Oriented and Sustainable Housing*. Berlin, Germany: Jovis, 2013.

Laidler, Harry W. *History of Socialism: An Historical Comparative Study of Socialism*. New York: Routledge, 2000.

Le Blanc, Paul. "The Third American Revolution: How Socialism Can Come to the United States." In *Imagine Living in a Socialist USA*, edited by Frances Goldin, Debby Smith, and Michael Smith, 249–263. New York: Harper Perennial, 2014.

Lenton, Stephen. "Mulberry Family Scrapbook: An Intentional Community Presented as an Experiment in Creative Recordation." PhD diss., Union Graduate School, 1976.

Levitas, Ruth. *Utopia as Method: The Imaginary Reconstitution of Society*. New York: Palgrave Macmillan, 2013.

Lieberman, Hal. "Cogswells and a Utopian Community." *Cogswell Courier*, April 2000, 5–6.

Lindsey, Almont. *The Pullman Strike: The Story of a Unique Experiment and of a Great Labor Upheaval*. Chicago: University of Chicago Press, 1943.

Maloney, C. J. *Back to the Land: Arthurdale, FDR's New Deal, and the Costs of Economic Planning*. Hoboken, NJ: Wiley, 2011.

Maniaque-Benton, Caroline. *French Encounters with the American Counterculture 1960–1980*. Burlington, VT: Ashgate, 2011.

Manzella, Joseph C. *Common Purse, Uncommon Future: The Long, Strange Trip of Communes and Other Intentional Communities*. Santa Barbara, CA: Praeger, 2010.

Marschak, Beth, and Alex Lorch. *Lesbian and Gay Richmond*. Charleston, SC: Arcadia, 2008.

Matthews, Mark. *Droppers: America's First Hippie Commune, Drop City*. Norman: University of Oklahoma Press, 2010.

McCamant, Kathryn M., and Charles R. Durrett. *Cohousing: A Contemporary Approach to Housing Ourselves*. Berkeley, CA: Ten Speed Press, 1998.

McMillen, Neil R. *Dark Journey: Black Mississippians in the Age of Jim Crow*. Urbana: University of Illinois Press, 1990.

McNally, Dennis. *A Long Strange Trip: The Inside History of the Grateful Dead*. New York: Broadway Books, 2002.

Melton, J. Gordon "The Theosophical Communities and Their Ideal of Brotherhood." In *America's Communal Utopias*, edited by Donald E. Pitzer, 396–418. Chapel Hill: University of North Carolina Press, 1997.

Mikkelsen, Michael Andrew. *The Bishop Hill Colony: A Religious Communistic Settlement in Henry County, Illinois*. Baltimore: Johns Hopkins University Press, 1892.

Miles, Malcolm. *Urban Utopias: The Built and Social Architectures of Alternative Settlements*. London: Routledge, 2007.

Miller, Donald L. *City of the Century: The Epic of Chicago and the Making of America*. New York: Simon & Schuster, 1996.

Miller, Timothy. Foreword to *Leaving New Buffalo Commune*, by Arthur Kopecky, xiii–xvi. Albuquerque: University of New Mexico Press, 2006.

———. *The Quest for Utopia in Twentieth-Century America*. Syracuse, NY: Syracuse University Press, 1998.

———. *The 60s Communes: Hippies and Beyond*. Syracuse, NY: Syracuse University Press, 1999.

Misiroglu, Gina. *American Countercultures: An Encyclopedia of Nonconformists, Alternative Lifestyles, and Radical Ideas in U.S. History.* New York: M. E. Sharpe, 2009.

Morgan, Michael. *Pirates and Patriots, Tales of the Delaware Coast.* New York: Algora, 2005.

Morhart, Hilda Dischinger. *The Zoar Story.* Dover, OH: Siebert, 1967.

Nichols, John. *The S Word: A Short History of an American Tradition . . . Socialism.* London: Verso, 2015.

Nordhoff, Charles. *The Communistic Societies of the United States.* New York: Harper & Brothers, 1875.

Noyes, John Humphrey. *History of American Socialisms.* Philadelphia: J. B. Lippincott, 1870.

Oved, Yaacov. *Two Hundred Years of American Communes.* New York: Routledge, 1987.

Ownby, Ted, and Charles Reagan Wilson. *The Mississippi Encyclopedia.* Jackson: University of Mississippi Press, 2017.

Payne, Phillip G. *Crash!: How the Economic Boom and Bust of the 1920s Worked.* Baltimore: Johns Hopkins University Press, 2015.

Penix, Amanda Griffith. *Images of America: Arthurdale.* Charleston, SC: Arcadia, 2007.

Penner, James. *Timothy Leary: The Harvard Years: Early Writings on LSD and Psilocybin with Richard Alpert, Huston Smith, Ralph Metzner, and Others.* Rochester, VT: Park Street Press, 2014.

Pitzer, Donald E. *America's Communal Utopias.* Chapel Hill: University of North Carolina Press, 1997.

———. "The New Moral World of Robert Owen and New Harmony." In *America's Communal Utopias,* edited by Donald E. Pitzer, 88–134. Chapel Hill: University of North Carolina Press, 1997.

Piven, Frances Fox. "Welfare in a New Society: An End to Intentional Impoverishment and Degradation." In *Imagine Living in a Socialist USA,* edited by Frances Goldin, Debby Smith, and Michael Smith, 125–135. New York: Harper Perennial, 2014.

Plockhoy, Pieter. *A Way Propounded to Make the Poor in These and Other Nations Happy: By Bringing Together a Fit, Suitable and Well-qualified People unto One Household-government, or Little Common-wealth.* London: Black Spread-Eagle, 1659.

Randall, Emilius Oviatt. *History of the Zoar Society, from Its Commencement to Its Conclusion: A Sociological Study in Communism.* Columbus, OH: Fred J. Meer Press, 1904.

Rokicky, Catherine M. *Creating a Perfect World: Religious and Secular Utopias in Nineteenth-Century Ohio.* Athens: Ohio University Press, 2002.

Rosen, Joel Nathan. *From New Lanark to Mound Bayou: Owenism in the Mississippi Delta.* Durham, NC: Carolina Academic Press, 2011.

Sartwell, Crispin. *The Practical Anarchist: Writings of Josiah Warren.* New York: Fordham University Press, 2011.

Saxby, T. J. *The Quest for the New Jerusalem: Jean de Labadie and the Labadists, 1610–1744.* Boston: Martinus Nijhoff, 1987.

Schneider, Herbert Wallace, and George Lawton. *A Prophet and a Pilgrim: Being the Incredible History of Thomas Lake Harris and Laurence Oliphant; Their Sexual Mysticisms and Utopian Communities Amply Documented to Confound the Skeptic.* New York: Columbia University Press, 1942.

Shantz, Douglas H. *An Introduction to German Pietism: Protestant Renewal at the Dawn of Modern Europe*. Baltimore: Johns Hopkins University Press, 2013.

Shipley, Morgan. *Psychedelic Mysticism: Transforming Consciousness, Religious Experiences, and Voluntary Peasants in Postwar America*. Lanham, MD: Lexington Books, 2015.

Siméon, Ophélie. *Robert Owen's Experiment at New Lanark: From Paternalism to Socialism*. New York: Palgrave Macmillan, 2017.

Smith, Michael Steven. "Law in a Socialist USA." In *Imagine Living in a Socialist USA*, edited by Frances Goldin, Debby Smith, and Michael Smith, 53–58. New York: Harper Perennial, 2014.

Soleri, Paolo. *What If? Collected Writings, 1986–2000*. Berkeley, CA: Berkeley Hills Books, 2003.

Soleri, Paolo, and Scott M. Davis. *Paolo Soleri's Earth Casting for Sculpture, Models and Construction*. Salt Lake City, UT: Peregrine Smith, 1984.

Spann, Edward K. *Brotherly Tomorrows: Movements for a Cooperative Society in America, 1820–1920*. New York: Columbia University Press, 1989.

———. *Hopedale: From Commune to Company Town, 1840–1920*. Columbus: Ohio State University Press, 1992.

Sreenivasan, Jyotsna. *Utopias in American History*. Santa Barbara, CA: ABC-CLIO, 2008.

Stack, Sam F. *The Arthurdale Community School: Education and Reform in Depression Era Appalachia*. Lexington: University Press of Kentucky, 2016.

Steinmetz, Hiram Erb. "Peter Miller and Michael Witman: A Revolutionary Episode." *Journal of the Lancaster County Historical Society* 6, no. 3–4 (1901): 46–49.

Stephenson, George Malcolm. *The Religious Aspects of Swedish Immigration: A Study of Immigrant Churches*. Minneapolis: University of Minnesota Press, 1932.

Stevens, Errol Wayne. *Radical L.A.: From Coxey's Army to the Watts Riots, 1894–1965*. Norman: University of Oklahoma Press, 2009.

Stevenson, Douglas. *The Farm Then and Now: A Model for Sustainable Living*. British Columbia: New Society Publishers, 2014.

Stockwell, Foster. *Encyclopedia of American Communes, 1663–1963*. Jefferson, NC: McFarland, 1998.

Stone, Elaine Murray. *Dorothy Day: Champion of the Poor*. New York: Paulist Press, 2004.

Strawser, Cornelia J. *Business Statistics of the United States 2012: Patterns of Economic Change*. Lanham, MD: Burnan Press, 2013.

Strom, Jonathan, Hartmut Lehmann, and James Van Horn Melton. *Pietism in Germany and North America 1680–1820*. New York: Routledge, 2016.

Sutton, Robert P. *Communal Utopias and the American Experience: Religious Communities, 1732–2000*. Westport, CT: Praeger, 2003.

———. *Communal Utopias and the American Experience: Secular Communities, 1824–2000*. Westport, CT: Praeger, 2004.

———. *Les Icariens: The Utopian Dream in Europe and America*. Urbana: University of Illinois Press, 1994.

Turner, Charles Henry Black. *Some Records of Sussex County, Delaware*. Philadelphia: Allen, Lane & Scott, 1909.

Tyler, Alice Felt. *Freedoms Ferment*. Minneapolis: University of Minnesota Press, 1944.

Unohoo, Coyote, Rick and the Mighty Avengers. *Morning Star Scrapbook*. Occidental, CA: Morning Star Ranch Tribe, 1973.

Vallet, Emile, and H. Roger Grant. *An Icarian Communist in Nauvoo: Commentary*. Springfield: Illinois State Historical Society, 1971.

Versluis, Arthur. *The Secret History of Western Sexual Mysticism: Sacred Practices and Spiritual Marriage*. Rochester, VT: Destiny Books, 2008.

———. "Sexual Mysticisms in Nineteenth Century America." In *Hidden Intercourse: Eros and Sexuality in the History of Western Esotericism*, edited by Wouter J. Hanegraaff and Jeffrey J. Kripal, 333–354. New York: Fordham University Press, 2011.

Wagner, Jon. "Eric Jansson and the Bishop Hill Colony." In *America's Communal Utopias*, edited by Donald E. Pitzer, 297–318. Chapel Hill: University of North Carolina Press, 1997.

Walker, Liz. *EcoVillage at Ithaca: Pioneering a Sustainable Culture*. Gabriola Island, BC: New Society, 2005.

Washington, Booker T. "A Town Owned by Negros," *World's Work* 14 (July 1907): 9125–9134.

Watkins, T. H. *The Great Depression: America in the 1930s*. Boston: Little, Brown, 1993.

Wells, Lester Grosvenor. *The Skaneateles Communal Experiment: 1843–1846*. Syracuse, NY: Onondaga Historical Association, 1953.

Wilson, Marie, and Michel Sarda. *Arcosanti Archetype: The Rebirth of Cities by Renaissance Thinker Paolo Soleri*. Fountain Hills: Freedom Editions, 1999.

Winship, Michael P. *Godly Republicanism: Puritans, Pilgrims, and a City on a Hill*. Cambridge, MA: Harvard University Press, 2012.

Wolf, Edwin. *Germantown and the Germans*. Philadelphia: Library Company of Philadelphia, 1983.

Young, William H., and Nancy K. Young. *The 1950s*. Westport, CT.: Greenwood Press, 2004.

Zicklin, Gilbert. *Countercultural Communes: A Sociological Perspective*. Westport, CT: Greenwood Press, 1983.

Zimmerman, Nadya. "Performance of an Anti-Commercial Culture." In *Rock Music*, edited by Mark Spicer, 77–100. London: Routledge, 2011.

INDEX

ABOUT THE AUTHOR

MARK S. FERRARA is associate professor of English at State University of New York and author of several books, including *Palace of Ashes, Sacred Bliss*, and *New Seeds of Profit*. Ferrara lives with his wife in an intentional community dedicated to sustainable living and experiential learning.